汉语流行口语
最新版

Popular Chinese Expressions
—Latest Edition

李杰群 李杰明 高永安 马骏鹰 编著

Jian Leng（冷健）　　C.L. Shannon

谷平湖　　Andrew Gluckman 翻译

华语教学出版社

First Edition 2007

ISBN 978-7-80200-100-8
Copyright 2007 by Sinolingua
Published by Sinolingua
24 Baiwanzhuang Road, Beijing 100037, China
Tel: (86) 10-68320585
Fax: (86) 10-68326333
http://www.sinolingua.com.cn
E-mail: hyjx@ sinolingua.com.cn
Printed by Beijing Songyuan Printing Co. Ltd.
Distributed by China International
Book Trading Corporation
35 Chegongzhuang Xilu, P.O. Box 399
Beijing 100044, China

Printed in the People's Republic of China

论中国人的面子／代序

　　本书的前身是我们在2000年写的《汉语流行口语》，那本小书出乎意料地受到欢迎，不仅在国内多次印刷，而且还先后在日本、韩国、俄罗斯面市。与此同时，也有不少外国朋友提出批评意见。问题集中在分类上：缺乏逻辑，相互交叉。"其实你们的落脚点都在'面子'上，为什么不从'面子'出发来分类呢？"经过近几年的教学实践，同留学生反复讨论，我们决定从"面子"切入，对原书进行大手术。

　　什么是"面子"？

　　"面子"是一个社会心理学意义上的人的感觉，是一个历史学意义上的人的价值，是一个人类学意义上的人的仪式，是一个语言学意义上的人的表达。

　　"面子"是一项科研课题。中国人一直在研究，外国人一直想了解，因为它是双方顺畅交流的必要前提。

　　当然，前人对此已多有建树。但是，纯粹从话语的角度来进行解析的，以本书为先（真有面子）。如果不从话语这个面子的最后的根破起，仅在意识、心理等方面对面子进行批判，那是不可能取得成效的。因为面子意识与面子心理早已成为我们民族的生理遗传基因。一个汉族人，还没有生下来，就已经被放置在面子的网络之中！所以除了封口以外，很难找到别的疗法了。

　　可是我们至今尚未得到一个具象的、可以量化的关于面子的定义；一个判断面子属性的标准。这大概是因为不管怎么说也说不清楚面子的内涵和外延。为此我们找到两个实例。

　　第一个是两千年前的西楚霸王项羽。

　　项羽的祖上是战国时代楚国的贵族，家里有钱有势——有面子。秦始皇统一中国后，原先各诸侯国的贵族失去了一切——没有了面子。项羽当然很不甘心，一天，他巧遇秦始皇出游，看到皇家车仗的威严盛大，他发誓要"取而代之"。项羽的"争要面子"也从此开始了。

　　不久，天下大乱，具有超人力量的项羽成了百战百胜威名远扬的楚霸王，他率领各诸侯国的起义军，灭掉秦国，得到了全国第一的"面子"。这时的项羽决定要回到家乡去光宗耀祖，而放弃了中原逐鹿的大好时机，他说："富贵不归故乡，如衣绣夜行，谁知之者！"这种有了面子就要"讲面子"的做法，被一个有见识的人讥讽为"沐猴而冠"，意思是猴子虽然戴上人的帽子，它仍然还是猴子——比喻项羽表面上轰轰烈烈，却成不了大事。项羽闻听后立即烹杀了那个胆敢损毁他面子的人。然而那个人并没有看错，项羽在之后的战争中逐渐处于劣势，面子越来越小，直至被对手汉王刘邦团团围住，一败涂地，脸面全无。

尽管如此，项羽在事实面前仍然不承认失败，他说："此天之亡我，非战之罪也。"为了证明不是自己不会打仗，而是上天不帮助自己，他又几次冲入汉营，凭借匹夫之勇，杀伤汉军无数——用以挽回面子。

当他退到乌江岸边，有人劝他渡江回根据地重新发展时，他考虑的还是自己的面子："天之亡我，我何渡为！且籍与江东子弟八千人渡江而西，今无一人还，纵江东父兄怜而王我，我何面目见之？纵彼不言，籍独不愧于心乎？"是啊，项羽宁可死了，也不能去面对八千子弟兵的妻儿老小，因为那是最没面子的！他再次杀回汉营，在寡不敌众的情况下，体面地自刎而死，完成了"死要面子"的最后一幕。

没有面子争面子；有了面子讲面子；讲了面子丢面子；丢了面子找面子；找不回面子也要死要面子。项羽的人生之路，生动地展示出关于面子的全过程。

帝王项羽爱面子，平民百姓同样爱面子。这就是我们要介绍的第二个人物——鲁迅先生笔下的阿Q。他和面子的关系就更有趣了。因为到了清朝末年，中国的国势已经弱得不能再弱了。如果说项羽的面子是强势中的真面子，那么阿Q的面子就是弱势下的虚面子了。

比如，阿Q同别人争吵时，常说："我们先前——比你阔得多啦！你算是什么东西！"——这是说大话撑面子。再如，阿Q没钱找女人，就去摸小尼姑的脸，还说："和尚动得，我动不得？"——这是欺负弱小挣面子。当他被别人痛打之后，总是说："儿子打老子！"——这是假托大辈儿找回面子。当他被押赴刑场，已经吓得心惊胆战时，居然还能说出"过了二十年又是一个……"的豪言壮语，博得看客的一片喝彩声。——阿Q也完成了他"死要面子"的最后一幕。

从项羽到阿Q，我们社会的历史与心理的特征，保持着一定的惯性。为了抓住要领，本书以"面子"为话题，展开讨论。因为"面子"是中国人文化心理的内核，是第一生存意义，是基本话语基因。要学习中国语言，要了解中国社会，不明白"面子问题"是不行的。

我们把有关面子的短语分成四大类：给自己面子、给别人面子、不给自己面子、不给别人面子。每大类中又分为三小类：主动的情况，即：我方强于对方（在强势中）；一般的情况，即：双方地位均等（在均势中）；被动的情况，即：我方弱于对方（在弱势中）。分类是不可能尽善尽美的，有的语条可以在多个类别中使用，我们只择其一类解析，相信读者在理解之后，自会灵活运用。每小类中的语条按音序排列。全书序号为：1、1.1、1.1.1……。

对每一条话语又从两个角度进行分析。一是话语脉络，即在同一语义表述上，列出古语——古代汉语；雅语——现代书面语；对话——当代口语；类语——当代口语中的近似说法。一是话语情境，即通过对话尽量具象出特定氛围，然后，再详细诠释中国文化心理在该情境中的思维走势、动机缘由和利害取舍。由此，就形成了：语条、对话、语境、古语、雅语、类语的"六合一"的体例模式（本着宁缺毋滥的原则，有个别空缺）。

本书由李杰群、李杰明主编，参加编写工作的还有高永安、马骏鹰先生。

限于水平，有不妥之处，望读者赐教。

李杰群　李杰明

2006 年 5 月

于北京西郊红果园

Assessing Chinese' Face / Preface

This is the second edition of *Popular Chinese Expressions*. The first edition published in 2000 and reprinted in 2001 and again in 2004, was surprisingly well received. It not only sold well in China, but also in Japan, Korea, and Russia. During this time, we have received many letters from our foreign readers, some criticizing and others offering suggestions. The critical questions concentrated on the system of classification we used in grouping the phrases: stating that they were not logical and occasionally overlapped. The correspondence from our readers asked: "Why don't you categorize all phrases by feature topics' concerning face, since the fundamental philosophy of the book is about 'face'?" Through further teaching experience and discussion with our students, we decided to reorganize the phrases as they relate to the concept of "face", and undertook a major restructuring of the original book.

What is "face"?

It is multifaceted. The concept of "face" is a human sense perception related to social psychology, it is a human value from a historical perspective, a human custom with formal and informal rituals from the view of anthropology, and a human testimonial as viewed through its expression in language.

"Face" has been a subject of research for many years among Chinese. Foreigners have worked extensively toward understanding it, since "face" is an essential condition to an unhindered cultural exchange between East and West.

Of course, there have been many books about this topic, but this book is the first to analyze "face" from the perspective of language. Since language is the root and origin of human "face", we sought to create something distinct from those books that only describe "face" from the view of human consciousness and psychology. We think the concept of "face" has become a kind of cultural 'genetic factor' in our country, especially among those of Han ancestry. Everyone is captured within a web of connections concerning their "face" before they are even born. To reformat our spoken language is the best way to cure this predicament.

But we haven't found an exact definition and measurement for this term yet, because the concept of "face" has a very rich connotative meaning and an almost infinite number of explanations. Hence, we are using two examples here to better define this term.

The first example is a story about Xiang Yu, the Conqueror (232-202 B.C.).

Xiang Yu was born of a noble family in the Chu State, during the Warring States Period (475-221 B.C.) with money and power, so he had a lot of "face". Since all the dukes and nobles lost their power and money after Qin Shi Huang, the first emperor of Qin unified China, they lost "face". Xiang Yu, of course, was not going to take his defeat lying down. One day, he saw Qing Shi Huang on a tour and the carriages were exceptionally ornate and large. He was jealous and swore that he would "take it over". From then on, Xiang Yu began to compete for his own "face".

Soon there was a great disorder throughout the country. Xiang Yu proved to be a superman in mental and physical strength. He led the rebellious armies from all the States and defeated Qin and won power and his "face" back. At this time, Xiang Yu decided to go back home and bring glory to his ancestors and give up the opportunity to take control over the Central Plains of China. He said: "If a person has wealth and honors and doesn't go back home, it is no better than wearing fine cloths in the dark, nobody will see it." He was particularly concerned with "face", and showing off the signs of that "face". One of his companions's ridiculed him, saying that: "Even if a monkey wears a human hat, it is still a monkey." Xiang Yu killed him because he insulted his "face". But this companion was correct, and Xiang Yu's force was gradually reduced to absolute inferiority. Ultimately he was completely surrounded by Liu Bang and suffered a huge defeat. He lost all his "face" in the end.

Under these circumstances, Xiang Yu couldn't admit his mistakes. He said: "I am not vanquished through battle, but through the force of heaven." In order to prove this and his ability to fight, he rushed into the Han military camp and killed many enemy soldiers to save his "face". When he drew back to the Wujiang River, one advisor urged him to cross the river and go back to his base camp to fight again. He still considered his face and said: "Why should I cross the river, if it is the heavens that want to kill me! I led eight thousand soldiers to this place and all of them are dead now. Even if their parents, wives and children all forgive me; I don't have the face to stand before them. Even if they don't say anything to me, how could my heart be quiet?" So, he went back to the enemy camp to fight again. Since he fought against hopeless odds, he respectably committed suicide by cutting his throat in the end. Xiang Yu preferred to commit suicide rather than face his solders' families. He is a perfect example of the process where a person dedicates his life in the struggle for face, gives in to the excessive display of face, loses face and dies in his determination to save face.

But, just as a general or government minister cares about face, common people also care about their face. This brings us to the second person we want to introduce: Ah Q, the main character in Lu Xun's book of *The True Story of Ah Q*. His story is more interesting than Xiang Yu's. Xiang Yu wanted to project a real face under strong and powerful conditions, but Ah Q wants an empty face during a period when the nation was weak at the end of the Qing Dynasty.

For example, Ah Q's often quarreled with others and countered them by saying: "Previously we were much richer than you, you count as nobody!" This boast is used to maintain his face. Another example concerns the fact that Ah Q didn't have enough money to own a woman, so he touched a little nun's face and said: "Why can you be touched by a monk, and not by me?" This sentence is used to take advantage of weaker people in order to maintain his face. When people would beat him, he would always yell "A son is beating his father!" Here he falsely acts as if he belongs to an older generation to recover his face. When he was taken to the execution ground and was shaking with fright, he still had some brave words to save his face: "Twenty years after today, there will be another ...." His action won everyone's acclaim. Thus, Ah Q also finished his life with a "dead determination to save face".

From these two examples, we can see how it is that Chinese people would even today hold to these characteristics of our social history. In order to grasp this essence, we launch a discussion around the topic of "face" in this book. If you want to learn the Chinese language and understand Chinese society, you have to first, understand the "face problem", because "face" is the nucleus of Chinese cultural psychology and the key to survival in Chinese society.

We classified all the phrases into four categories: saving your own face, giving other people face, failing to retain your own face, and denying other people face. Under each category, we further divided the topics into three subtitles: stronger than others, equal to others and weaker than others. The classification is not perfect; since many phrases can be used under more than one title we put them under what we believe was the most suitable one. We believe the reader can use these phrases with some flexibility after understanding them. Each phrase is alphabet-ordered as 1, 1.1, 1.1.1 ...under the subtitles.

Each phrase is analyzed from two angels: language sequences and language contexts. Language sequence includes how this phrase was used in ancient communication, in contemporary written usage, contemporary oral language and all comparable phrases. Language context is given through conversations providing all the specific circumstances of use, and then providing explanatory notes explaining the Chinese cultural background, motivations, and gains and losses. The content of the book includes phrases, conversations, contexts, ancient language usages, and similar phrases (note, there may be content missing for a few phrases).

Compilers are Li Jiequn and Li Jieming. Associated Compilers are Gao Yong'an and Ma Junying.

Li Jiequn, Li Jieming

May 2006

Hongguoyuan, Xijiao, Beijing

作者简介

李杰群

四川成都人，1948年生。1982年毕业于首都师范大学中文系。现任北京广播电视大学中文系教授。中央广播电视大学《简明古代汉语》主讲教师。从事古代汉语、言语交际教学与研究工作。主要论著有：《250字闯北京》《汉语流行口语》《〈商君书〉虚词研究》《古代汉语》《非言语交际概论》《公共关系实用语言》《连词"则"的起源和发展》《"甚"的词性演变》《上古汉语程度副词考辨》《〈马氏文通〉的作者不容混淆》《〈孟子〉总括副词辨析》等。

李杰明

四川成都人，1953年生。1984年毕业于北京大学图书馆系。1986年毕业于北京高等教育自学考试中文系。现任北京舞蹈学院学报、院报编辑。首都师范大学、北京理工大学、北京工业大学对外汉语教学兼职教师。从事文化艺术、对外汉语教学与研究工作。主要论著有：《250字闯北京》《汉语流行口语》《文明服务语言艺术》《唐宋八大家鉴赏辞典》《中国文学名著故事大观》《关于视听说课》等。

高永安

河南驻马店人，1966年生。2004年毕业于北京大学中文系，文学博士。现任中国人民大学对外语言文化学院讲师。从事对外汉语和汉语史方面的教学与研究工作。主要论著有：《语言符号任意性的汉语阐释》《日本留学生学习汉语时的几个特殊的语音问题》《〈字汇〉音切的来源》《〈墨子〉对虚词的研究》《宣城方言的早期形式》《中华字典》《非言语交际概论》等。

马骏鹰

河北张家口人，1973年生。2002年毕业于浙江师范大学中文系，文学硕士。现任北京广播电视大学讲师。从事中国古代文学、对外汉语教学与研究工作。主要论著有：《王逸〈渔父章句〉校记》《读韩愈〈答刘秀才论史书〉札记》《读〈史记·东越列传〉》《250字闯北京》等。

Authors' Short Biography

Li, Jiequn was born in Chengdu, China, in 1948. She graduated from the Department of Chinese, Beijing Normal University in 1982. She is Professor of Chinese in Beijing Radio and TV University. She is the main lecturer for "Concise Ancient Chinese Language" in Beijing Radio and TV University. Her research interests are ancient Chinese language and language communication. Her publications include *250 Chinese Words to Get You Around Beijing, Popular Chinese Expressions, Shang Jun Shu (Function Words), Ancient Chinese Language, An Introduction to Non-Language Communication, Practical Language in Public Relations, The Origin and Development of A Conjunction Word - "Ze", Tracing the Characteristic of A Word: The Evolvement of Part of Speech of the Character 其, Examining Adverbial Words in Ancient Chinese, Who was the Author of "Ma Shi Wen Tong" Differentiation and Analyses of Adverbial Words in "Mencus"*, and so on.

Li, Jieming was born in Chengdu, China, in 1953. He graduated from the Department of Library Studies, Peking University in 1984 and passed the examination for the self-taught from the Department of Chinese, Beijing Higher Education in 1986. He is the editor of *Journal of Beijing Dance Institute*, and teaches Chinese as a foreign language at Beijing Normal University, Beijing Technology Institute, and Beijing Industry Institute. His research interests are cultural arts and teaching Chinese as a foreign language. His publications include *250 Chinese Words to Get You Around Beijing, Popular Chinese Expressions, Civilized Service and Arts of Language, Dictionary for Appreciation of Eight Masters in Tang and Song Dynasties, Famous Chinese Literature Stories, About Audio-Visual-Speak Education*, and so on.

Gao, Yong'an was born in Zhumadian, Henan, China in 1966. He received his Ph.D. in literature from the Department of Chinese, Peking University in 2004. He is a lecturer at the Institute of International Languages and Culture, People's University. His research interests are Chinese Language teaching as a foreign language and the history of Chinese education. His main publications include *Linguistic Notation and Chinese Explanation, The Problem of Several Chinese Pronunciations for Japanese Students, The Origin of Tone for "Glossary", The Research of the Function Words for*

"Mo Zi", The Early Style of Xuancheng Dialect, Chinese Dictionary, An Introduction to Non-Language Communication, and so on.

Ma, Junying was born in Zhangjiakou, Hebei, China in 1973. He received his Masters in Literature from the Department of Chinese, Zhejiang Normal University. He is a Lecturer for Beijing Radio and TV University. His research interests are Chinese ancient literature and Chinese Language teaching as a foreign language and Chinese history education. His main publications include *Collating Wang Yi's "Yu Fu Zhang Ju", Reading Notes of Han Yu's "Da Liu Xiucai Lun Shishu", Interpretation of "Shiji - Dong Yue Lie Zhuan", 250 Chinese Words to Get You Around Beijing*, and so on.

目录
Contents

13

2. 给别人面子   gěi biéren miànzi   114

2.1 在强势中   zǎi qiángshì zhōng   114

2.2 在均势中   zài jūnshì zhōng   127

4. 不给别人面子 bù gěi biéren miànzi　230

4.1 在强势中 zài qiángshì zhōng　230

给自己面子
Saving Your Face 1

1.1
在强势中
Stronger than Others

1.1.1>

比较忙
[pretty busy]

😊 对话 Conversation

① A：老李呀，昨天好几个单位来人都没找到你！

Mr. Li, several organizations tried to contact you yesterday. Where have you been?

B：哎呀！我最近比较忙，一个人管几十个单位，只能抓主要的，别的就顾不上啦！

Oh, I have been very busy recently. I am supervising so many divisions. One person can only do so much.

② A：喂，听说你有好几个女朋友！怎么安排得开呢？

I heard you have several girlfriends now. How can you handle it?

B：噢，我最近是比较忙，有什么办法，是她们喜欢追我！

You are right. I am too busy to take care of all of them. But they like to chase me around. What can I do?

👉 语境

　　忙，表明有事情做，有钱赚，很有"面子"。在①中，老李是领导，是重要人物，忙得很有"面子"。在②中，先生是女生追求的对象，说明他非常有魅力，很体面。

 **Context**

"Busy" in this example means that there are always things waiting for you to do. Therefore, you have more opportunity to make money and have more power and status. In conversation (1), Mr. Li is a leader and an important leader has to be busy. In conversation (2), Mr. A is being chased by several girls at the same time. He says it must be because he is charming and attractive.

古语：兢兢业业，一日二日万几。// 《尚书·皋陶谟》
雅语：日理万机
类语：事儿太多

1.1.2>

不是我说你
[busybody]

对话 Conversation

① A：你干吗整天把嘴搁在我身上？
   Why do you always find faults with me?

B：不是我说你，你这一身毛病没个人说行吗？
   You have so many problems (defects). Am I the only person who tells you this?

② A：不是我说你，全班这么多人，哪个喜欢你呀？
   I have to tell you, is there anyone else who likes you enough in our classroom?

B：你少管我。

Stop nagging me.

 语境

　　这话一般出自心眼好，但是唠唠叨叨的人之口。有意思的是，说者明明知道听者非常不愿意听，但是，出于关心、爱护、责任，更出于习惯，原本不想说，想了半天还是得说。如果真的不说，大概就会憋出病来。碰到这样热心肠的好朋友或者长辈，除了听着也没有其他的办法。其实大家都差不多，谁说谁呀！

 Context

　　A busybody usually has a kind heart, but talks too much. A busybody knows people don't want to listen to them, but they have to speak out about whatever is on their mind. They feel this shows their love, concern and responsibility. If you meet friends or older persons who are this way, often the only polite choice is to listen.

古语：居，吾语女。// 《论语·阳货》
雅语：出于好心
类语：我是关心你

跟你说你也不懂

[Even if I try to explain it, you wouldn't understand.]

☺ 对话 Conversation

① A：您这首歌有点深，能不能解释一下？

Your song must contain some deeper meaning. Can you explain it to me?

B：嘿嘿，跟你说你也不懂。

Well, you're right. But even if I explain it, you wouldn't understand.

② A：我跟她的感情吧，跟你说你也不懂！

You would never understand the feeling between her and me, even if I tried to explain it to you!

B：我是过来人了，都懂。你要是不想说就算了。

I have been there too. If you don't want to tell me about it that is fine, you don't have to make any excuses.

 **语境**

　　这话有些欠礼貌，可是有的时候还真想说，听人家说的时候也挺爽。因为知识、年龄、价值观等方面的差异是无法避免的，所以不可能都沟通，更不可能都理解。孔子说，对于低水平的人，不要讲高水平的话。所以，在①的情况下，也就只好这么说了。另外，这话还有不想说出心里话的意思，如②；那就不是礼貌不礼貌的问题，而是信任不信任的问题了。

这样，在①中是我懂你不懂，你没面子。在②中是即使你懂也休想帮我懂，不让你有面子。

 ## Context

    Although these conversations sound very impolite, they cannot be avoided in real life. This is because people come from different age groups, knowledge levels, and value systems. As Confucius advised, don't speak in high ideological sentences to people who understand the world in more simple terms. For conversation (1), the answer is reasonable; moreover, there may be some secret that cannot be shared. B definitely knows more about the music than A, and shows it off by rudely dismissing A's interest. In conversation (2), A is not only very impolite, but also shows he doesn't trust B. B knows A understands what's going on, but doesn't want to hear A's opinion. A insults B.

古语：中人以下，不可以语上也。//《论语·雍也》
雅语：对牛弹琴
类语：说也白说　白费唾沫

1.1.4>

好嘞　好吧　好的
[okay, okay, okay]

☺ 对话 Conversation

① A：哎，别睡了，要查票了！（两个人掏出月票）
Excuse me, please show me your tickets! (Two people show their monthly passes).

B：（售票员对众人）好嘞，请收好，好嘞，好嘞……
(Ticket seller says to everyone) Okay, please put your passes away.

② A：（男）这个星期六总该去见爸爸妈妈了吧！
Anyway, we must visit my parents this Saturday.

B：（女）……，好吧。
Okay!

③ A：老板，该办的事都办好了，我们明天回总公司。
Boss, we've finished all the things that we were supposed to do. We should go back to the head office tomorrow.

B：好的，好的好的好的。
Okay, okay, okay.

 **语境**

在汉语口语中，好多的"好"字并没有赞扬的意思，在①中售票员用"好嘞"表示查过了你的票。②中的"好吧"一般是势态稍强的人用，表示经过考虑，答应了对方的请求，并在语气中流露出一些让步的味道。③中的"好的"多为领导在电话里听取下级汇报时用，意思是知道了；另外，如果领导连用了多个好的，那就是让你收线，别打了。

Context

In spoken Chinese, "okay" doesn't imply "good" or "praise" (as it often does in English). In conversation (1), the ticket seller uses "okay" to state that they have finished checking everyone's tickets. In conversation (2), B says "okay" after considering the situation, agreeing with A's assessment and conceding that they should visit the parents. Conversation (3) usually happens when the leader listens to their officers' report. "Okay" means that he heard it. But when the leader repeats "okay" several times, it means he heard you, he understands, and he wants you to stop talking.

古语：太后曰："诺，恣君之所使之。" //《战国策·赵策四》
雅语：就这样吧
类语：歆

1.1.5>

好说好说
[No problem.]

☺ 对话 Conversation

① A：老李呀，我女儿刚进你们公司，今后请多关照！

　　Mr. Li, my daughter just started working at your company, please look after her.

　B：好说好说。

　　No problem!

② A：小红啊，明天有个实习生去你那，你带带她。

　　Xiao Hong, a trainee will report to your department. Could you please train him/her?

　B：好说好说。

　　That can be easily arranged.

☞ 语境

　　这句话在早先的交际场合中有"可以商量""好商量"的意思。如今变成了"打保票""没问题""你放心吧"的意思。不论在早先，还是在如今，这句话都属于那种顺口说出来的"口水话"，即：不负责任的应酬语言。如在①和②中，虽然两个B都答应得挺好，但是对于这种白添麻烦的事，他们肯定是会心生反感，敷衍了事的。

 Context

Traditionally, this phrase meant "we can discuss this" or "it can be easily discussed". Now, however, it means "no problem", "nothing to worry about", or "the outcome is guaranteed". In either sense, this phrase occurs in the exchange of a few polite words in many social contexts and does not imply any responsibility. In conversations (1) and (2), although B answered A politely, they understand that the request involves some more work or trouble. B may or may not comply with the request, but in order to maintain the relationship and be polite, they give this perfunctory response.

古语：敬诺 //《战国策·赵策》
雅语：尽管放心
类语：包在我身上

1.1.6>

今晚我请
[It is my treat.]

😊 对话 Conversation

① A：明天是我生日，今晚我请大家吃饭。
　　Tomorrow is my birthday. I am inviting everyone to dinner tonight.

　 B：太棒了，我们去哪儿吃？
　　Excellent, where will we eat?

② A：昨晚是你请，我们又喝酒又唱卡拉OK。今晚该我请了，咱们先蹦迪，后桑拿。

You treated us to drinks and karaoke last night. Tonight it's my turn. We will go dancing first and then go to a sauna.

B：好啊！

Great!

 ## 语境

花钱请人去吃喝玩乐，是有效的交际方式之一。在朋友、同学之间，一般是谁有喜事谁请客，谁请客谁有"面子"。客人越多，主人越有"面子"，如①。在其他社会交往中，一般是谁求人谁请客，谁请得到重要人物谁有"面子"。当然也有请来请去的情况，但千万可别忘记，吃了人家一顿，要还人家一顿，如②；要不然就"没面子"了。

 ## Context

Inviting your friends to eat, drink, or to a party is a very effective way of maintaining your status among them. In general, people enjoy occasions when their friends and classmates pay the expenses. The person entertaining others gains status or face, and the more guests that show up the more status one receives. This is the case in conversation (1). For other social occasions, usually the person who asks others to help should pay for the entertainment. If some important people attend, the person paying gains even more face. Of course people often treat each other for some reasons. But, as conversation (2) demonstrates, always remember to return the favor.

古语：旦日飨士卒 // 《史记·项羽本纪》
雅语：我做东
类语：我买单

就这么定了
[That's settled.]

☺ 对话 Conversation

① A：局长啊，要不要再研究研究？

   Boss, should we discuss this more later?

  B：算了，就这么定了！

   We don't have to, I've decided already.

② A：校长您看，会开了10天，这件事还是定不下来！

   Dean, our meeting has lasted over 10 days and we still cannot reach a decision.

  B：谁说的？就这么定了！

   Who says? It's already settled.

 ## 语境

　　这句话在各种会议上都是很难听到的。因为一般人没有资格说，能说的人又都很慎重，所以，很多事情也就不容易"定"。只有到了实在不能再拖下去的时候，"第一把手"才会说出这句"结束语"，并承担一切责任。

Context

One does not often hear this phrase during a meeting. In general, the ordinary workers cannot make decisions, and leaders are very cautious about making decisions. Hence, there are a lot of things that cannot be decided upon easily. Only when time has run out to make a decision will the director be forced to use this phrase to close the deliberations and commit to all the responsibilities involved in whatever choice they eventually make.

古语：吾计决矣 //《资治通鉴·六十五卷》
雅语：就这样决定了
类语：就这么着吧

1.1.8>

举手之劳
[That's easy for me.]

☺ 对话 Conversation

① **A**：主任，这个老大难问题群众已经反映了很多年，不好解决啊！
Boss, people have been unable to solve this problem for years. What should we do?

B：是吗？对我来说，不过是举手之劳。
Is that true? Solving this is nothing for me.

② **A**：他老说什么举手之劳，可他就是不举那只手！
He always said that this problem was easy to solve, but he never got around to solving it.

B：想让他举那只手，比登天还难。
You're right, solving it would be harder than flying up to the sky.

语境

　　这是具有超级实力的人喜欢说的很有面子的话。因为他们手中有权，手里有钱，手下有人，社会上有关系。所以，无论对老百姓是多难的事，在他们看来，不费吹灰之力就能办到。当然，他们绝不会也不可能真说真干；否则，他们也就不会坐在那里说这种局外人的话了。一个时时刻刻都在为人民付出"举手之劳"的人，是最辛苦，最值得尊敬的人，他们永远没时间吹这种牛。

 Context

　　People too full of self-confidence use this phrase, because they have power, money, labor and connections. It is true that something that might be very hard for common people to solve would be easier for them. But often they never really solve the problem the way they promise. They brag about what they can do, but never get things done. A person who is intent on getting things done has to work hard and has no time to brag about themselves. It is these kinds of people who are worthy of our respect.

古语：天下可运于掌 //《孟子·梁惠王上》
雅语：易如反掌
类语：这算什么

看我的
[I can do it.]

😊 对话 Conversation

① A：哎呀，我怎么修不好这扇窗户！
　　Oh well, I can't repair this window.

　 B：让开，看我的！
　　Get out of the way, let me see if I can do it.

② A：这块石头真重，谁也搬不动。
　　This stone is so heavy that no one could remove it.

　 B：这算什么，看我的。
　　No problem for me, I can move it.

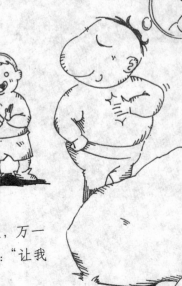

 语境

　　当看到别人做不了，或者做不好一件事时，有的人喜欢为自己挣点"面子"。尽管别人没有请他帮忙，他对自己也没有十分的把握，可是，他自然会一边说"看我的"一边努力去做。当然，他很有可能做好。但是，万一做不好，那可怎么办哪！如果只说："让我试试"，多聪明啊。

Context

Some people like to gain respect or face when they see that other people cannot accomplish one kind of task or another. Even though nobody asks them for help and they are unsure of their ability, they insist on trying it. Sometimes it is possible for them to do it. But even if they cannot, what can they lose by trying? They are usually smart to say, "Let me try!"

古语：唯余马首是瞻 // 《左传・襄公十四年》
雅语：易如反掌
类语：我来吧

1.1.10>

来电

[electrical shock]

😊 对话 Conversation

① A：老李呀，你干吗老盯着那个漂亮姑娘啊？

Mr. Li, why are you staring at that beautiful girl?

B：哎呀！多少年没这么来电了！

My God! It has been years since I was startled by a beautiful woman.

② A：我一看见他就脸红心跳！

My face turns red and my heart beats faster when I see him.

B：那就是来电了！

That is just like electrical jolt to your system.

语境

男女之间的感觉是非常微妙的，说不清楚的。有的人一辈子都没有碰到过让自己心动的人，那真是白活了。可是我们一直缺少一句专门比喻那种一见倾心、失魂落魄的话语，所以，当"来电"一出现，就立刻被大家毫不犹豫地接受了。需要区别的是，"来电"只是瞬间感觉，和传统的"一见钟情"不一样，它没有什么长期的、永远的考虑。仅仅是人们在性心理上的自由和放纵，是那种想象中的浪漫。希望大家都有"来电"的幸运，都能点亮自己的生命之灯。

Context

The feelings between a male and a female are very delicate and hard to explain. Some people never meet someone who could interest them all their life. This is really too bad. But even when we do meet someone who sparks our interest, we often lack a word to describe the moment of excitement when two people first meet and are jolted out of their ordinary existence. So, when the word "electrical shock" was used to describe this, people accepted it right away. There is one thing that should be remembered when people describe their experience as an "electrical shock", and that is the feeling that comes fast and is gone just as fast. It is, therefore, different from the traditional description of "two people falling in love at first sight". That phrase means their love would last forever. The jolt of an "electrical shock" is usually used to describe a sexual impulse. This kind of romance is more in their imagination. Still, we wish more people could experience this kind of feeling and momentary shock in their life.

古语：众里寻他千百度，蓦然回首，那人却在灯火阑珊处。
      // 辛弃疾《青玉案》
雅语：心有灵犀
类语：有感觉　对上眼儿了

1.1.11>

下不去手

[don't have the heart to]

😊 对话 Conversation

① A: 老大，老二做了那么多坏事，炸死他是应该的。

Old brother, Lao Er has done so many bad things; he deserves to be blown up.

B: 应该是应该，还是有点下不去手啊！

Even though he deserves it, I still don't have the heart to kill him.

② A: 我们的儿子太不听话了，你教训他一次吧。

Our son doesn't listen to us at all. You should teach him a lesson.

B: 我早就想揍他，就是下不去手。

I have long wanted to beat him, but I just don't have the heart to do it.

③ A: 你吃鸡吗？要吃就帮我杀了它。

Would you like to eat chicken? If so, please help me kill it.

B: 哎哟，那我可下不去手！

My dear, I simply don't have the heart to do that!

👉 **语境**

　　"下手"特指开始迅速，有力的行动。一般来说，是黑社会的专用词，如在①中。其他人，比如警察，就不用"下手"，而用"动手"。"下

37

不去手"的意思，是完成了下手的准备以后，因为感情上的原因，心里有些不愿意看到下手的结果，如在①、②中。在③里，B 只是因为胆小，所以下不去手。

Context

To "start on a task" means to begin something rapidly and powerfully. The phrase often has a special use for the criminal syndicates as seen in conversation (1). For the other people, like police, the phrase usually used is "get to work". When they said that they don't have the heart to do something, it means they know they should do it, but hesitate for a number of reasons. It could be that they don't want to see the results. Conversation (1) and (2) both provide examples of this kind of hesitation. In conversation (3), B is simply too cowardly to see a chicken slaughtered.

古语：吾不忍其觳觫 //《孟子·梁惠王上》
雅语：于心不忍
类语：狠不下心来

1.1.12>

先这样
[Don't do anything yet.]

☺ 对话 Conversation

① A：老板，股票的行情变化不大，您看……?

Boss, there's not much change in today's stock market prices, any ideas?

B：先这样。

Don't do anything yet.

② A：领导，关于老李的去留，背景比较复杂，您看……？

Boss, Old Li's background is rather complicated, should we keep him or let him go?

B：先这样。

Don't make any decision about that yet.

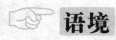 ## 语境

这句话一般来讲是"上级"的专用语，专门用在各种情况还不清楚，领导心中还没有思路，因此，还不能做出决定的时候，如在①中，是"待机"的状况。还有一种情况，是领导不想介入比较复杂的关系，因此，宁可不处理，也不找麻烦，如在②中，是"远离"的状况。虽然两者不同，但结果都是保持原样。下级听到这句话时，不要再说什么。

Context

This sentence is reserved for leaders to use when they are unclear about the situation or don't know how to deal with a problem. Hence, they delay the decision. In conversation (1), the boss is waiting for a more advantageous opportunity. In the other example, the leader doesn't want to get involved in what appears to be a difficult relationship. As we can see in conversation (2), he would rather leave it along, instead of getting involved in more trouble. The leader doesn't want to touch this thing. Although these two cases are different, the results are the same — stay true with the original statement. When subordinates hear this sentence, they should just keep quiet.

古语：分据要害之地，以固维持之势。// 《晋书·杜预传》
雅语：保持现状
类语：放一放再说

有的是
[have plenty of]

 **对话 Conversation**

① A：你说请我去"马克西姆"吃牛扒，你的钱够吗？

You promised to invite me for a steak at Maxim's. Do you have enough money?

B：钱？有的是！

Money? I have plenty of money.

② A：您说帮我学英语，您有时间吗？

You promised to help me with English. Do you have time?

B：别的没有，时间，有的是。

I don't have much of anything else, but I have plenty of time.

☞ **语境**

"有的是"的意思：一、非常多。二、不是宝贵的。在①中，B好像是个大款，听他的口气，身上最少也有几万。当然，也有可能是吹牛。在②中，B好像是个老师，老师是挣不着大钱的，因此说"别的"没有；在时间上呢，还是比较灵活的，但也谈不上"有的是"。所以，当你听人说"有的是"的时候，别太相信。

☞ **Context**

This phrase means to have a lot, even though what you have might not be valuable. In conversation (1), B has a lot of money, over ten thousand yuan at the least. Of course, it is possible that B is just bragging. In conversation (2), B is like a teacher and teacher doesn't make much money. So B says that he doesn't have anything else, but B does have some flexible time to help A. However, B may not have as much time as the phrase suggests. When you hear someone say "plenty", don't always believe it a hundred percent.

古语：绰绰有裕 // 《诗经·小雅·角弓》
雅语：不计其数
类语：多的是

1 给自己面子
Saving Your Face

1.2
在均势中
Equal to Others

包在我身上

[Just leave it all to me.]

对话 Conversation

① A：晚上你买菜、做饭、接孩子啊！

Will you shop, do the cooking and pick up the child this evening?

B：包在我身上。

Sure, just leave it all to me.

② A：我刚来北京，什么都不懂，还要找工作，找房子，找爱情……

I just moved to Beijing, so I don't know what's going on yet. But I have to look for a job, find a place to stay, and find a lover.

B：包在我身上。

Don't worry, just leave it all to me.

语境

汉语口语中用"包"字的地方不少。大概意思均为"全部、彻底、周到、保证"之类，而且总是拍着胸膛说出的。但恳请听者及有时听有时也说的人，都不要信以为真，自欺欺人。"吹牛"是很多人尤其是男人的特点。"吹"的目的，当然是为了有"面子"。在①中事情不困难，但话讲得太满，难保全部兑现。在②中，就肯定是说大话了。可叹这些吹牛的人只顾一时"面子"上好看，但"吹"过之后，也就忘了。如无特殊理由，倒也不必提醒。

☞ **Context**

The idea of "taking on all the jobs" is used in many situations. It means a fundamental promise to complete something, to be thorough, thoughtful, or guarantee something. When people use this phrase and promise something, you shouldn't necessarily believe it. They can deceive themselves as well as others. Men like to brag about their ability to take care of it all in order to keep their face. In conversation (1), these are small things and are not hard to complete, but there are perhaps too many jobs so it is possible that he will not be able to fulfill his promise. In conversation (2), B talks big. Sadly these people will forget what they promised very quickly. If there are no specific reasons, you shouldn't remind them at all.

古语：舍我其谁也 // 《孟子·公孙丑下》
雅语：没有问题
类语：擎好吧　我办事你放心　交给我吧　不算什么

1.2.2>

别价
[Don't be that way.]

☺ 对话 Conversation

① A：老李呀，今儿这顿饭我结了啊！

　　Old Li, I am going to pay for this evening's dinner!

　 B：别价呀！别价别价，说好了我请客的！

　　No, don't be that way. We've agreed that this is my treat.

② A：老李啊，你的论文还没够数，所以职称的事我们也没替你报名。

　　Old Li, since you don't have enough degrees to qualify for a higher position, I didn't enter your name in the application.

　B：别价！等了5年了，够不够也得报啊！

　　Please don't be that way, I have waited for five years. Even though I don't have enough degrees, I would like to apply for a higher position.

 ## 语境

　　这句话的意思是：我不同意这样。在用法上大概有两种：一种是礼貌地争抢。如在①中：中国人在饭馆吃完饭后抢着付钱的场面，早已成为一种景观。外国人横竖不明白，中国人不得不照旧，因为这是"面子"问题，谁也不能露出想"白吃"的意思来。一种是愤怒的制止，如在②中，不少知识分子为了职称睡不着觉，个别人甚至要死要活。在那种时候说出的"别价"，当然是异常坚决的了。

Context

　　This sentence means that the speaker does not agree. It has been used here in two occasions. The first use is a polite competition common among Chinese, as in conversation (1) where two people vie with each other to pay for a meal at a restaurant. These competitions have become a sightseeing event for foreigners. Foreigners don't understand, but Chinese remain unchanged. This is because Chinese people like to keep their faces, they don't want other people to think of them as being cheap. Another occasion would be to strongly disagree in order to stop someone from doing something. We see this in conversation (2), where so many scholars lose sleep over a desperate competition for professional rank and titles. In this case, "don't" implies a very strong disagreement.

古语：急击勿失 //《史记·项羽本纪》
雅语：不要不要
类语：那哪成啊

1.2.3>

别拦着我
[Don't try to stop me.]

😊 对话 Conversation

① A：老李啊，有事慢慢商量嘛，不一定上法院。

Old Li, this can be settled through discussion. You don't have to go to court.

B：别拦着我！上法院就完了？我还得去电视台呢！

Don't try to stop me! Going to court is just the beginning. I will speak out on television!

② A：老李啊，你想开点，别干傻事！

Old Li, please don't be so stubborn about it and do something silly.

B：别拦着我！我一定要死给他们看！

Don't try to stop me! I will fight to the death and then they'll see!

 **语境**

　　当两方面发生矛盾冲突时，有的人喜欢用"扩大事态"来吓唬对方。这种做法的前提是：自己什么都不怕，对方却有一些顾虑。在①中，B说要去这去那，是想通过公开曝光让对方没"面子"。在②中，B用的是"最后一招"，通过"要自杀"来争取大家的同情，迫使对方让步。当然，真

想死也不怕死的人比较少。说"别拦着我"，就是希望有人阻拦。要不然怎么下台呢？

 Context

When people have conflicts, some like to "ramp up the situation" in an effort to scare the other party. If you want to do so, the premise behind such a move should be that you are not afraid of anything, but the other party has some misgivings. In conversation (1), B wants to take the matter to the "court" of public opinion and embarrass the other party. In conversation (2), B threatens to commit suicide in order to win sympathy from the public and force the other party to give way. Certainly, there are not many people who want to die like this. When they say "don't try to stop me even to my death", they hope that someone will stop them before it gets that far. If not, how can they get out of an embarrassing situation?

古语：大王必欲急臣，臣头今与璧俱碎于柱矣。//《史记·
　　　廉颇蔺相如列传》
雅语：不要阻止我
类语：别管我

1.2.4>

怪不得呢
[No wonder...]

☺ 对话 Conversation

① A：哎！老李因为贪污罪被抓走了！
　　Hey, Old Li was arrested for embezzlement.

B：怪不得呢！我一直纳闷，他买奔驰车的钱是从哪儿来的！

No wonder! That explains why he was able to buy a Mercedes-Benz.

② A：你们快来看哪！小红的妈妈是日本人！

Come here quickly and look at this! Xiao Hong's mother is Japanese!

B：怪不得呢！我说她的日语怎么那么好！

No wonder she could speak fluent Japanese.

 ## 语境

生活中可能有些人和事让人纳闷，有的人不大注意，有的人却喜欢提出问题，寻找答案。如果后来事实说明了某些原因，那么那些喜欢猜想的人，就会觉得很有"面子"。因为，他们早就注意到了什么。

 ## Context

In daily life, there are some people or some things that make you wonder about. Some people don't pay much attention, but others like to ask questions and seek answers. For the second group of people, if the final facts explain their original thoughts, they feel some satisfaction because they paid attention to it long ago.

古语：怪道呢，原来爬上高枝儿去了，把我们不放在眼里。

// 《红楼梦·二十七回》

雅语：难怪

类语：我说呢

还行

[not too bad]

对话 Conversation

① A：老李！好久不见，最近身体好吗？
Old Li, I haven't seen you for a while, how is your health?

B：噢，还行。
Oh, not too bad.

② A：老李呀，你们公司的经营状况怎么样？
Old Li, how is your company doing recently?

B：啊，还行。
Ah, it's not too bad.

语境

这是一句很灵活，很巧妙的答话。一、它很"中庸"，可好可坏。二、信息量是零。三、99%的评估类问话都可以用它回答。四、问话人不好再问。比如在①和②中，A都想得到一些真实的情况，可是在"还行"面前，A很难继续追问，所以只好打住；因为很多人说"还行"的含意是：不想与你具体谈。

Context

This is a flexible and clever answer for a number of reasons. First, because it is neutral, it can be good or bad. Second, because it contains no real information. Third, because it can be used for ninety-nine percent of the questions most people ask. And fourth, because it can often stop people from asking any further questions. For example, in both conversation (1) and (2), A would like to gain some more detailed information about the situation, but cannot continue to ask after A answers "not too bad", because this sentence means they don't want to go into any detail about the situation.

古语：古人贵朝闻夕死，况君前途尚可。//《世说新语·自新》
雅语：马马虎虎
类语：还可以　还成　还过得去

1.2.6>

看怎么说了
[That depends.]

对话 Conversation

① A：老李，你对这件事有什么看法？
　　Old Li, what do you think about this thing?

　B：这件事啊，看怎么说了。
　　It depends on how you look at it.

② A：老李啊，听说你支持老张他们！
　　Old Li, I have heard that you support Old Zhang and his group.

　B：没有的事，那得看怎么说了。
　　Not necessarily, it depends.

语境

发生一件事情，总有各方面的因素。分析一个问题，也有不同的角度。所以，有时一个人会这样说，换个地方，他又会那样说。这也是正常的，如在①中。但是有的人不是这种情况，或者吞吞吐吐，或者见人说人话，见鬼说鬼话，看风使船。这种人表面上看挺公平，实际上一是显示自己看问题很全面，二是谁也不想得罪。这就有点问题了，如在②中。俗话说：做人难。大概指的就是不能轻易地表明态度吧。

Context

There are various factors that determine what happens. There are also different angles from which to analyze a situation. Thus, it should come as no surprise that someone could speak one way about something from one perspective and a different way from another perspective. This is the case in conversation (1). But some people "speak one word and swallow the next word" or speak according to circumstances. They want to show that they examine the question in its entirety, and at the same time, offer offence to no one. This is the case in conversation (2). When people say that it is hard to get along with everyone, it could mean simply that you cannot let other people know what you think about things.

古语： 但摸棱以持两端可矣 //《旧唐书·苏味道传》
雅语： 换言之
类语： 话说回来

另想着儿吧
[Try another way out of difficulty.]

😊 对话 Conversation

① **A：老板，人家不同意咱们的方案。**
Boss, they don't agree with our proposal.

B：那就另想着儿吧。
Then we'll have to try another plan.

② **A：老大，他对吃喝玩乐不感兴趣。**
Boss, he is not interested in any kind of entertainment.

B：奇怪，那就另想着儿吧。
That's strange! Let's think of some other way out of this.

 语境

　　"着儿"原来指下棋的一步。在①中指计划，在②中指伎俩。虽然不同，意思都是：换一条路走。在社会上的各种人事关系中，有的"着儿"是对的，有的"着儿"是错的。有时是需要的，有时是不需要的。很多人把心思放在"着儿"上，使简单的事情复杂起来，却忘记了根本的东西。

 Context

　　This phrase was used for playing chess. It means "plan" in conversation (1) and "trick" in conversation (2). Although they are different, they are all attempts to find another way out of a difficult situation. There are "correct" ways to deal with personal connections and "wrong" ways as well. Sometimes we need plans and tricks and sometimes we do not need them. There are a lot of people who think too hard about planning strategies to deal with others. They make a simple thing more complicated and overlook the basic nature of human relations.

古语：宜别图之 // 《资治通鉴·六十五卷》
雅语：改弦易辙
类语：换个方式

1.2.8>

哪能啊
[How can that be true?]

对话 Conversation

① A：老李呀，听说你 20 年来一直对我有意见？
Old Li, I heard you have complained about me for the past twenty years?

B：哪能啊，我根本不了解你。
How can that be true? I even don't know you very well.

② A：哎，听说明年地球得爆炸！
Hey, I heard that the earth is going to come to an end next year!

B：哪能啊！你听那些干吗？
How can that be true? Why do you listen to this kind of news?

 语境

"哪能啊"，是"不可能"的意思，但是也有不同的情况。在①中，老

李对自己的老同事说"根本不了解",这本身就是"不可能"的。所以,老李在这里是用反问的口气在否认事实,目的是避免矛盾。②中的情况比较简单,地球肯定早晚会毁灭,但是那不是哪个人可以预料的。所以,明年的爆炸绝对是不可能的。

 ## Context

This phrase means that something is "highly unlikely" to be true. But it can also be used for other situations. In conversation (1), it is impossible for Old Li not to know a lot about his colleague of twenty years. So, he answered the question with a question in order to deny complaining and avoid a problem. Conversation (2) is simple, the earth will end some day but no one is able to predict it. Hence, it is impossible to know it will end tomorrow.

古语:不可,吾既已言之王矣 // 《墨子·公输》
雅语:绝无可能
类语:怎么会呢

1.2.9>

那有什么难的
[It's not that hard.]

😊 对话 Conversation

① A:哎,考研可难了!尤其是英语和政治!
　　Oh, I heard that the examinations for graduate school are very hard, especially the ones for English and politics.

　 B:那有什么难的,只要下功夫。
　　It's not that hard if you study well; you must put in a lot of effort in it.

② A：做买卖太难了，谈来谈去也成不了一笔。

It is too hard to make a business deal.

B：那有什么难的，只要你有诚意。

It's not that hard if you show your good faith.

 ## 语境

　　每个人的面前都有困难，其中最可怕的，就是自身的畏难情绪。考研难，做生意难，做女人难。可是做男人就容易吗？前几年连找公共厕所还难呢！如果你把所有的难都当困难看，那就没法活了。①B的话很对，老老实实地做学问，踏踏实实地做人，再难也不难。

📖 Context

Everyone has to face some difficult situations, but the biggest fear comes from a lack of confidence. Passing examinations for graduate school is hard, doing business is hard, and being a woman is also hard. But, it is not easy to be a man either. At one time it was even hard to find a public W.C. in China. If you call all of these things difficulties, you cannot live in the world. In coversatoin (1), B's answers are correct. You can overcome all of life's difficulties if you do things honestly and sincerely and in a through going manner.

古语：同恶相求，如市贾焉，何难？//《左传·昭公十三年》
雅语：不过如此
类语：那算什么

你怎么不早说呀
[Why didn't you tell me earlier?]

☺ 对话 Conversation

① A：帮我搞两张"天鹅湖"的票好吗？

Can you find two tickets for Swan Lake?

B：你怎么不早说呀！刚才我手里还有10张！

Why didn't you ask me earlier, I had ten tickets a short while ago?

② A：这件事情要是照我的意思做就好了！

It would be better if we did it my way.

B：你怎么不早说呀！现在说什么也没用了。

Why didn't you say that earlier? It is not useful to say that now.

 ## 语境

　　这是一句在"事后"经常用的话。在①中，B手里已经没有票，他不说抱歉，反倒怪A说晚了，还得让A知道，他是很有办法的人。在②中，情况更复杂。几个领导商量事情，总有不同意见，也只能用一种，后来事情没做好，肯定有人说②中A的话。其实，可能是A当时没说；或者可能是A说了，B们没重视；也可能是虽然说了，但是没有坚持。反正大家都在推卸责任。A是要表明自己早就正确，B是讨厌A说那种不负责任的话。

 **Context**

    This is a sentence usually used after something has already happened. In conversation (1), B doesn't have any more tickets, but B doesn't feel sorry about it because A didn't tell him he wanted some earlier. B would still like A to see that he is a very capable person. Conversation (2) is a more complicated case. Several leaders meet together and usually disagree with each other. If something didn't get completed as well as it could have, one of them would complain much as A complains in the example. In fact, there are several possibilities: one is that A didn't say anything in the beginning; second, that A said something, but no one listened; and third, that A said something but didn't insist on others following his suggestions. However, everyone in this example is shirking responsibility and shifting the blame onto others. A wants to show that he was correct from the beginning. B is disgusted by A's late complaint.

古语：吾既已言之王矣 //《墨子·公输》
雅语：何不早说
类语：你早干什么来着

1.2.11>

求人不如求己
[It would be better to do it by yourself instead of asking for other people's help.]

☺ 对话 Conversation

① A：你为什么自己修理水龙头?
    Why did you fix the faucet by yourself?

B：嗨，找人修又麻烦又花钱，求人不如求己。

It's better to do it yourself than depend on others for help or spend money to have it done.

② **A：我们的国家没有国际上的帮助不行。**

Our country cannot get along without the help of other countries.

B：不对！求人不如求己。

I disagree with that approach. It's better to depend on our own resources.

 ## 语境

　　自己有了麻烦，碰到困难，首先想到的是什么？是马上找朋友帮忙，还是自己想办法克服。这个问题很重要。如果你什么事都麻烦朋友，那么再好的朋友也会烦。如果你自己通过坚持和努力，最后克服了困难，那么你会得到大家的称赞，得到真正的"面子"。当然，我们需要外部的支援，但是自己的坚持和努力才是根本。

 ## Context

　　This is an important issue. When you have difficulty or trouble, the question is whether you should first try to overcome the thing by yourself or ask others for help. If you ask for help from your friends all the time, they will become tired of you. If you try hard and overcome the problems on your own, you will receive praise and win status. Of course, we need the support of others, but we should try our best to accomplish things ourselves first.

古语：君子求诸己，小人求诸人。//《论语·卫灵公》

雅语：自力更生

类语：我自己能行　我不想麻烦别人

受不了
[I can't stand it.]

对话 Conversation

① B：北京的污染太严重了，真受不了！

The pollution in Beijing is so bad that I can't stand it.

A：正在治理，过两年就好了

They are making efforts to improve it. It should be better in a couple of years.

② B：半年吃不到可口的食物，真受不了！

It has been half a year since we've had anything tasty to eat. I can't stand it anymore.

A：你会习惯的。

You'll get used to it.

③ B：他每天半夜两点唱卡拉 OK，我受不了了！

He sings karaoke until two o'clock in the morning. It's unbearable.

A：忍着点吧。

You'd better put up with it.

语境

为什么大家喜欢用这句话呢？一是让人受不了的事情还比较多；二是自己身上的毛病也比较多，所以有些本来受得了的情况，到了他们身上也就成了难以忍受的事，这第三也许更重要，那就是经常表达"受不了"，大概会给旁人造成一种印象，即：这个人是比较高贵的和比较有个性的。当然，表达"受不了"之后该怎么做，那是另外的事，另有一句话叫做：受不了也得受。

 ## Context

    Why do people still like this phrase? One reason is that there are still many things that we feel we can't put up with. A second reason is that we all have some weaknesses concerning one thing or another and are unable to endure the hardships associated with them. A third reason may be the most important one. If someone always says they "can't stand something", it may be to impress others with their elite character. Of course, the question is what you are going to do to deal with the reality after you've already said you "can't stand it". The other side of this phrase is that "even if you can't stand it you have to put up with it."

古语：君将不堪 //《左传·隐公元年》
雅语：无法忍受
类语：太难受了　挺不住了

1.2.13>

说句公道话
[Be fair.]

对话 Conversation

① A：老李总是找我麻烦，我恨死他了。
Old Li is always looking for trouble, I hate him.

B：说句公道话，老李也是为了工作。

Be fair, his actions also contribute to the work.

② **A：是他的车撞了我！**

His car ran into me!

B：谁让你逆行的？

Why did you go in the wrong direction?

C：说句公道话，你们俩都有责任。

Be fair, you both bear some of the responsibility.

 ## 语境

讲这句话的条件，是两个人有矛盾，请你来裁判谁对谁错。"公道"是"公正"的意思，指你要站在中间，不能偏向一方，如在①中。但是，主持公道是很难的。在②中，C就不能，或者不想明辨是非。他说"都有责任"，大概是想从双方都得到好处吧，如果你碰上这种法官，那就倒霉了。

 ## Context

This phrase is usually used to restore some balance to a disagreement. Whoever would judge who is right and who is wrong has to be just and fair and cannot be partial to either side. This is the case in conversation (1). But, it is very hard to be fair for conversation (2). C can't make a clear decision about who is right or wrong, so he says that both parties have some responsibilities. He may want to take some advantages from both sides. It would be bad luck to experience this kind of judge.

古语：楚将伐齐，鲁亲之，齐王患之。张丐曰："臣请令鲁中立。"//《战国策·齐一》

雅语：平心而论

类语：说句良心话

说真的
[Tell the truth.]

😊 对话 Conversation

① A：说真的，你到底爱不爱她？
Tell the truth, do you really love her?

B：不骗你，我每天都想她。
I am not kidding you, I think of her every day.

② A：说真的，你喜欢这个地方吗？
Tell me the truth, do you like this place?

B：说实话，谈不上喜欢。
To tell the truth, I don't like it.

③ A：说真的，你的汉语水平怎么样？
Tell me the truth, how is your Chinese?

B：我发誓，所有留学生里我是最好的。
I swear that I'm the best of all the international students.

👉 语境

在汉语口语中，"说真的"这类话比较多。为什么呢？是不是因为"说假的"的时候更多呢！很多人习惯在交谈的时候"绕弯子"，绕来绕去，离题越来越远。这时其中一方有些着急，就会逼问，另一方也只好亮出底牌，例如在①和②中。可是还是有"不真"的情况，例如在③中，就好像还是假的。所以这句话实际上只是起到强调的作用。

 # Context

    This sentence is used quite often in Chinese conversation. The reason is that people tend to stray from the subject under discussion. Sometimes one party will feel anxious and force a direct answer by using this phrase. The other party will have to tell the truth or "put their cards on the table". This is the case for both conversation (1) and (2). But, sometimes you still can't get the real answer. Just as in conversation (3), you are unsure whether what is said is the truth. Hence, this just functions to accentuate whatever is said.

古语：握手出肺肝相示 // 韩愈《柳子厚墓志铭》
雅语：实话实说
类语：说心里话　说实话　不骗你　我发誓

1.2.15>

听说
[I heard that...]

😊 对话 Conversation

① A：听说，经理的妻子跟别人跑了！
    I heard that our manager's wife has run away with another.

  B：听谁说的？
    Who told you this?

② A：听说李老师的论文是请人写的！

I heard that someone else wrote Professor Li's thesis.

B：别瞎说。

That's sheer nonsense!

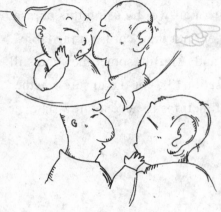

☞ **语境**

有的人不仅喜欢"小道消息""内部新闻"，更习惯于议论同事、朋友们的私生活，并添油加醋地再转告其他人。凡此种种，没有人会说是自己"亲眼看到的"！又要有面子，又怕负责任，这是人之常情。"知情"有面子，"乱讲"要负责。两全其美的办法，就是用"听说"来交待"信息源"，推卸"主要责任"。一旦追查紧了，就一口咬定是从厕所那一边听说的。

 Context

Some people not only like to pay attention to rumors and insider stories, but also like to talk about other people's private lives. And when they do, they exaggerate the rumors they spread. In almost all of these cases, nobody can give an eyewitness account of the incident. They want to keep their face and are afraid of being held responsible for the story. It's only human nature and satisfies both parties. If anyone asks the source of the rumor, you can say you do not know. If they want to trace a rumor to its source, you can state categorically that you heard it while in the washroom.

古语：臣闻之 // 《孟子·梁惠王上》

雅语：据说

类语：人家都说

1 / 给自己面子 Saving Your Face

1.2 / 在均势中 / Equal to Others

1.2.16>

我认了
[I accept it as unavoidable.]

😊 对话 Conversation

① A：你那天买的股票，一直跌到今天！
   The stocks that you bought the other day dropped sharply.

   B：我认了！
   I cannot change anything now!

② A：你和那个男人在一起不会幸福的！
   You won't be happy if you stay with that man!

   B：我认了！
   Whatever!

③ A：你这样生活下去怎么行呢？
   You cannot live like this.

   B：我认了。
   There is no other way around it.

👉 语境

　　"我认了"这句话在①中，是不认输也不行，但是并没有失去信心。在②中是固执，意思是：我自己的事，谁也别管。在③中表示：只能这样，没有别的办法。这三种用法不一样，目的都是为了保住"面子"。但是，也使事情更麻烦。

☞ **Context**

In conversation (1), B has to admit his loss, but still trusts in the future. In conversation (2), B persists in her own opinion and doesn't want to hear anything. In conversation (3), there is the only way; there is no other way around the situation. Even though the three cases are different, they are all about keeping one's face. Sometimes, this attitude can make the situation worse.

古语： 此乃天也 // 《资治通鉴·六十五卷》
雅语： 听天由命
类语： 没脾气　这是天意　我认头

1.2.17>

无所谓
[It doesn't matter.]

☺ **对话 Conversation**

① A：昨天你借给我的自行车丢了。
　　I lost the bicycle that you lent me yesterday.

　B：无所谓。
　　It doesn't matter.

② A：老板说你不会做事，要辞退你。
　　The boss said you aren't qualified for this job and he's going to fire you.

B：无所谓。

I don't care.

 语境

　　很多人喜欢用"无所谓"来表示自己的老练，其实说这话是为了保持自己的"面子"，是要向身边的人显示自己根本不会被某事伤害。人们在生活中都会碰到不愉快的事情，可能在意，也可能不在意。但是，较多的情况是不太舒服或很不舒服。这时，不少知情者会暗自高兴！为了装作没有受伤，为了不被别人笑话，就有了这句遮羞的"无所谓"。

 Context

　　Many people use this sentence to show they are experienced. In fact, they are using this phrase to maintain their faces and show off their strength. Nothing could hurt them anymore. In our life, people normally run into some unhappy things, some people take them to heart and others don't. Even the people who don't take these things to heart are still somewhat uncomfortable, or very uncomfortable about it. Under these circumstances, the people who know the truth can be secretly happy. This sentence is created for people who want to avoid other people laughing at them and to cover up their embarrassment.

古语：无伤也。// 《孟子·梁惠王上》
雅语：无关紧要
类语：不在乎　没关系

走着瞧
[Wait and see.]

😊 对话 Conversation

① **A：你已经输了三盘棋，还不服气吗？**
   You've already lost three games in the set. Do you still want to play?

　B：别高兴得太早了，走着瞧！
   Don't celebrate too early, just wait and see.

② **A：看你小小年纪，我就饶了你吧。**
   You look so young, I'll let you off this time.

　B：少来这一套，走着瞧！
   Cut it out, just you wait and see!

👉 语境

　　"走着瞧"这句话，经常用在某事已经失败，但不愿承认，并宣布以后还要决战的场合。为什么输了以后还嘴硬呢？又是"面子"问题。如果输了以后说"走着瞧"，那就表示将来还会赢，会把暂时丢了的"面子"，加倍地找回来。

👉 Context

　　Someone who has suffered a loss or defeat usually uses this sentence. They refuse to admit they've lost and promise another more decisive battle later. Why are people so stubborn and reluctant to admit defeat? It is related to their "face" and dignity. If you lose once but still say "wait and see", it shows that it is still possible to win later. And if you do, then, you also win back your dignity and face.

古语：子姑待之 // 《左传·隐公元年》
雅语：来日方长
类语：等着瞧　骑驴看唱本

1 给自己面子
Saving Your Face

1.3
在弱势中
Weaker than Others

1.3.1>

爱谁谁
[no matter who or what]

☺ 对话 Conversation

① A：老李，你的做法真的不好，所以大家都反对。

Old Li, Your way of doing things is really not very good, so we all disagree with you.

B：爱谁谁！我就这样。

It doesn't matter whether you agree with me or not, this is just my way.

② A：老李，别在马路上躺着了，汽车会轧死你！

Old Li, please don't lie on the street, a car will run you over and kill you.

B：爱谁谁！警察来了也没用！

No matter who tries to stop me, even the police, I will still lie here.

☞ 语境

"爱谁谁"，是"不管他是谁（我也不怕）"的意思。这是一句无赖专用语，在①中，B的坚持只是为了自己的"面子"。在②中，B已经无赖到疯狂的程度，好像天老大，他老二似的。当然，我们也不用担心，因为警笛一响，B的酒就全醒了。

☞ Context

This sentence means that the speaker is not afraid of anybody or anything. It is specially used when someone acts shamelessly. In conversation (1), B says this to keep his face. In conversation (2), B is not acting rationally and is not afraid of anything. Of course, we don't have to worry about B. The police siren will soon sober him up.

古语：毛遂按剑而前曰："王之所以叱遂者，以楚国之众也。
今十步之内，王不得恃楚国之众也，王之命悬于遂
手。吾君在前，叱者何也？"//《史记·平原君列传》
雅语：不管他是谁
类语：爱谁是谁

1.3.2>

板儿板儿的
[It is guaranteed.]

☺ 对话 Conversation

① A：我让你做的事儿怎样了？
How is the project?

B：老板放心，板儿板儿的！
Don't worry boss. It's guaranteed.

② A：这件事非常复杂，你都考虑好了吗？
This thing is really complex. Have you taken everything into account?

B：我的领导呀，当然是板儿板儿的！
Boss! Of course, it's all under control.

 语境

这句话有两个出处：一指"响板"，是用音乐节奏比喻事情安排好了。

二指"木板上钉进钉子"，是用无法改变来比喻事情已经落实。两种比喻的意思都是肯定。这句话一般是回答上级的询问时用。但是，如果你是上级，请别轻信。因为这句话里很可能有夸张的成分，因为很多人只是自我感觉良好，没有逻辑推理与事实根据。

 ## Context

    This phrase has two sources: one is from castanets; using musical rhythm to assure that everything has been settled on time. The second source is from driving a nail into wood, and means something is certain. This is especially used when people answer to higher authorities. But if you are in higher position of responsibility, please don't readily believe this response. It is an inflated use of language based more on how people feel, and not on an analysis of the facts.

古语：破操军必矣 // 《资治通鉴·六十五卷》
雅语：毫无疑义
类语：没问题　搞定　拿下

1.3.3>

别跟我过不去啊
[Please don't make things difficult for me.]

😊 对话 Conversation

① A：老李同志，别跟我过不去啊！这十个公章能不能少盖两个？
    Comrade Li, please don't make things more difficult for me. Can't you just stamp the letter with eight official seals?

  B：不成！一个都不能少！
    No, I have to stamp the letters with all ten seals.

② A：老李呀，咱们过去虽然有点矛盾，也别跟我过不去啊！

Old Li, although we had some disagreements before, please don't make things difficult for me.

B：怎么会呢？这是公事公办！你这事绝对不行！

Business is business. I have to follow the rules.

 ## 语境

这句话，是受到某种对待后表示不满用的。意思是：不要给我出难题。换句话是：你就让我"通过"吧。这句话的背景大概有两个。一、刁难性的。如在①中：谁都害怕四处盖公章，所以A求老李照顾一下，老李当然不会让A那么省事。二、报复性的。如在②中：老李是等到了一个收拾A的机会。①中的A多跑几趟也就成了。②中可就没那么简单了，老李永远也不会让A"过去"。

 ## Context

Someone who is not content with the way someone else is handling things would use this sentence. It means: don't make things harder or more troublesome. There are two backgrounds for its use: Situations where someone deliberately makes things difficult, as in conversation (1). No one likes official seals everywhere on a document, so A asks Old Li to stamp it fewer times. Of course, Old Li won't make things simple for A. But, if A visits Old Li many times, the task can be achieved. The second situation is one of revenge. In conversation (2), Old Li has been waiting for an opportunity to punish A for earlier problems. Here it is impossible to avoid the resulting difficulties, no matter how hard A might try.

古语：相逢狭路间，道隘不容车。// 古乐府《相逢行》

雅语：心存芥蒂

类语：别和我作对　　放我一马吧　　您高抬贵手

1.3.4>

不甘心
[won't give up]

对话 Conversation

① A：你就比他慢半步，没得第一！

You were only a half step too slow to win first place.

B：唉！我实在不甘心！

Oh, I really can't accept failing.

② A：听说老李等了她一辈子！

I heard that Old Li has been waiting for her all his life.

B：是啊，老李是死不甘心哪！

You're right. Old Li won't give her up.

语境

"甘"有"满意"和"自愿"两种意思。在①中，B失掉金牌，很不服气，认为再比一次肯定赢，这是为了"面子"。在②中，老李只有等到所爱的人，心里才能舒服，那是自我的选择。

Context

This word has two meanings: "Contented or satisfied with" and "be willing to". In conversation (1), B was just a little too slow to win the gold medal and he is not satisfied with failing. B thinks he will win if he has another chance. This response also restores some of B's dignity. In conversation (2),

Old Li will wait until someone he loves comes to him. This is his choice and he is willing to wait for love.

古语：不忍为之下 //《史记·廉颇蔺相如列传》
雅语：死不瞑目
类语：不服气　不甘休

1.3.5>

不是故意的

[I didn't do it on purpose (it was an accident).]

☺ 对话 Conversation

① A：哎呀，把你的裙子弄脏了，我可不是故意的。
　　My God, I dirtied your skirt. I didn't do it on purpose.

　B：没关系。
　　No problem.

② A：对不起，我和你的女朋友好了，但真不是故意的。
　　I am sorry I dated your girl friend. But I didn't do it intentionally.

　B：……！

 语境

　　"故意"是"有意"，"不是故意的"就是"无意"的。在①中，因为没看见，或者不小心，这可以原谅。在②中，A明明知道那是B的女朋友，还那么做，这就不是"无意"，而是"有意"，甚至"蓄意"了。不管是有意的还是无意的，做了错事，然后又用这句话来逃避责任。都会让人看不起，是最没有"面子"的无赖行为。

 # Context

"Intentional" is when someone makes a conscious decision to do something. "Unintentional" is when someone does something they do not intend, like an accident. In conversation (1), A either didn't see or was careless, so this incident can be easily forgiven. In conversation (2), it is obvious that A knew that the girl was B's girlfriend, but he still took her out on a date. This is not an innocent accident but an intentional action to hurt B. No matter whether an action is intentional or not intentional, if someone does something wrong and uses this sentence as a way of shirking responsibility, it is wrong.

> 古语：夫我乃行之，反而求之，不得吾心。//《孟子·梁
> 　　　惠王上》
> 雅语：误会
> 类语：我不知道啊　一不小心　一不留神

1.3.6>

凑合点儿吧
[to make do with it]

☺ 对话 Conversation

① A：大中午的，就吃方便面哪！

It's lunchtime, do we have to eat these instant noodles?

B：没钱了！你凑合点儿吧。

Since we don't have any money, they will have to do.

② A：亲爱的，先凑合几年吧，以后我们会有房子、车子和你想要的一切。

　Dearest, please don't ask for too much this year. I will buy whatever you want, like a house and a car, when I have money.

　B：对不起，我一天也过不下去了！再见吧。

　I'm sorry; I can't stand this kind of life anymore. Goodbye.

 ## 语境

　　每个人都有理想，要实现，就得努力。在努力的过程中，什么都是苦的。面对艰苦，你要忍受，当你习惯了忍受，你就懂得了生活，同时明白了"凑合"。这么长历史，这么多人，那么多麻烦，那么多矛盾，不"凑合"，行吗？理想呢？在天堂。到了天堂，还得"凑合"。

Context

　　Everyone has dreams, but you have to work hard to make them real. It could be a painful process with many difficult circumstances. If you learn to be tolerant and work hard, you will begin to understand life. At the same time, you will understand what it is to "make do with it". Over a long history, there are many people, many troubles, and many conflicts. We have to learn how to make do with whatever we have. Dreams may be in heaven, but even there one may have to make do with what they have.

古语：吾子忍之 // 《左传·成公二年》

雅语：苟且偷生　得过且过

类语：别要求太高　将就点吧　这就不错了

1.3.7>

放不下
[cannot relinquish]

😊 对话 Conversation

① **A：我死以后，别的都好说，就是家产放不下！**
I really can't give up my family property after I pass away.

  B：你要是跟葛朗台似的，就不要死。
If you want to be Grandet, you just have to live forever.

② **A：我可以不当领导，但是很多工作放不下呀！**
I don't have to be a leader, but there are a lot of responsibilities that I can't relinquish control over.

  B：你永远当领导，永远有事情做。
If you keep these responsibilities, you will always have to be a leader.

👉 语境

　　"放不下"专门指不愿意放弃自己的金钱、权力之类。就像在①和②中，因为得来不易，所以放弃更难，这是可以理解的。可是谁都有走下坡路的那一天，放不下，也得放。中国有句俗语：该放手时须放手。还有一句格言：生不带来，死不带去。都是很有道理的。

👉 Context

　　This phrase means that someone doesn't want to give up their money or power. In conversations (1) and (2), since the possessions and power have not come easily, it is difficult to give them up. This attitude is understandable, but everyone has to get older and relinquish things from their earlier life. Even though you don't want to give up anything, you have to. There are some good Chinese sayings that come from this idea. When it is time to give up, you should give up. Human beings are born with nothing, and when they die, they will not take anything with them either. These are profound truths.

古语：忍不能予 //《史记·淮阴侯列传》
雅语：死不瞑目
类语：不放心　撒不开手

1.3.8>

你少管我
[Please don't try to control me.]

😊 对话 Conversation

① A：小红，你每天都回来那么晚，妈妈不放心！
Xiao Hong, Mom is very worried about your coming home so late every night.

B：妈——，你少管我！
Mom, please don't try to control me.

② A：小红，那个老家伙不是好人，你别理他！
Xiao Hong, that old guy is not a good person, you shouldn't talk to him.

B：你是我的什么人？你少管我！
Who are you? Please don't tell me what to do.

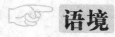 **语境**

在①中，是女儿对妈妈说。在②中，是姑娘对男朋友说。

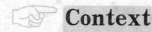 **Context**

In conversation (1), a daughter responds to her mother's concern. In conversation (2), a girl responds to her boyfriend.

古语：有复言令长安君为质者，老妇必唾其面！//《战国策·
　　赵策四》
雅语：不劳费心
类语：你管得太多了吧　　你省点心吧

1.3.9>

挤对谁呢
[Stop badgering me.]

😊 **对话 Conversation**

① A：老李呀，你走路怎么一拐一拐的，是不是有一条腿短哪？
　　Old Li, you walk with a limp. Is one leg shorter than the other one?

　B：挤对谁呢？你腿脚才有问题呢！
　　Stop badgering me. It must be your leg that has a problem!

② A：老李呀，你很少下馆子吃饭吧？
　　Old Li, I see you cannot afford to eat at restaurants very often.

　B：挤对谁呢？昨儿我刚在长城饭店大吃了一顿！
　　Stop badgering me. I had a feast at the Great Wall Hotel just yesterday.

语境

"挤对"是欺负人的意思，多指用语言来让对方没"面子"。在运用方式上，很有一些讲究。比如，你不能明说，而要"暗说"。如在①中，A表面上关心老李的健康，其实是故意气老李。在②中，情况更典型：是用"话里有话"来"挤对"人。话里的意思：你是舍不得下馆子吃饭的小气鬼！老李听出了这个意思，所以立刻反击。注意：用语言"挤对"人是一种艺术，它的最高水平是：被"挤对"的对象还没什么反应，可在场的人都听出来了，脸上也都带出来了。

Context

This sentence is used when someone tries to find fault with you. The person criticizing is trying to make the other person lose "face" through words. However, this must usually be used very carefully. For example, you cannot be too explicit, but cover the criticism in an underhanded way. In conversation (1), A is only superficially concerned with Old Li's health, and makes Li angry on purpose. Conversation (2) is a typical case, A is insinuating that Old Li is cheap, but never says so. The insinuation is designed into the remark. Old Li caught on at once, and he strikes back right away. Using phrases and sentences like this to insult others is an art. Even though everyone understands the insulting insinuation, because the listener has to keep his or her dignity, they can't respond directly.

古语：嫂蛇行匍伏，四拜自跪谢。苏秦曰："嫂，何前倨而后卑也？"嫂曰："以季子之位尊而多金。"苏秦曰："嗟乎！贫穷则父母不子，富贵则亲戚畏惧。人生世上，势位富贵，盍可忽乎哉！"// 《战国策·秦一》

雅语：讽刺

类语：糟改谁呢　埋汰谁呢

可话又说回来
[Let's go back to the original topic.]

😊 对话 Conversation

① A: **老李啊，你和大家的矛盾，要跳出来看，从大局去想，不要太小心眼啦。**

Old Li, we have to resolve your disagreement with everyone. You should open your mind, take the whole situation into account.

B: **领导啊，你刚才讲得不少，可话又说回来，谁对谁错你只字没提呀！**

Boss, you said a lot of things. But let's go back to the original topic, you haven't mentioned who's right who's wrong yet.

② A: **老李啊，我又进一步谈的那几点，你认为怎么样？**

Old Li, I made some further points here, what do you think?

B: **领导啊，你讲的都对；可话又说回来，我也不全错呀！**

Boss, what you said is correct. But let's go back to the original topic, you can't say all the mistakes are mine.

 语境

　　"话又说回来"，表明"话说远了"。目的是"回到原本的话题上来"。这里面可能有两个"弯子"。在①中，领导上升到一定的高度来谈问题。因为，如果局限在具体细节上，那双方的矛盾就不仅难以缓解，反而容易激化。可惜老李水平低，只求个对错。在②中，领导大概是客气地指出了老李的错误，同时也给他留了点"面子"。但是老李仍然要把话"说回来"，要用自己的"小对"，来掩盖自己的"大错"，并平衡整个结论。现在我们明白了："话又说回来"的意思，几乎等于是：一、坚持自己的看法。二、坚持让别人理解或接受自己的看法。

 ## Context

This sentence is used when you have wandered away from the original topic of the conversation and is designed to pull you back on topic. It is not a straightforward situation. In conversation (1), the leader tries to solve the problem at a more abstract level rather than concentrating on all the details because he knows the issues will become more acute, if they emphasis the details. Unfortunately, Old Li just wants to know the details of who is right and who is wrong. In conversation (2), the leader politely pointed out Li's mistakes, at the same time trying to save his dignity. But Li still wants to deny his mistakes and indulge in sophistry. Hence, we understand that this sentence means: one, persist in one's own opinion; two, persist in convincing other people to accept your own opinion.

古语：夫子欲之，吾二臣者皆不欲也。//《论语·季氏》
雅语：归根究底
类语：这话看怎么说了

1.3.11>

豁出去了
[I'm desperate.]

对话 Conversation

① A：你已经输了全部现金，别再赌了！
You've lost all your money, please don't make any more wagers!

B：不行！把住宅也押上，我豁出去了！

No, I am going to put the deed to my house to cover another bet, I'm desperate!

② **A：我们已经被包围了三天，不突围不行了！**

We have been under siege for three days. We have to break out!

B：豁出去了！宁可战死，不能饿死！

It's desperate! It would be better to die fighting than starve to death.

 **语境**

当人说"豁出去了"时，都是要拼命的心态，是抱着最后一线希望，希望能够在特别不利的条件下，突然取得极大的胜利。应该说，这种勇气是让人激动的。但是，如果没有做好充分的准备，如果一条"后路"也没有，那么最好不要轻易地"豁出去"。因为，这种例子成功得很少。

 **Context**

When people use this sentence, they are ready to risk it all to do something. It is their last hope. They hope to win some great success under adverse conditions. We could admire their courage, but if you don't have adequate preparation and room for maneuver, you would be better not to risk everything, because not many people can succeed under desperate circumstances even if they risk their lives.

古语：于是张良至军门，见樊哙。樊哙曰："今日之事何如？"良曰："甚急。今者项庄拔剑舞，其意常在沛公也。"哙曰："此迫矣，臣请入，与之同命。" // 《史记·项羽本纪》

雅语：孤注一掷

类语：拼了吧

了不得了

[What a terrible disaster!]

☺ 对话 Conversation

① A：了不得了！教学楼着火了！
　　What a terrible disaster! The school building is on fire!

　B：快跑！晚了就出不去了！
　　Run fast! We won't get out if we're slow!

② A：可了不得了！大街上全是人！
　　It's terrible! The streets are full of people!

　B：是吗？快去看看！
　　Really? Quick, take a look!

☞ 语境

　　"了不得了"这句话，一般用在坏消息的前面，目的是要引起别人的注意。在这种情况下，"了不得了"与"不得了了"都有夸张的意思，可以通用。但是，"不得了"还有称赞的意思，"了不得"却没有。不少人喜欢夸大事实。好像因为是自己首先看到的，就应该是重大的事情，就一定要让大家都知道。所以，听到这句话时，请保持冷静。

☞ Context

This sentence is usually used when something bad happens in order to get people's attention. Under these kinds of circumstances, 了不得了 and 不得了

了 are often an exaggerated use of language, but 不得了 can be used for good news too. Some people like to exaggerate. It seems that if they see something first, they want to emphasize how important it is to know about. When you hear this sentence, please keep calm until you know what is going on.

古语：甚急 //《史记·项羽本纪》
雅语：十万火急
类语：不好了　出事了

1.3.13>

没法说
[I don't know how to tell you.]

😊 对话 Conversation

① A：请你说说被非礼的经过。
　　Please tell us how that guy insulted you.

　B：没法说！
　　I don't know how to tell you.

② A：你们说输球输得冤，冤在哪儿了？
　　You said that you couldn't lose this game. Can you tell me why?

　B：没法说。
　　I don't know how to describe it.

语境

在①中,"没法说"是不好意思说的意思。如果当众详细讲述那种经过,那么以后就很难见人了。在②中,"没法说"是对既成事实非常不满意,但是又拿不出充足的理由。从①中可以看出,不好意思说的原因,是怕丢"面子"。从②中可以看出,非常不满意的原因,是已经丢了"面子",还要死命维护。

 ## Context

In conversation (1), "can not tell" means that the speaker is too embarrassed to describe the incident. If she gives the details of how she was insulted, she will lose some status in other people's eyes. A is embarrassed and afraid to loose face. In conversation (2), B is very unhappy that his team lost the game, but he doesn't have any reason to explain why they didn't win. A has already lost face, but still tries to maintain his dignity.

古语:事未易一二为俗人言也 // 司马迁《报任安书》
雅语:千头万绪
类语:说不清楚　怎么说呀

1.3.14>

哪儿啊
[That's not true.]

对话 Conversation

① A:老李呀,你没上过学吧?
Old Li, I guess you've never been to school before.

B：哪儿啊！我们家几代都是读书人。

That's not true! My family have been scholars for several generations.

② A：老李啊，从来没有女人追过你吧?

Old Li, I've never seen any girl chasing after you.

B：哪儿啊！好几个开电梯的都对我有意思。

That's not true. Several of the girls who operate the elevators are chasing me now.

 语境

这句话的意思是：你说的不对，你的话距离真实情况很远。在①中，因为老李在言行上比较粗俗，所以被认为没受过教育，老李当然要马上解释清楚。在②中，没被女人追过的男人，是最没"面子"的男人。老李绝不能接受那种事实，仔细想想，开电梯的漂亮妹妹可不少！只要曾经有过点想象中的眉来眼去，老李就算没白活！

 Context

This sentence means that whatever the speaker said about you is not right, and is far from the truth. In conversation (1), Li's uncouth behavior has caused people to think he hasn't received much education. Of course, Li should explain his real background. In conversation (2), it is embarrassing when a man has no girlfriend. Old Li cannot accept this situation. There are many pretty girls operating the elevators. So if Li has exchanged love glances with one of them, he can defend his honor as a man.

古语：否 //《孟子·公孙丑上》

雅语：不对

类语：根本不是那么回事

拿下
[capture]

☺ 对话 Conversation

① A：**皇上，您的意见不对！**
Majesty, your opinion on this is wrong!

B：**你敢反对我！（对卫兵说）给我拿下！**
How dare you oppose me! (To guards) Take him away!

② A：**已经打了三天，那个山头还在敌人手里！**
This battle has lasted for three days and the hill top is still in enemy hands.

B：**军长放心，今晚我一定把它拿下来！**
Please don't worry, Commander. I will capture it tonight!

③ A：**我让你办的事怎么样了？**
The thing I asked you to do, how is it going?

B：**领导，我克服重重困难，刚刚拿下！**
I had to overcome a lot of problems, boss, but I just finished it.

☞ 语境
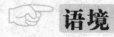

　　这个词原来是皇帝、长官用的，意思是把下边的人抓起来，押下去问罪。如在①中。现在变成：(一)、一种保证：一定要解决问题。如在②中。(二)、一种汇报：问题已经解决了。如在③中。说这句话时，有居高临下的胜利者的感觉，所以，这句古代官场用语，被人们从古装电视剧中重新发现并流行起来。

 # **Context**

    This word was originally used by kings (his majesty) and commanders and meant to take people into custody, like a criminal, just as in conversation (1). Later, this phrase is used in two ways: the first is when people promise to solve a problem, as in conversation (2). The second use is to report that the problem has been solved, as in conversation (3). When people use this phrase, they feel like they are the victors and can look down on other people. This bureaucratic language from ancient times has been borrowed from television programs and has found its way into popular use.

古语：执虞公 //《左传·僖公五年》
雅语：大功告成
类语：搞掂　摆平　OK

1.3.16>

那又怎么样
[So what?]

☺ 对话 **Conversation**

① A：老李，你还赖在简易房里？推土机可要来了！
    Old Li, why do you hang on to this simple house and refuse to clear out, the bulldozers are on the way!

  B：那又怎么样？不给单元楼，我死也不搬！
    So what? If they don't give me an apartment, I'd rather die than leave it.

② A：老李，你居然敢跟领导吵架！

　　Old Li, how could you dare to quarrel with boss?

　B：那又怎么样？他还能把我吃喽！

　　So what? What can he do, bite my head off?

 ## 语境

　　"那又怎么样"，是一句比较无赖的话，它的逻辑推理是这样的："如果我这样"，"那他会怎么样"？"就算他想那样"，"他也不敢那样"，"因为他不能怎么样"，"所以我还这样"。碰上这种好像连死都不怕的人，大概有两种办法：一是惹不起就别惹，早早地躲得远远的；二是如果你敢"摸老虎屁股"，那就得下决心"恶治"。如在①中，叫推土机顶到老李的门上，你再看他怎么样。

 ## Context

　　"So what" is a rude response. Its logical interpretation is even if I say or do something, no one can dare to kill me for it, so I will do whatever I like. If you meet the kind of person who isn't afraid, you have two options: if you don't dare provoking them, just avoid them; or if you decide to risk provoking them, you have to teach them a lesson. For example, in conversation (1), if the bulldozers are coming, Old Li will have no other way but to be shoved out of the house!

古语：休道您兄弟不伏烧埋，由你便直打到梨花月上来。//
　　　康进之《李逵负荆》
雅语：我就这样
类语：怎么着

你放心
[No doubt about it!]

对话 Conversation

① A：你会永远爱我吗？
Will you love me forever?

B：你放心。
You can trust me.

② A：那件事能成吗？
Can that thing be achieved?

B：你放一万个心，绝对没问题！
Please rest assured, we have absolute confidence in our success!

 语境

"放心"的反面是"担心"。"你放心"的意思，是我一定会实现你的愿望，所以，请你把心放在原来的地方。如果一个人经常为各种事情担心，那么听到对方说"你放心"，他会很舒服。

 Context

The reverse of this phrase is "to worry". "Please don't worry" means that I am sure to achieve your wish, there is no doubt about the outcome. If someone is always worried, he should feel some comfort in hearing this guarantee.

古语：君无疑矣 //《商君书·更法》
雅语：没有问题
类语：我发誓　我保证

1.3.18>

你这话什么意思
[What do you mean by that?]

😊 对话 Conversation

① A：小红，你有男朋友吗？
　　Xiao Hong, do you have a boyfriend?

　B：你这话什么意思？
　　What are you getting at?

② A：小红，张老板可是有老婆孩子的人。
　　Xiao Hong, Boss Zhang has already married and has children.

　B：你这话什么意思？
　　Why are you telling me this, what's your point?

 ## 语境

　　这句话的意思是：不明白对方到底是什么意思，是希望对方把话说明白。如在①中，A可能是想同小红交朋友；也可能是想给小红介绍朋友；还可能是……在②中则可能是指责小红在充当第三者；还可能是……小红虽然心虚，但是，表面上嘴还挺硬，用这句话来维护自己的"面子"。

☞ Context

This sentence implies that you are unsure of the other party's meaning and ask them to provide some further explanation. In conversation (1), A probably wants to be Xiao Hong's boyfriend, or find her a boyfriend, or something else.... In conversation (2), A is probably criticizing Xiao Hong by referring to a third party's marriage, or something else.... Although Xiao Hong has a guilty conscience, she obstinately refuses to admit any shortcoming. She uses this sentence to maintain her dignity.

古语：此言何谓也？ //《孟子·滕文公上》
雅语：不明就里
类语：你到底想说什么

1.3.19>

实话实说
[to speak frankly]

☺ 对话 Conversation

① A：老李呀，你觉得我刚才的讲话怎么样？
　　Old Li, how was my speech just now?

　B：老赵呀，我实话实说，不怎么样。
　　Old Zhao, Let me be frank with you. It was so so.

② A：快说！是不是你干的？
　　Hurry up, did you do this?

B：实话实说，真的不是我干的。

To be blunt, I really didn't do this.

 ## 语境

这话本来有被强迫时才说出真实情况的意思。后来有了"说实话、办实事"的倡导，又作为中央电视台的栏目名称，就成了完全的好话，但是要做到实话实说，还是比较困难的，因为那太容易得罪人，如①。另外，由于这话的使用率太高，所以几乎变成了正文之前的发语词，作用仅在赢得对方的信任，至于后面说的是不是实话，那就不一定了，如②。

 ## Context

This phrase implies that someone feels compelled to tell the truth. Currently, the popular meaning of this phrase is that everyone should speak the truth and handle their affairs in a down-to-earth manner. It has also come to mean praise since it is used as the title of a program on CCTV. In real life, it is hard to speak frankly. Sometimes it causes offence to the listener, as in conversation (1). On the other hand, people often use this phrase at the beginning of their comments to gain trust. But you can never be sure whether they speak the truth or not, as seen in conversation (2).

古语：所谓诚其意者，毋自欺也。// 《礼记·大学》

雅语：恕我直言

类语：有啥说啥

谁怕谁呀
[I am not afraid of anyone.]

☺ 对话 Conversation

① A：听说拳击冠军要找你玩玩？

I hear you will have a boxing match against a champion!

B：来吧！谁怕谁呀！

It's fine, I'm not afraid of him!

② A：明天参加比赛的都是金牌运动员！

All the past gold medal athletes will participate in the competition tomorrow!

B：好啊，谁怕谁呀！

Good, I am not afraid of them!

☞ 语境

这是句提高自己勇气的话。从①和②中看出：B不是特别有力的人，却挺勇敢，至少是"嘴硬"。可惜，这句话现在已经没有了正义的标准。只是表示：我不怕他。

☞ Context

This sentence is used to build up one's courage. In both conversations (1) and (2), B is not very strong but tries to be brave, at least displays a "big mouth". Unfortunately, this sentence has lost its original meaning as a criterion for justice. It now usually means simply, "I am not afraid of him."

古语：独畏廉将军哉 //《史记·廉颇蔺相如列传》
雅语：无所畏惧
类语：他算老几　有什么了不起

1.3.21>

谁认这个头啊
[No one would accept the blame.]

😊 对话 Conversation

① A：小红啊，刚才老板问是谁把复印机弄坏的，你怎么不言语啊？
　　Xiao Hong, Why didn't you say something when the Boss asked who broken the copy machine just now?

　B：谁认这个头啊？反正那么多人都用过，老板不会找到我头上来。
　　No one would admit that. Besides, there are so many people using the copy machine, the Boss can't possibly know that I was the one who broke it.

② A：老李呀，厕所里有人大便后没冲水！你知道吗？
　　Old Li, someone didn't flush after using the toilet?

　B：别问啦，谁认这个头啊！看上去个个都跟人似的，其实全是嫌疑犯！
　　There is no use asking who it was because no one would admit it. They all look innocent enough, but everyone is suspect!

语境

"认头"专指低头认错。很多人做了错事以后，从不主动承认，而且还用这句话来解嘲。在①中是小红弄坏了设备，怕老板扣她钱，所以假装没事人。在②中，八成是老李没冲水，可他不但不坦白，还用这句话把嫌疑推到大家的身上。说实话，不敢承认错误，确实是我们的一大毛病。在第一次，大概是怕丢"面子"，可是次数多了以后，就完全是道德品质问题了。什么时候，我们才可以把"当众认错"作为最大的"面子"呢？

Context

This sentence means you should admit it if you made a mistake. Many people never take responsibility for mistakes and try to explain things away when confronted with the facts. In conversation (1), Xiao Hong broke the equipment and is afraid the boss will deduct part of her salary. So, she feigns ignorance. In conversation (2), it is possible that Li is the one who didn't flush the toilet. But he is not only dishonest, he also shifts the responsibility on to others. In fact, it is a real shortcoming if you cannot face your mistakes. You probably do so to save your face the first time. But it gradually became a question of morality. When can we make the responsibility of acknowledging one's mistakes in public the best model to preserve one's "face"?

古语：又没烧糊了洗脸水，有什么不是？ //《红楼梦·五十九回》
雅语：死不认账
类语：不是我干的

谁说不是呢
[You're right.]

😊 对话 Conversation

① **A：这么多人骑车，没人修车怎么行呢！**

There are so many people riding bicycles; they need someone to repair them!

B：谁说不是呢！

You're right about that!

② **A：你的工作一直很好，应该涨工资了吧？**

You've been working very hard; you should get a raise.

B：谁说不是呢！

I agree with you!

③ **A：等我们退休以后，早上打打拳，下午写写书，晚上散散步，多好啊！**

After I retire, I will practice *taiji* in the morning, write in the afternoon, and take a walk in the evening. It would be an ideal life.

B：谁说不是呢！

Who wouldn't agree with that?

 语境

　　在①中，B 听了 A 的话，觉得很有"面子"，但想到还有不少人看不起修车的，又有些委屈。他想：修车的应该受到大家的尊重。在②中，B 的心

里有怨气，他想：自己对工作那么认真，可是为什么没人给长工资呢？在
③中，A和B都盼望着退休以后的生活，两个人的想法完全一致。用反问语
气来表明同意，这是强调的方法。但有这种习惯的人，往往有不满的情绪。

☞ **Context**

In conversation (1), when B heard A's comments he felt better. When he thought
that there were still many people who looked down on his job he felt like no one
respected him. He feels that his work should be appreciated. In conversation (2), B is
full of complaints because his salary hasn't increased. In conversation (3), A and B
are looking forward to retiring and enjoying a relaxing life. B answers A's comments
in the form of a question to emphasize his agreement. When people answer a question this way, they are usually discontented with their current circumstances.

古语：其谁曰不然 // 《左传·隐公元年》
雅语：我也这样认为
类语：可不是嘛

1.3.23>

说不清楚
[can't explain it]

☺ 对话 Conversation

① **A：这事挺复杂，一句两句说不清楚。**
This thing is quite complicated; I can't use one or two sentences to
explain it.

B：别着急，慢慢说。
No hurry, tell me slowly.

② A：这事挺麻烦，我也——说不太清楚。

This thing is troublesome, I can't explain clearly.

B：噢，那就算了。

Oh well, that's ok.

③ A：这事啊……我——也，说不太清楚。

About this thing..., I don't know how to explain to you.

B：你要怎样才能说清楚呢？

Is there any way I can help you to explain it?

 ## 语境

当"说不清楚"这话出现时，怎么才知道它属于哪一种情境呢？在
①中是一件比较棘手的事，A的语气是烦燥的，他发现自己抓不住要点。
在②中是托辞，但你能听出A的冷静。在③中是A想让你更感兴趣，语
气是飘乎、闪烁的。在①中，是不能把自己想说的说出来，其原因或是
迷失了本来的目的，或是发现行为与目的之间存在矛盾。在②中，说不
清楚的意思是不想说清楚，是逃避。在③中，说不清楚的目的是吊人胃
口，是增加筹码的引诱。

 ## Context

This sentence can be used in several circumstances. For example, in conversation (1), it is a sticky business. A feels irritated and can't grasp the main
points. A cannot explain the situation because A either lost track of its purpose
or found the conflict between the facts and the goal too complicated. In conversation (2), A avoids explaining the situation, but you can see A is very calm.
A doesn't want to explain the situation and wants to escape from the effort of
trying to. In conversation (3), A would like to attract the listener's interest and
his voice is both inviting and unsure. This sentence is used to raise attention
and lure the listener into the dialogue.

古语：是诚何心哉 //《孟子·梁惠王上》

雅语：一言难尽

类语：说不好　不好说　说不明白

1.3.24>

听我慢慢说嘛
[Please be patient and hear me out.]

 **对话 Conversation**

① A：老李呀，你甭说了，你的意见不就是……

Old Li, you don't have to continue, I know what you are going to say...

B：领导呀，您别着急，事情复杂着呢，听我慢慢说嘛！

Boss, you shouldn't be in such a hurry. These things are very complicated. Please be patient and hear me out.

② A：老李呀，你的心思你不说我也知道，还是不说的好！

Old Li, I can read your mind before you open your mouth. You'd better not say anything.

B：小红呀，不说不知道，我对你的感情可不是一天半天，你还是听我慢慢说嘛！

Xiao Hong, if I don't tell you, you'll never know that I have had feelings for you for a long time. Please be patient and let me tell you slowly.

 **语境**

在言语交际中出现的问题，总是双方的。首先是说的人比较罗嗦，绕的弯子比较大，所以听的人容易着急，最后不得不打断说者的话头，如

在①中。然后是听的人比较武断，以为听上两句就知道是怎么回事。用不着再浪费时间去听废话，如在②中。从对话策略上看，双方均应提高。从一般礼貌上说，还是听者应该多耐点心，因为不让人把话讲完是非常不礼貌的，也是最容易得罪人的。

 # Context

The problems involved in communicating fall on both speaker and listener. In conversation (1), someone who is always long-winded makes the listener impatient and causes them to cut the speaker off. In conversation (2), the listener makes an arbitrary decision and thinks she has understood everything after listening to just one or two sentences. She doesn't want to waste her time listening to more nonsense. In regards to communication, both parties should increase their skills and strategies. One also should be polite and patient, stopping other people's sentences short is bad manners and makes them angry.

古语：王徐徐答曰 // 《世说新语·品藻》
雅语：娓娓道来
类语：别打岔

1.3.25>

 # 我不是那种人
[I'm not that kind of person.]

对话 Conversation

① A：老王，我听说一个地下赌场，咱们去玩一把吧！
Old Wang, I heard there is an underground gambling house. Should we go?

B：对不起，我不去那种地方，我不是那种人。

I'm sorry. That's not the kind of place I would go to, I'm not that kind of person.

② A：老李，我听说你在王府井和人打架，被警察拘了半宿。

Old Li, I heard that you fought with someone at the Wangfujing market and were arrested by police and spent half the night in jail.

B：你省了这份心吧，我不是那种人，也干不出那种事。

You don't have to worry for me. I'm not that kind of person and have never done anything like that.

③ A （警察拿着证据问小偷）：你干这行有多久了？

(Holding the evidence, the police questions the thief): How long have you been a thief?

B （小偷）：您说什么呢，我根本就不是那种人。

(Thief): What are you talking about? I'm not that kind of person.

 语境

　　解除别人的怀疑，解释发生的误会，本来是需要证据的。可是在交际中这句话却很有用，好像说这句话的人自有一定之规，是不会发生偶然性的失误的。在①中，从来不赌的人可以讲这句话。在②中，从不打架的人也可以讲这句话，因为他人的一贯行为可以作证。在③中就不行了，那明明是在说瞎话呢。

 ## Context

You need evidence to disprove people's suspicions and explain any misunderstanding they might have about you. But people usually use this sentence as a typical response to excuse their occasional faults. In conversation (1), the person who never engaged in gambling can say so. In conversation (2), the speaker has never fought and can also claim that he is not that kind of person because of his past consistent behavior. But in conversation (3), the speaker uses the sentence to tell a lie.

古语：管仲，曾西之所不为也。// 《孟子·公孙丑上》
雅语：我以人格担保
类语：我不会干那种事　　我是那种人吗

1.3.26>

我是男人
[I'm a man.]

☺ 对话 Conversation

① A：（女）外面有好多坏人在砸门，咱们快逃命吧！
　　(Woman): There are a lot of bad people pounding at the door, let's run for our lives!

B：……，我是男人，跟在你们娘儿们后边跑，不合适吧？
　　I'm a man. It's not right for me to follow a woman, isn't it?

② A：（男足教练）我真受不了你们这种踢输了就哭的毛病！

(Male soccer coach): I can't stand your habit of crying every time you lose a game.

B：（众球员）我们是男人，我们不哭了。

(Team members): We're guys, we shouldn't cry!

 ## 语境

男人本来就没什么特殊的，可是有的男人自己却好像很了不起似的，经常用我是男人这句话来激励自己。说句玩笑话，①中的男人要是觉得在后面跑没面子，那完全可以先跑嘛。②中的男人们的眼泪就更不值钱了。因为现在的男人确实都有点"输不起"的软弱性，而把"我是男人"这句话挂在嘴上，恰恰说明了男人们越来越"女性化"的普遍现象。

 ## Context

Comparing to women, men are not special. But men with a bit too much pride usually use this sentence to inspire themselves. If the sentence is used in a kidding way, as in conversation (1), where the man thinks he shouldn't run off following the woman, he could run off first. In conversation (2), the losing players' tears are useless. Males are afraid of failure and lack vitality nowadays. The use of this kind of sentence all the time is evidence of more and more "feminization" of manhood.

古语：如丈夫何 // 《春秋公羊传·定公八年》
雅语：堂堂须眉
类语：男子汉大丈夫

我这不是来了吗
[Ok, I'm here.]

☺ 对话 Conversation

① A：嗯，该来的差不多都来了。咦，老李怎么还没来？

Ok, most people who ought to be here are here, but where is Old Li?

B：（老李喘着粗气跑进来坐下）我这不是来了吗！

(Old Li runs in breathing heavily and sits down) OK, I'm here!

② A：打麻将就怕"三缺一"，这老李可真急死人！

I'm really worried about when you are going to get to play mahjong, we are still waiting for one of the four people to show up!

B：说谁呢？我这不是来了吗！

Who are you talking about? I'm here.

语境

　　有的人迟到后极少讲"对不起"，或只强调客观原因，比如：堵车、有事、忘带了东西等等，反正不是故意耽误大家的时间。更有甚者，还倒打一耙，说出这句"我这不是来了吗！"好像批评他的人有错，他倒是被人冤枉了似的。

☞ Context

Some people when they are late, rarely say "sorry", and usually give some objective reason for being late: traffic, busy, or that they forget something.

They want others to know that they are not wasting the time of those waiting for them on purpose. Moreover, they use this sentence to reverse their guilt and instead blame the people who criticized them. They make it seem that they are the one being treated unfairly.

古语：与老人期，后，何也？ // 《史记·留侯世家》
雅语：姗姗来迟
类语：我不是在这呢吗

1.3.28>

（要个）说法

[ask for a final decision]

😊 对话 Conversation

① A：你的官司已经拖了三年，还打吗？
　　Your lawsuit has been going on for the last three years, are you going to continue with it?

　B：当然，死活得要个说法！
　　Of course, either life or death, I have to have a decision!

② A：老李的麻烦事，上边有说法吗？
　　Regarding Old Li's trouble, have the higher authorities given the final word yet?

　B：上边什么都不说，这也算一种说法吧。
　　No, I haven't heard anything yet. But no news is good news.

语境

　　"说法" ＝上级的指示＝法院的判决。这句话原来是陕西方言,经过导演张艺谋之手、演员巩俐之口,在电影《秋菊打官司》之后,进入流行口语。那部电影提出了一个老问题:权力大?还是法律大?一个农民被村里的小领导打了,他的妻子从乡里告到省里,最后得到了公正裁决。但是,其中有一个县级领导的帮助,要不然,那个"说法"还得继续要下去。

Context

A final word is same as higher authorities' direction, or a court's decision. This sentence originally came from the Shannxi dialect. After the release of director Zhang Yimou and actress Gong Li's film, "Qiu Ju Goes to Court", this sentence has become popular in spoken language. That film raises an old question: which is bigger, power or the law? A peasant was beaten by a village leader and his wife files a lawsuit and pushes it from the village to the provincial level. In the end he gets his justice, but there is a county leader who helped them every step of the way. Without this help, it wouldn't be easy to get the final word you want to hear from the higher authorities.

古语:且告诉我们评评理 // 《红楼梦·二十六回》
雅语:谁是谁非
类语:分个青红皂白

也就这样了
[This way is good enough.]

😊 对话 Conversation

① A：领导啊，您看我的准备工作还有什么问题？
Leader, are there problems with our preparation?

B：挺好，也就这样了。
They are fine, this way is good enough.

② A：老李啊，听说你还有几个大目标要实现？
Old Li, I heard that you still want to achieve several big goals?

B：哪儿啊，我都快70岁的人了，也就这样了。
How can I achieve anything? I'm almost seventy years old. What I have achieved now is good enough.

👉 语境

在很多情况中，人们总是希望把事情做到最好，得到十全十美的结局，可是有的时候是没有那种必要，有的时候是没有那种能力。在①中，领导认为虽然不够完美，但是已经过得去了，也好不到哪儿去了。在②中，老李认识到人生的局限性，表现出比较灰心的情绪。

👉 Context

People often hope to finish something perfectly and be professional. But in real life, it is not always necessary to be perfect or you may not be able to reach that level anyway. In conversation (1), the leader thinks that although they didn't finish the work perfectly, it is fairly good and cannot be much better. In conversation (2), Old Li realizes that there is only a limited amount of things you can do in a life span. He is discouraged by this.

古语：吴公差强人意，隐若一敌国矣。//《后汉书·吴汉传》
雅语：比较令人满意
类语：不错了　可以了

1.3.30>

一不留神
[looked away for an instant]

😊 对话 Conversation

① A：哎，你在找什么呢?
　　　Hey, what are you looking for?

　　B：嗨，刚买了只猫，我那儿做饭
　　　呢，一不留神，它就没了!
　　　Sigh, I bought a cat. I looked away
　　　for an instant to cook, and the cat
　　　disappeared.

② A：跟了半天儿，一不留神，还是被目标给甩了！

I followed that guy for half a day. I looked away for an instant and the suspect escaped.

B：目标太狡猾了，你也嫩点儿！

Your target is too sly and you are a little immature.

 ## 语境

"神"在这就是"注意力"。你在干什么，你的"神"自然也就"留"在那里。可是，当你稍不注意，马上就出了问题，这说明什么呢？是你的注意力过于集中，一些重要的细节被忽视了。在①中，"神"都在饭上，猫就跑了。在②中，跟着，跟着，目标忽然就不见了。这就是"脑袋不够用"了。怎样才能都留着"神"呢？这就需要科学地安排程序，避免忙乱中肯定会出现的"一不留神"。

 ## Context

People need to pay attention when they do things. If your attention wanders, problems can appear right away. This means when you concentrate on one thing, you will ignore other important details. In conversation (1), while B's attention was on the cooking board, the cat ran away. In conversation (2), B followed the suspect, but he escaped and B was not quick enough to catch up with him. How can we pay attention to everything? We need to objectively balance our activities to avoid problems during the rush and muddle of everyday life.

古语：俯仰之间，已为陈迹。// 晋·王羲之《兰亭集序》
雅语：眼错不见
类语：一眨眼的功夫

2 给别人面子
Give Other People Face

2.1
在强势中
Stronger than Others

大腕儿

[the star of the show]

 对话 **Conversation**

① **A：老李，你先入席吧！**
Old Li, please take your seat first!

   B：哎哟！那哪成啊！您是大腕儿，当然是您先请！
No, I can't sit first. You're the star, you should be seated first.

② **A：老李呀，你这个电影，想请谁来演呢？**
Old Li, who are going to cast in the leading role in your next movie?

   B：还是请大腕儿吧，要不然上座率高不了。
I'll cast a well-known star so the box office will be higher.

☞ **语境**

　　这个词本来是戏曲界的，写做"大蔓儿"，是借植物的粗大的茎，来比喻行会中有"面子"、有势力的人物。这个词头些年被影视界重新使用，也被全社会接受后写成"大腕儿"，使人联想到过去政界的"铁腕"。可是，"大腕儿"不管有多大的影响，基本上还是个人身份，只不过社会关系比较多，有些号召力，身价也特高而已。

☞ **Context**

This word originally comes from the local operas. This was a figure of speech, using a plant's big stem to represent a powerful or popular person. It was re-used by film and television circles first, and then accepted by the public and changed to "highhanded person". People easily associate this name with an ironhanded person in politics. But, even a "highhanded person" has a lot of influence. Although it is only the power of their name, they have more social contacts, mass appeal, and a higher social status.

古语：炙手可热势绝伦 // 杜甫《丽人行》
雅语：头面人物
类语：大牌明星　龙头老大

2.1.2>

话不能这么说
[That's not altogether correct.]

😊 对话 Conversation

① A：哎，老王多好啊，又有钱，又厉害！
Oh, Old Wang is wonderful! He is very wealthy and strong!

B：老李呀，话不能这么说，你知道老王的钱是从哪儿来的吗？
Old Li, it's not that simple. Don't you know where his money comes from?

② A：咱们老板今天这么说，明天那么说，一点儿准儿也没有！
Our boss says one thing today and another thing tomorrow. I don't know which one is right.

B：话不能这么说，情况是在不断变化的嘛。
That's not altogether true. It is the circumstances that change all the time.

语境

很多人不知道怎样表示不同意，其实这句话就挺好。既表明了反对的态度，语气也比较和缓。在①中，老李非常羡慕老王。②中的情况反映了不少人对领导的逆反心理。其实当领导真的不容易，他们经常不得不根据发展变化了的情况，做出新的决定。

Context

Many people don't know how to express disagreement. In fact, this sentence is perfect. It not only expresses disagreement, but also adopts a mild attitude. In conversation (1), Old Li worships Old Wang very much. Conversation (2) reflects workers' antagonistic attitudes toward their leadership. As a matter of fact, it is not easy to be a leader. He always has to make new decisions based on the changing circumstances around him.

古语：马谡言过其实，不可大用君其察之 // 《三国志·马良传》
雅语：言语偏激
类语：你说的有点过了

2.1.3>

美女
[pretty woman]

☺ 对话 Conversation

① A：快过来吧，这儿有大美女等着你呢!
　　Come here quick! There is a pretty woman waiting for you.

B：真的？ 我马上就到！
Really? I'll be there immediately.

② **A：怎么刚来就走啊？**
Why are you leaving, you just
got here?

**B：这就是你说的美女？ 比大猩
猩还可怕！**
Do you think she's pretty? She
looks worse than a gorilla.

 ## 语境

"美女"在现如今更多地成为一种对
女性的溢美之词，多少还带有一点讨女人高
兴的意思，到底美不美倒也没人太计较。听到这称
谓，女人一般都会美滋滋的；不过，真要碰见一特丑的女人，就别这么
叫了，因为反倒会被误以为你在讽刺她。

 ## Context

　　Nowadays, when people call a woman who meets with "the beauty", you
don't take it to heart. Because they give her excessive praise just in order to
please her. You don't mind whether the woman is really beautiful or not.
Generally, when women hear this title, they are very appreciated. If you meet
a woman who looks ugly, you'd better not call her beauty. Otherwise, she
thinks you're mocking her.

古语：静女其姝 //《诗经·静女》
雅语：倾国倾城
类语：大美人　靓女

2.1.4>

那可没准
[I can't promise (Uncertain).]

😊 对话 Conversation

① A：小红，晚上七点，我在北京饭店等你，一定来啊！

Xiao Hong, I will wait for you in the Beijing Hotel at 7:00 pm.
Be sure to be there, OK?

  B：哟！那可没准！

Oh, I can't promise you that.

② A：咱们的协议书已经签字，就等着贵公司汇款了！

We have signed the agreement and are waiting for your company's remittance.

  B：协议归协议，资金什么时候到位，那可没准！

An agreement is an agreement, but I'm not at all sure when the money will be here.

③ A：明年春天咱们就结婚吧！

Let's get married next Spring!

  B：那可没准！

I'm not so sure about that.

👉 语境

　　"那可没准"，是"说不准""不能肯定"的意思。应该讲这是一种托词，基本上倾向于"不"，最起码听的一方不要抱什么希望。在①中，A

先生的邀请好像比较突然，小红小姐有点吃不准，就用这话来表示推辞。在②中，缺钱的一方很着急，出钱的一方还要看一看。B先生用这句话，表示资金不会马上到位，希望对方保持冷静。③中的B还不想结婚，直接拒绝怕伤害对方，用这话给对方留点"面子"。

 ## Context

　　This phrase means that the speaker is "uncertain", "not sure". It could also be a way of making an excuse and/or very close to saying "no". At least for the listener, the phrase does not offer much hope. In conversation (1), when Mr. A suddenly invites Xiao Hong, Xiao Hong is uncertain about the situation and uses this sentence to make an excuse. In conversation (2), the party that is short of money is getting anxious, but the party that owes the money still wants to wait and see. Mr. B uses this sentence to ask A to keep calm and not to get too excited. In conversation (3), B doesn't want to get married yet, but she is afraid to hurt the other person's feelings by sayings "no". She uses this sentence to keep both parties' dignity.

古语： 飞卫曰："未也，必学视而后可。" // 《列子·汤问》
雅语： 未必
类语： 说不准　说不好　再说吧

2.1.5>

我对你很有信心
[I have confidence in you.]

 ## 对话 Conversation

① A：李教授，您看我能完成这项科研课题吗？
　　Professor Li, Do you think that I can finish this research project?

B：没问题，我对你很有信心。
I think you can. I have confidence in you.

② A：小红，你肯定能考上北京大学！我对你很有信心。
Xiao Hong, I am sure that you will be admitted to Beijing University. You have my full confidence.

B：爸，我可没有十分的把握。
Father, I am not quite sure.

③ A：小红，咱们还是吹了吧，你跟着我会一辈子受苦的。
Xiao Hong, let's stop dating. If we are together, you will have a rough time all your life.

B：别这么说，你一定会成功的，我对你很有信心。
Please don't say this, I have confidence in you and you will be successful.

语境

　　这是一句流行不久的时髦话，在①中，是教授用这句话来鞭策自己的学生。应该说多数能够起到激励作用。可是也不一定，因为信心这东西不是别人可以给的，如果你自己确实缺少实力，那是不可能拥有信心的。另外，如果外来的"信心"太多，还会起负作用呢，比如中国足球。

Context

　　This sentence is becoming very popular. In conversation (1), the professor uses this sentence to encourage his student and in most cases, it should inspire the student's further efforts. But the outcome is not 100% guaranteed because self-confidence cannot be given by other people. If you don't have the strength, it is impossible to have confidence. On the other hand, too much "faith" in you from others may work in a negative way, for example, look at Chinese Soccer teams.

古语： 与（仲长统）交友者多异之 // 《后汉书·仲长统列传》
雅语： 寄托厚望
类语： 你能行

2.1.6>

再说吧
[Let's talk about it later.]

☺ 对话 Conversation

① **A：** 李老师，我什么时候去找您求教？
Professor Li, when should I come to see you for advice?

B： 再说吧。
Not now, we'll talk later.

② **A：** 这笔买卖你还做不做？
Do you still want to make this deal?

B： 再说吧。
Let's leave that decision for later.

 ## 语境

此语多为推卸之辞，如果误以为是还有下文那就错了。如闻此语，应另想办法或再次明确请求。中国人基本上没有说"不"的习惯，所以如果遇到想拒绝，又不好意思直说的时候，就用"再说吧"来缓和气氛，给对方留个"面子"，有保持联系，以后还可以谈的意思。

 ## Context

This sentence is mostly used to avoid something or someone. It would be a mistake to think that there will be good news about this matter later. If you hear this response, you should try to find another way around the issue or ask again with a more specific question. Most Chinese don't like to say "no", hence, if they feel like refusing something they are shy to say so directly. They usually use a sentence like this to ease the tension. They want to keep other party's dignity, and keep in touch and talk later.

古语：先生休矣 // 《战国策·齐策》
雅语：再考虑考虑
类语：先放一放吧

2.1.7>

这回看你的了
[We're counting on you.]

☺ 对话 Conversation

① A：老李呀，去了三拨人！都没做成这笔生意，这回看你的了！
　　Old Li, I have sent three teams to deal with this business but none of them got it done. I'm counting on you to do it this time!

B：感谢领导信任，我一定圆满完成！

Thanks for your trust, boss. I will bring the matter to a successful conclusion.

② A：老李呀，这个苦差事，谁都不干，这回看你的了。

Old Li, no one wants this difficult job. We're relying on you to do it.

B：啊？都不干您就叫我干哪！

Oh? You're asking me to do something because no one else will do it!

语境

这句话大概出现在两种情况里。在①中，是很多人都没完成的任务，要找能干的人去做。这属于"恳求"和"拜托"。在②中，是最苦最没好处的事，总得找个人干，还得让他心情舒畅地去干。于是，就用这句话来表示"委派"和"鼓励"。

Context

This sentence is probably used in two different situations. In conversation (1), a number of people tried before but were unable to get the job done and the leader has to find a capable person to do it. Here the leader has to solicit someone and put his trust in their ability to do the job. In conversation (2), the hard job no one wants to do must be completed anyway so the leader uses this sentence to express his trust and encouragement.

古语：平原君与楚合从，言其利害，日出而言之，日中不决。
十九人谓毛遂曰："先生上。" //《史记·平原君列传》
雅语：拜托　辛苦
类语：全仗你了

跩
[show off]

😊 对话 Conversation

① **A：我儿子上哈佛了！**
My son has enrolled in Harvard University!

B：真的？这回该你跩了！
Is that true? This time you can boast!

② **A：前一段特别跩的那老李，怎么见不着了？**
Why don't I see Old Li anymore? He had a very big head a few days ago.

B：他的公司破产了，再也跩不起来了。
His company went bankrupt and he can't show off anymore.

👉 语境

跩，本是北方人说鸭子走路时左右摇晃的词，等到瞧见米老鼠的朋友唐老鸭，才知道这种走相具有世界意义。有的人在自以为了不起的时候，常常会改变自己平时走路的姿势，表现出得意洋洋的劲头儿，透露出一种希望被人注意，被人夸赞的心理。当人们从旁看到这种状态时，就用"跩"来进行描述。由此，这是一条褒贬兼具，说者和听者都比较过瘾的时下口语。

☞ **Context**

This word originally comes from people's description of the way a duck waddles in Northern China. After we saw Mickey Mouse's friend, Donald Duck, we realized that there is an international significance associated with this kind of walk. When someone is puffed-up with pride, they usually change the way they walk. They are flattered by others and hope to get even more attention and praise. When people observe someone under this abnormal condition, they use this word to describe them. Because this word can be explained as both praise and censure, no matter who uses it or listens to it, both sides enjoy it to the full.

古语：春风得意马蹄疾 // 孟郊《登科后》
雅语：大摇大摆
类语：不会走道了

给别人面子 2
Give Other People Face

2.2
在均势中
Equal to Others

差不多
[just about right]

对话 Conversation

① A：你看，这样做可以吗？

Could you please take a look, can this be done this way?

B：差不多。

That's just about right.

② A：这双鞋他能穿吗？

Can he wear these shoes?

B：差不多。

They're OK.

③ A：他们俩谁高？

Who is the taller of the two?

B：差不多。

They're about the same height.

④ A：她们俩谁漂亮？

Between the two of them, who is more beautiful?

B：差不多。

They are about the same.

⑤ A：两个城市的物价呢？

Which city's price is better?

B：差不多。

The prices are similar.

⑥ **A：考试能通过吗？**

Can you pass the examinations?

B：差不多。

Just about.

⑦ **A：你看咱们能赢吗？**

Can we win this game?

B：差不多。

Maybe we can.

 ## 语境

模糊，是既古老又时髦的艺术。长度、高度、程度、结果……各种应该具体回答的问题，都变成了"两可"的"差不多"。"差"是比较之后的评价，如果"差"的"不多"，如果就"差一点"，那到底是怎样呢？何况，谁也没听明白是"谁差"，到底"差多少"？这就是语言的水平。

可能是无法明确回答，可能是不想明确回答，可能是礼貌性的应付，可能是不想得罪人，也可能就是"一样"。反正这是一句不会承担任何责任的妙语。

 ## Context

Being vague is a skill that was used in traditional art as well as in modern art. All the questions of length, height, grade, and results... can all be answered directly, but when someone is vague they claim not to know which to choose between two options, so both will do. When we say "difference", the answer should come from a comparison of the options. If there is not much difference or only a little difference, no one knows what the final analysis is based on? Much less, noboby understands which option falls short or how much it falls short of the standard. This use of language is a skill.

It is very possible that when people use this phrase they are unable to provide a definite answer, because they do not know, they would prefer not to give a direct answer, or they politely take a perfunctory attitude so as not to offend anyone, or it could be that the choices are really the same. However, with this answer one doesn't have to take any responsibility.

古语：齐其庶几乎 // 《孟子·梁惠王下》
雅语：相差无几
类语：没什么区别　说不好　几乎一样

2.2.2>

得了
[(1) finished (2) that's enough (3) hold on]

对话 Conversation

① A：师傅，我的车修好了吗？
　　Mister, is my car ready to go?

　B：早就得了。
　　It was finished a long time ago.

② A：昨天的电影很好。
　　The movie yesterday was very nice.

　B：得了！我一点也不喜欢。
　　Hold on a minute; I didn't like it at all.

③ A：这孩子太不听话，我要打他一顿。

This child doesn't listen to me at all, I want to spank him.

　B：得了得了，和孩子生那么大气干吗？

Hold on. How can you be so angry with a child?

 语境

　　在①中是"修好了"，表示一件事情完成了——这是原义。在②中是反驳的前奏，有"别说了"的意思。在③中是平息事件的专用语，是"算了"的意思。有趣的是在②中，用它打断对方谈话，跟着予以反驳。按说这里出现的，不该是"得了"，应该是"不！"可是直接说"不"的情况很少，否定的意思就被"打住"的语句给代替了。

 Context

In conversation (1), the car "is fixed" and thus one thing has been finished. This is the original meaning of the phrase. In conversation (2), it was used before any disagreement and asks the other party to stop giving their opinion. Conversation (3), is a special use designed to calm things down. The most interesting case is conversation (2). It uses this phrase to stop another's conversation and refute an assertion. B uses "hold on a minute" instead of "no", because people don't like to use "no" nowadays.

古语：可矣 // 《左传·隐公元年》

雅语：大功告成

类语：完了　好了　打住　算了　行了

2.2.3>

干吗去
[What are you up to?]

☺ 对话 Conversation

① A：老李，干吗去了？
Old Li, what are you up to?

B：噢，去长城饭店吃饭！
Ah, I went to the Great Wall Hotel for dinner!

② A：老李，干吗去？
Old Li, what are you up to?

B：噢，没事，随便走走。
Ah, nothing, I'm just going to take a walk.

③ A：老李，干吗去？
Old Li, what are you up to?

B：哎，买点儿东西去。
Ah, I am going to buy something.

☞ 语境

　　五十年代到八十年代，最常用的见面语有两句。第一句是"你吃了吗"，随着生活水平的提高，这句话过时了。第二句是"干吗去"，这句话还在用。在①中，老李的回答是不合适的。因为很快会有很多人猜想老李是发了大财，那是比较麻烦的，除非你希望那样。在②中和③中，老李的回答是合适的。因为问的人本来就是"打招呼"，不是一定要知道你去哪儿，去干什么。所以你大可不必伤脑筋去回答，只要含糊过去就行了。或者，还有一个办法，就是你先看见对方，并且抢先发向："老张，干吗去？"

Context

From the 1950's to the 1980's, people usually used these sentences as a way of greeting when they saw each other. The first one was "have you eaten?" This sentence is out-of-date now since our standard of living has risen. But people still use the second sentence: "What are you up to?" In conversation (1), Li's answer is inappropriate. Because other people will immediately think that Li has become rich. Only if you want people to think this is so would you answer this way, but it could cause some trouble for you. In conversations (2) and (3), Old Li's answer is suitable. Because when people meet and ask this question it only means "hello". They don't really care where you are going or what you are going to do. So you don't have to feel troubled. Or you can try to be the first to ask this question when you see someone.

古语：何之 //《孟子·梁惠王上》
雅语：您好
类语：上哪儿去呀　干什么去呀

2.2.4>

看上了
[I'm fond of it.]

🙂 对话 Conversation

① A：听说有很多人给你介绍了女朋友，怎么样？
I heard that many people are trying to find you a girl friend, How is it going?

B：没怎么样，我都看上了。

So far, I'm fond of all of them.

② **A：你是看上了，人家呢？**

You're fond of them, are they

also fond of you?

B：人家都看不上我。

None of them are fond of me.

③ **A：昨天我看上了一套衣服。**

I found a suit that I really
like yesterday.

B：看上了就买呗！

If you like it you should
consider buying it.

☞ **语境**

　　这句话的意思是：眼睛看到了，心里很喜欢。一般用在男人与女人之间，如在①、②中。可惜的是，一方看上另一方，没有用，要双方互相看上才行。这句话也用在喜欢一件东西上，如在③中。那比较容易，花钱就行了。

☞ **Context**

　　This phrase is used when you see someone or something that you know you will like, but it usually refers to a male and female relationship. This is the case in conversation (1) and (2). Unfortunately, just because one party is fond of the other does not mean there is a relationship unless the other feels the same way. This phrase can also be used when someone likes something as seen in conversation (3). That is easy to understand, you should spend some money to buy it if you like something.

古语：武王使玉人相之//《韩非子·和氏》

雅语：相中了

类语：看中了

2.2.5>

了不起

[amazing]

 对话 Conversation

① A：你知道老王帮助穷孩子上学的事吗？

Do you know that Old Wang is helping poor children go to school?

B：听说了，真了不起！

Yes, I heard about it, he's wonderful!

② A：小刘会六门外语！太了不起了！

Xiao Liu can speak six foreign languages! That's amazing!

B：了不起是了不起，就是中文太差！

That may be amazing, but his Chinese is still poor!

③ A：小张开了一辆奔驰，特了不起的样子。

Xio Zhang is driving a Benz and he looks conceited.

B：有什么了不起，那车是他女朋友的！

That's nothing; the car belongs to his girl friend!

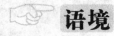 语境

"了不起"这句话，专门用来赞扬。当然，说的是他人，不是自己。

有趣的是，现在已经很少听到谁赞扬谁；或者说，较少有人想向好人学习，较少有人为他人高兴。如果有人赞扬在先，那么一定有人讽刺在后。就像在②和③中那样。

 ## Context

This phrase is especially used to praise an action or event. Of course, you should use it to praise others rather than yourself. It is interesting that we hardly ever hear people praising others these days. Perhaps only a few people are happy about or want to learn from other people's achievements. If they give someone some praise, they usually follow it with a sarcastic remark.

古语：善哉 //《庄子·养生主》
雅语：实属不易
类语：真不错

2.2.6>

你再考虑考虑
[You should reconsider it.]

☺ 对话 Conversation

① A：离婚可是件麻烦事，你再考虑考虑。
Divorce is a serious matter, you should reconsider.

B：嗯。
Okay.

② A：是回国，还是留在这，我拿不定主意。

I cannot decide if I should go back to China or stay here.

B：你再考虑考虑吧。

You should think it over a little more.

 ## 语境

当哈姆雷特说"生存还是死亡，这是一个问题"时，他不是在讲道理，而是在选择。选择的过程，应该是考虑的过程。可惜，99%的人跟哈姆雷特一样，只在两条道路上进行选择，错！如果你有第三条路，或者更多，那才是真正的考虑呢。

 ## Context

When Hamlet says: "To be or not to be, that is the question." he is not explaining a principle but making a choice. The process of making a choice involves thinking the thing over. Unfortunately, ninety-nine percent of people are just like Hamlet who is only able to choose between two options. They are wrong! If you could find a third way or even more ways, that comes from really thinking things over.

古语："今吴、蜀未定，军旅在外，愿陛下动则三思，虑而
　　　後行，重慎出入，以往鉴来，言之若轻，成败甚重。"
　　　//《魏志·杨阜传》
雅语：再斟酌斟酌
类语：你再琢磨琢磨　　你再好好想想

2.2.7>

你自己好好儿想想吧
[You need to look at yourself.]

😊 对话 Conversation

① **A：** 为什么我一个好朋友都没有呢？
　　Why haven't I even one good friend?

　B： 你是怎么对待他人的，你自己好好儿想想吧！
　　How do you treat others? You'd better look at yourself first.

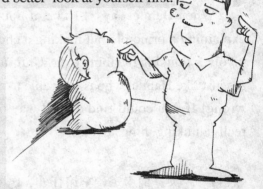

② **A：** 我的老婆、孩子不要我了，
　　我的情人又跟别人跑了，
　　你说，这是怎么回事呢？
　　My wife and children have
　　all left me and my lover ran
　　away with someone else.
　　What is going on?

　B： 那谁知道啊！你还是自己好好儿想想吧。
　　Who knows! You'd better look at yourself for the answer.

👉 语境

　　有人老是觉得自己对，并且坚持自己的思想和生活方式，到了混不下去的那一天，他才会找个人问：这是为什么？答案当然只能是：你自己好好想想吧。其实，孔子早在两千多年前就"每天三次检查自己"，及时改正错误。可惜，今天不少人习惯了把所有的问题推给时代、环境、政府、家庭、他人和命运什么的，完全忘记了自我批评的好处，等到无路可走的时候，就算知道了问题在哪，也晚了。

 Context

Some people think that they are always right and persist in their own ideas and life style. One day when they realize they are a failure, they will ask why? Of course, the answer can only be: "You'd better look at yourself." In fact, two thousand years ago, Confucius said, "Everyone should examine themselves three times per day," so they can correct their mistakes immediately. Unfortunately, many people now blame all their mistakes on modern times, the environment, government, family, other people, and fate. They absolutely forget the benefit of self-criticism. When they realize they have no way out, it is too late.

古语：见不贤而内自省也 //《论语·里仁》
雅语：你应该做自我批评
类语：你还是问问自己吧

2.2.8>

牛
[good for you]

☺ **对话 Conversation**

① A：昨天我一个人踢进四个球！
　　I kicked four goals yesterday!

　B：牛！
　　Good for you!

② **A：我再喝一瓶 XO，就可以打倒泰森。**
If I drink one more XO, I can knock out Mike Tyson.

B：牛什么呀！
Don't brag!

③ **A：去年我一共赚了 200 万。**
I made two million last year.

B：够牛的！
Good for you!

 ## 语境

　　此语原为贬意，近年来偏于褒意。在①中A是宣布自己的成绩，B是真心称赞。在②中A是说大话，B在嘲笑他。在③中A在炫耀财富，B在拍马屁。

　　吹牛是手段，目的是有"面子"。如果想让对方高兴，就要想办法吹捧他。因此当称赞、评价、鼓励某人某事时，均可用此语来表示"特别好"的意思。

 ## Context

This phrase was used as an insult, but now it is used as a compliment. In conversation (1), A announces his achievement and B sincerely praises him. In conversation (2), A is bragging and B is laughing at him. In conversation (3), A shows off his wealth and B flatters him.

People brag to gain "face". If you want to keep the bragger happy, you should find ways to flatter them. When you praise, assess, or encourage someone or something, you can use this phrase to mean "very good".

古语：踔厉风发 // 韩愈《柳子厚墓志铭》

雅语：登峰造极

类语：牛气

太棒了

[Great!]

😊 对话 Conversation

① A：咱们买的股票都升值了！

All the stocks we brought increased！

B：太棒了。

That's great.

② A：我要去哈佛大学读博士！

I am going to Harvard University to study toward a PhD.

B：太棒了。

That's great.

③ A：今天天气不错。

It's a beautiful day today.

B：太棒了。

It's a great day!

👉 语境

　　这句话表示赞赏，使用率很高。但是在不同情况下，意思也不一样。在①中，是正常的高兴。在③中，是没有意义的口头禅。在②中，有可能是虚假的称颂，因为听到别人的好消息，有的人会嫉妒，极少为别人高兴。所以，当有人给你"戴高帽子"时，在你很舒服、很得意时，一定要想一想，他为什么这样做？我们知道中国人是最要"面子"的，可是他为什么要把"面子"给你呢？或许是有所图。此言此法，无论对谁都是管用的，就看你给对方"戴"的合适不合适了。

 ## Context

This phrase indicates appreciation, so people use it a lot. But it can be used under different circumstances with different meanings. In conversation (1), it is used for normal happiness. In conversation (3), it is used as a common saying. In conversation (2), B offers an artificial congratulation to A. Because people are usually jealous of the good news of others and only a few are happy for them, when you hear people's praise and begin to feel comfortable, you should ask why before you feel too proud of yourself. We all know that Chinese people care a lot about "face", when people easily give you "face", they may have some hidden intentions. It is very useful to use this phrase to praise others, but you have to use it in the appropriate way.

古语：善哉！// 《庄子·养生主》
雅语：太好了
类语：没的说了　了不起

2.2.10>

雄起
[Go, go!]

☺ 对话 Conversation

① A：这些家伙今天怎么了？输了球也不着急！
What is going on with them today? They seem flat when the other team scores a point!

B：咱们一起喊：雄起！雄起！
Let's all yell: "go, go!"

② **A：这小伙子很有前途！**
This young guy shows promise!

B：再过两年一定雄起！
He will be excellent in two years.

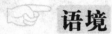 ## 语境

"雄"指男性，"起"指勃起。这句话一开始是四川足球迷的专用语，后来流行全国。意思变成"要努力""要拼搏""要像个男人"。多用在鼓励的场合，也作为小公牛刚发育时那种状态的比喻。

"雄起"的感觉是每一个男人和女人的追求，显示着生命的力量。可惜，不知道什么原因，无论是在体育竞赛场上，还是在99%的普通家庭生活中，都已经阴盛阳衰。这使男人很没面子，更被女人看不起！终于，"雄起"成了恢复"第一性"的呼唤。

 ## Context

This phrase originally meant "a male having an erection". It was especially used by soccer fans in Sichuan Province and is becoming widely popular now. It means to "work hard", "go all out in work", and "work like a man". It is usually used in encouraging situations or description of the early growth of a calf.

Males and females all subscribe to the phrase "hard work" and demonstrate the strength of life today. We don't know when it began, but females are now much more successful than males in sports and within ninety-nine percent of ordinary families. This makes females look down on males and, thus, males lose "face". Finally, this phrase becomes a call to return to a more balanced relationship between male and female.

古语：崭然见头角 // 唐·韩愈《柳子厚墓志铭》
雅语：春光乍泄
类语：加油

2.2.11>

有话好好儿说

[keep cool or calm down]

☺ 对话 Conversation

① **A：** 要是照你说的办，非得亡国灭种！你到底安的什么心？

If we do as you say, our country will be conquered and our people subjugated! What are you up to?

B： 老李呀，有话好好儿说嘛，没那么严重吧？

Old Li, please calm down. It's not that grim.

② **A：** 他……他……，我……我……

He... he.., I... I...

B： 别急，有话好好儿说，把他干的坏事都告诉警官！

Please calm down and speak slowly. Tell the police all the bad things he did.

 语境

　　如今真是口语时代，很多电影的片名，都直接采用一句口语。例如：张艺谋的《有话好好说》。关于"好"字，有很多种用法。一是好坏的"好"。二是"可以"。例：好吧，好说。三是"特别"。例：好冷，好热等等。可是这个"好好儿说"的"好"，并不在其中。于是就有了"好"的新用法，是"慢慢儿"的意思，除了"好好说"，还有"好走"可以证明。一些急性子的人，说话快得要命，别人一时没听懂，他就急得要打架。所以，应该让每个人都"有话好好儿说"。

 # Context

The trend today is toward a more colloquial language. Many films are using idiomatic phrases as their titles. For example: Zhang Yimou's "Keep Cool". There are many ways to use the word "good". One way is to judge whether something or someone is good or bad. A second way is whether something is acceptable or agreeable. A third way is to indicate the degree of something or someone, e.g., "very cold", "very hot", etc. But the phrase "keep cool" is not one of them, it is a new usage and means "calm down". It not only means "speak slowly", but also means "go safely". This expanding meaning may be explained by some Chinese who are quick tempered. They speak very fast and if the other party doesn't understand, they want to argue with them right away. Hence, it is important to ask everyone to keep cool.

古语：虽无丝竹管弦之盛，一觞一咏，亦足以畅叙幽情。//
　　　王羲之《兰亭集序》
雅语：心平气和地说
类语：别着急慢慢儿说

"缘" 来是你
[It was meant to be.]

😊 对话 Conversation

① A：难道我们前世有缘？
Were we related in a former life?

B：嗯，"缘"来是你！
Yes, we were meant to be!

② A：刚才那姑娘让我怦然心动！
That girl made my heart tremble with excitement!

B：这不就是"'缘'来是你"的感觉吗？
Is this the way fate feels?

 语境

　　"缘"字代表一种古老的关于人际关系的模糊理念。对男女之事来说，其大意是有缘的人早晚要碰到，无缘的人永远不会在一起。"缘来是你"是语言游戏，即：和我有缘的人原来是你。不过，"缘"仅指相遇的机会，并不代表相爱的过程和结果。所以还得加一个"分"字，合成"缘分"。有的人是"有缘无分"，即：可以相爱却不能结婚。有的人"有分无缘"即：结婚多年并无感情。还有的人是"缘尽于此"，即：相爱了一段时间以后，什么感觉也没有了。总之，"缘"是一种可遇不可求的东西。

Context

"Fate" is a vague concept used to explain interpersonal relations in earlier times. The meaning is roughly that if a male and a female are fated to be together, they will be together sooner or later. On the other hand, if their destiny is not to be together, they can not be together. "It was meant to be you." is a play on words, meaning "it is you who have a destiny with me". "Fate" is only the opportunity to meet, not the process and result of love. Hence, people can be predestined to meet but not have the good fortune to be together, fall in love, or marry. In other cases, people may be married for many years that were never meant to be together forever. Some can only love for a short time and then lose their feeling for each other. After all, fate is something that happens to you, you can't choose it.

古语：众里寻他千百度，蓦然回首，那人却在，灯火阑珊
　　　处。// 辛弃疾《青玉案（东风夜放花千树)》
雅语：相见恨晚
类语：有缘

2.2.13>

在哪儿呢
[Where are/were you?]

😊 对话 Conversation

① A：老李！好久没见，在哪儿呢？
　　Old Li, long time no see, where have you been?

　B：老张啊，我在广东学习呢。
　　Old Zhang, I'm studying in Guangdong.

② A：喂——，在哪儿呢？

Hello, where are you?

B：噢，亲爱的，我在办公室开会呢！

Oh my dear, I'm in my office for a meeting!

 ## 语境

　　这是常用的电话用语。除了在①中是同事或两地之间朋友打招呼以外，这句话是妻子对丈夫、女友对男友的专用语。这句话里有关心，有询问，有猜疑，有焦虑，更有催促回家的命令。传统的爱是比较麻烦的，不能有什么个人隐私。她需要了解你的工作、行踪、朋友，尤其是你周边的异性。如果你在晚饭时间还没回家，那么请你做好准备，回答这句话时千万别犹豫。

 ## Context

This phrase is used commonly in telephone conversations. It is a unique way for a husband and wife, or girlfriend and boyfriend to show their concern, make enquiries, relate suspicions, explain anxiety and urge the other to come home, except in conversation (1) where the colleagues or friends say hello to each other. There are problems in traditional love relationships because you shouldn't hide anything from your lover. She needs to know about your work, your whereabouts, friends, and especially the friends who are of the opposite sex. If you didn't come home before dinner, you should be ready to answer this question without any hesitation.

古语：沛公安在 // 《史记·项羽本纪》

雅语：何处

类语：干什么呢　忙什么呢

真的
[Really.]

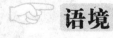 **对话 Conversation**

① **A：我考上哈佛大学喽！**
I have been admitted to Harvard University!

 B：真的？太棒了！
Really? That's great!

② **A：我发财喽！**
I've made a fortune!

 B：真的？几位数？
Really? How many digits?

③ **A：我写了一篇日记。**
I wrote an entry into my diary.

 B：真的？好。
Really? That's very good.

👉 **语境**

　　这是一句听者常用的话，可以表示很多意思。基本上包括相信与不相信两种。在①中是相信，同时有羡慕的意思。在②中是不相信，同时有嫉妒的意思。在③中出于礼貌，没有惊奇的意思。反正不管你听到什么消息，都可用这句话来回答。至于你到底是什么意思，就连好朋友也猜不出来，但你在礼貌上肯定是合适的。

☞ **Context**

This phrase can be heard frequently and expresses many meanings. Two basic meanings of this phrase show believing and not believing. In conversation (1), B believes A, and admires A's good fortune. In conversation (2), B doesn't believe A, and is jealous of A. In conversation (3), B is polite and shows no surprise. You can use this phrase on 'no-matter-what' kinds of information, and no one will know your real meaning, not even your good friends. But you surely display good manners by using it.

古语：嘻，善哉！//《庄子·养生主》
雅语：诚然
类语：是吗　哇塞

2.2.15>

最近忙吗
[Have you been busy recently?]

☺ **对话 Conversation**

① A：老李！最近忙吗？
　　Old Li, have you been busy recently?

　B：啊，啊，还可以。
　　No, not too busy.

② A：老张！最近忙吗？
　　Old Zhang, have you been busy recently?

B：噢，噢，老样子。

Oh, it's still the same.

 ## 语境

　　中国人打招呼的"第一句话"，原来是"吃了吗"。为什么这样问，是因为过去中国很穷，吃饭是最大的问题。所以，问这句话，最能体现对人的关心。改革开放以后，一般人的生活好多了，吃饭已经不是问题，人们每天忙来忙去，为的是做大事赚大钱。于是，这"第一句话"就自然地变成了"忙"和"不忙"的问题。在回答这句话时，请注意：不要太具体。因为，如果说"太忙"或者说"没事做"，都会引起猜想和一连串的为什么。所以，要回答得含糊一点。

 ## Context

Chinese people usually used "have you eaten" to say hello in earlier times. This is because China was poor and eating was the biggest concern. By using this phrase, you show that you care about others. After China's economic reform and opening toward the outside world, our standard of living has risen and eating is not the main priority anymore. People are very busy with major events and making money. Hence, it is natural to ask whether someone is "busy" or "not busy" when people meet each other. There is one thing that you should pay attention to! When you answer this question, you shouldn't give too much detail. If your answer is "too busy" or "nothing to do", it will lead others raise questions about you. You should give an ambiguous answer.

古语：亦无恙耶 // 《战国策·齐策四》
雅语：满面春风嘛
类语：怎么样

2 给别人面子
Give Other People Face

2.3
在弱势中
Weaker than Others

2.3.1>

不得了
[terrific]

 ## 对话 Conversation

① A：昨天的法国菜怎么样？
How was the French food yesterday?

B：哎呀！好吃得不得了！
My god! It was terrific!

② A：小红考上四所美国一流大学！
Xiao Hong has been admitted to four first-rate universities in the United States!

B：哇，真不得了！
Wow, that's terrific!

☞ **语境**

"不得了"可以表示程度很深，这里用于夸赞。在①中，法国菜特别好吃，"不得了"等于"太好了"，是虽然吃得很饱很舒服，但是还想再吃的意思。在②中，小红特别会考试，"不得了"等于"真棒"，考上一所就很了不起了，考上四所，实在是无人能比，出类拔萃。

☞ **Context**

"Terrific" can express a very extreme level of surprise and here is used to praise. In conversation (1), French food is extremely good. Even though B was fully satisfied with yesterday's meal, he still wants to have another meal like that one soon. In conversation (2), Xiao Hong has a lot of skill in taking entrance examinations. She must be extremely bright in order to be admitted to even one university, but she has been admitted to four universities. She stands out from the rest of the students.

古语：噫！甚矣哉！// 《庄子·在宥》
雅语：登峰造极
类语：太棒了　绝了

2.3.2>

不是开玩笑吧
[Are you teasing me?]

对话 Conversation

① A：明天我给你一万块钱买衣服！
I will give you ten thousand *yuan* to buy clothes!

B：不是开玩笑吧？
Are you teasing me?

② A：我想把自己所有的钱都送给穷人，一分钱也不给你留！
I want to give all my money to poor people and not leave you a penny!

B：不是开玩笑吧！
You must be teasing me now!

语境

　　在①中，B听到的消息太好了，她有点不敢相信，怕A是骗人，就用这句话来防止A改口。在②中，B听到的消息太坏了，她不愿意相信，她希望A是开玩笑，就用这句话来试探。总之，是要给对方留点"面子"。注意：中国人听到这句话时，99%都会回答：不是开玩笑。所以，在①中，B应该用这句话。在②中，B应该不说话。

 Context

　　In conversation (1), B heard some news that was so good she couldn't believe it. She is afraid that A is fooling her so she says this phrase to see whether A meant it. In conversation (2), B heard very bad news and she doesn't want to believe it. She hopes that A is teasing her and uses this phrase to discover the truth. In short, they all want to leave some "face" for the speaker. When ninety-nine percent of Chinese hear this phrase, they will answer "it isn't a tease." Hence, the answer in conversation (1) is correct, but in conversation (2) is wrong, B should keep silent.

古语：天子无戏言 // 《史记·晋世家》
雅语：君子一言　驷马难追
类语：你不是说着玩的吧

2.3.3>

可不是吗
[You can say that again!]

☺ **对话 Conversation**

① A：你这份工作挺不容易的！
　　Your job is very tough!

B：可不是吗!

You can say that again!

② A：我认为你的意见是对的。

I think that your opinion is right!

B：可不是吗!

You can say that again!

 语境

　　这句话，是肯定的意思。但是用生气的样子来说。因为，在一般人的眼里，大多数人看不起 B 的工作，如在①中。有比较多的人认为，B 的意见是错的，如在②中。所以，B 心里有气，当听到 A 的肯定后，B 很高兴，但同时又想：是啊，我一直是这么看，我的看法当然是对的，可其他人为什么不是这样看呢！B 用这句话，表示出自己的怨气。

 Context

This sentence confirms what was said, but is spoken with some frustration. In conversation (1), because everyone looks down on B's job, when A observes B's job, B is very pleased. It is the same in conversation (2), where most people think B's opinion is wrong, so when A thinks B is right, B is happy. At the same time, B knows that only one person agrees with him and doesn't understand why other people disagree with him. B uses this sentence to vent his frustration.

古语：不其然乎 //《论语·泰伯》
雅语：的确如此
类语：那当然啦　敢情

2.3.4>

酷毙了

[He is very cool.]

对话 Conversation

① A：你瞧见那歌手没有，高颧骨，塌鼻子，长头发，再加上声嘶力竭，真是要多难受有多难受！

Look, that singer has high cheek bones, a flat nose, long hair and shouts at the top of his voice when he sings! He makes me feel awful.

B：嘿，你还别说，现在最时兴的就是这样，叫"酷毙了"！

Hey, don't say that about him. He is very fashionable, very cool!

② A：哎！今天有三个一米九的老外来找小红！

Hey, three 1.9-meter tall foreigners came to visit Xiao Hong.

B：哇塞！我说她不一般吧，真是酷毙了！

Wow! I told you that she was out of the ordinary. This is so cool!

语境

"酷"，本有"特别""非常"的意思。近年来又有人发现它与英语的"cool"是"不谋而合"，于是，一时间广为流行。但是，这时的"酷"已不是一般的程度用语，而是对很多事、很多人都可以进行描述的万能的形容词。尤其是对比较丑、比较凶，好像"很男性化"的人和事，更觉用着很到位。比如①中的演员和②中的轰动性新闻。可是，"毙"又怎么讲呢？大概是"酷"得使人要死吧。

☞ **Context**

This word means trendy and extreme. Recently, we found another word that means something else but by coincidence, is pronounced similar to the word "cool" in English. This similarity makes the word more popular. This word is suitable for various things, especially for people or things that are unattractive, ferocious, or very manly or virile, e.g., the actor in conversation (1) and the sensational news in conversation (2). In Chinese, when they use the word "cool", they shout that something can be so "cool" that it can make you die.

古语：大王不以鄙陋寝容，愿纳以供箕帚之用。//《吴越
春秋·勾践阴谋外传》
雅语：喜怒不形于色　不苟言笑　冷若冰霜
类语：真叫酷　那叫一个酷　太酷了

2.3.5>

火得厉害
[flourishing]

☺ **对话 Conversation**

① A：听说，你的饭馆最近火得厉害?

　　I heard that your restaurant has really flourished.

　B：还行，总是坐得满满的。

　　It's okay, it's always full.

② A：听说，你的画廊火得厉害！

I heard that your gallery is flourishing.

B：哪儿啊！看画儿的挺多，买画儿的太少。

Who told you so! Many people come to look at the paintings, but not many of them are buying anything.

 ## 语境

　　"火"，是用正在燃烧着的火的感觉来比喻事业的兴旺，同时，也有"热闹"和"轰动"的意思。在①中，B赚到了钱，这是真的"火了"。在②中，B仅仅是制造了热闹，这是白"火"了一场。

Context

This word means a flaming fire and is used to describe something growing or flourishing. It also includes the meanings of bustling and sensation. In conversation (1), B is making money, so the business is really growing. In conversation (2), B says the gallery looks like it is bustling with viewers but he feels his efforts are wasted because no one buys.

古语：门庭若市 // 《战国策·齐策》
雅语：热闹非凡
类语：火了　火了一把　红红火火

2.3.6>

没您不成
[We can't do without you.]

😊 对话 Conversation

① A：我晚上有个应酬，我得
走了。
I've been invited out to dinner this evening. I have to leave.

B：怎么着老李！你没见这"三缺一"吗？没您不成！
How could you treat us like this! Don't you see that we can't play
mahjong without you.

② A：老李呀，明儿的新闻发布会我就不参加了，你主持吧。
Old Li, I cannot attend the news release tomorrow. You should
take charge of the conference.

B：那哪行啊？第一把手不在，还有什么信任度啊？没您不成！
How can you do this to me? No one will trust us if the director
isn't there. We can't have the conference without you!

👉 ## 语境

　　这是一句非常礼貌的客气话。在①中，打麻将得四个人玩，少一个
当然不成。在②中，重要的会议该有重要的人物，主要领导不出面，确
实也不成。虽然，讲这种话的人，只不过是要让听这句话的人高兴而已。
听这句话的人呢，感觉到自己对于他人的重要性，会觉得很有"面子"，
一般都会答应对方的请求。就算最后还是走了，那以后也说不出什么来。

所以，挽留一个人的时候，用这句话最合适。

 Context

This is a very polite and modest sentence. In conversation (1), they need four people to play mahjong and obviously need A in order to play. In conversation (2), an important meeting should be lead by the director. If the director can't attend the meeting it should be canceled. Although people use this sentence to make the person who will not be there happy, they will also feel that they are important and have more "face". The listener usually consents to their request. Even if they have to leave, they will not say anything later. Hence, you should use this sentence when you need to urge someone to stay.

古语：方蜀汉相攻，权在将军，举足左右，便有轻重。//
　　　《后汉书·窦融传》
雅语：非卿莫属
类语：你走了我们怎么办哪

2.3.7>

全仗您了
[We're all relying on you.]

对话 Conversation

① A：这件事求谁也没用，我们全仗您了。
　　There is no one else who can help us. We're all relying on you.

　B：包在我身上。
　　I'll take charge of the matter.

② A：这么大的麻烦，全仗您才给搞定了。

This problem has become too much trouble for us. We're all depending on you to settle it.

B：嗯，你们怎么谢我呀！

Okay, how will you thank me?

 ## 语境

"仗"是依靠的意思。按照传统，请人帮忙，不能同时请许多人。就像烧香拜佛似的，对每一座佛像都烧香是没有用的。理由：你不是特别重视我。心理："面子"给的不够。后果：会有新的麻烦。

 ## Context

This word means to rely or depend on someone. According to custom, you can't ask more than one person to help you with the same problem at the same time. It is much like burning incense and worshiping god, it wouldn't be very helpful to pray to every god because by doing so it would show that you didn't take any god seriously or give enough "face" or respect to them. Asking more than one person to help at the same time often results in new problems.

古语：恃此以不恐 //《左传·僖公二十六年》
雅语：全权拜托
类语：就指望您了　就这一柱香

是啊是啊
[Yes, yes.]

对话 Conversation

① A: 我觉得老李是完全错误的。

I think Old Li should take full responsibility.

B: 是啊是啊，老李太不对了。

Yes, yes. Old Li has gone too far this time.

② A: 我认为环境问题不是最主要的，有饭吃就行了。

I don't believe that the environmental problem is the most impor-tant issue. What we need is enough food to eat.

B: 是啊是啊，有饭吃是最主要的。

Yes, yes, enough food is more important.

语境

上级说什么，他就随声附和什么，这种人在汉语里叫"应声虫"。至于"应声虫"的目的，谁都能猜到，就不说了。可是，B是真的没有自己的看法吗？当然不是。如果B有一天当了领导，那他会比谁都固执。但是，到那时候，他是也喜欢"应声虫"呢？还是希望听到不同的意见呢？那就不知道了。

Context

Someone who agrees with the leader whether the leader is right or not is called a "yes man" in Chinese. Everyone understands what is on this kind of person's mind so we don't need to discuss it here. In both conversations, the question is whether B really has any opinions of his own? Of course, he does. One day, if he becomes the leader, will he be as stubborn as everyone else and will want to hear the "echo" or will he accept hearing opinions that differ from theirs? It is hard to know.

古语：曾子曰：唯。//《论语·里仁》
雅语：所见极是
类语：对对　没错

2.3.9>

帅呆了
[Very handsome!]

😊 对话 Conversation

① A：哇塞！你看对面那男孩，帅呆了！
　　Wow! Look at the boy opposite you. He's very handsome!

　B：是吗？我看帅的是人家，呆的是你！
　　Is that right? Well I think he's handsome and you're silly.

② A：哎，你的男朋友长得怎么样？
　　Hey, does your boyfriend look good?

　B：那还用说，绝对是帅呆了！
　　There's no question, he's extremely handsome!

语境

　　"帅"专门形容好看的男性。含意中有"英俊""挺拔""朝气""潇洒"等，好像京剧里的"小生"，或是美国男影星汤姆·克鲁斯。如今的"帅哥"比较少，有的女孩子却偏偏追"帅"，而不追"能力"、求"善良"。当然，作为"帅"的另一面，"酷"也挺叫座。于是，既不"帅"也不"酷"的，可就惨了。"呆"是"使人发呆"，就是碰到"帅哥"时，眼睛直勾勾地看，心里一片空白。注意！发这种呆的女孩，十个有十个失恋！

Context

　　"Handsome" is a special word used to describe a good looking male and includes traits like, bright, tall, energetic, stylish, etc, just like the young male role in a Beijing Opera or the American movie star Tom Cruse. Today, there are only a few extremely handsome boys around, but girls just pay attention to a man's looks, not their ability or kindheartedness. Of course, it will help his appeal if the boy is not that handsome but is 'cool'. Hence, it is sad for a man who is neither handsome nor cool. Sometimes girls stare at a handsome boy blankly. Please pay attention: this kind of girl is guaranteed to be disappointed in love.

古语：城北徐公，齐国之美丽者也。//《战国策·齐策》
雅语：一表人材
类语：美男子　俊小伙

听您的
[I'll take your advice.]

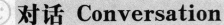

🙂 对话 Conversation

① A：这件事情，其他领导有不同意见。
Other leaders have different views on this matter.

B：我听您的。
I'll take your advice.

② A：我老了，我的看法可能过时了。
I'm getting old and my ideas may be out-of-date.

B：不，我们听您的，我们会认真考虑。
That's not true. We'll seriously consider what you say.

 ## 语境

这是一句上级、长辈和老师们喜欢听的话。在①中，B 的意思是：表示忠心，希望这位领导把他当做自己人，多加重用。在②中，B 的意思是：表示尊重，让老人觉得有"面子"。但是，事后不一定按老人的意见做。

Context

Higher authorities, older generations and teachers all like this sentence. In conversation (1), B shows his loyalty and hopes this leader takes his side and puts him in a more important position. In conversation (2), B respects the older generation and gives him a lot of "face" by saying so. But he may not necessarily follow the old person's suggestions later.

古语：惟命是从 //《左传·昭公十二年》
雅语：照办
类语：您说了算

3 不给自己面子
Don't Give Face to Yourself

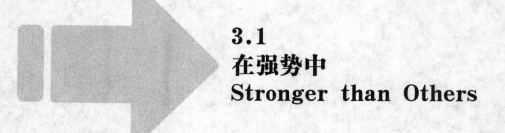

3.1
在强势中
Stronger than Others

别把我当人
[Don't be too polite to me!]

对话 Conversation

① A：老李！你可是贵宾！
Old Li, you're a distinguished guest!

B：干吗？别把我当人。
Why? Please don't treat me like a big shot.

语境

　　这句当代名言，出自作家王朔，影响非常大。表面上看，它的意思是：别对我太礼貌。实际上，里面包含有复杂的逻辑，流露出幽默的悲伤。按照传统交际理论，你尊重我，我也尊重你。王朔把话反过来说，因为你不尊重我，所以我也不尊重你。但是，其中还有几个"弯子"。如在①中，A很礼貌，B却那么说。为什么？答案：B受到过太多的不礼貌，已经变态。B的逻辑，可能由三个推理组合。(一)你们一直不把我当人，我习惯了。现在突然把我当人，我不习惯。所以，还是别把我当人。(二)你们一直不把我当人，我也从来没把你们当人。就算你们开始把我当人，我还是不想把你们当人。所以，别把我当人就对了。(三)被人当人很累，我怕累。不被人当人很轻松，我喜欢轻松。所以千万别把我当人。不管怎么说，这句话流行以后，真实的人——多了。

Context

　　This famous and influential remark comes from the author, Wang Shuo. On the surface, the sentence reads as "please don't be too polite to me". But, this sentence is also very complicated and expresses humor with a bit of sorrow thrown in. According to traditional ideas of communication, people should show respect toward each other. But, Wang Shuo turned this remark on its head, turning it into "if you don't respect me, then I don't have to respect you either." He didn't say it as straightforward as this, but there are still several different ways to understand this sentence, e.g., in conversation (1), A is very polite, but B asks impolitely, why? The reason could be that since B has been treated rudely all the time, this politeness is not normal. B's logic is: (1) you usually treat me bad and I am already used to it. Now you suddenly treat me so well, how can I get used to it? (2) You always treated me bad and my reaction was the same. Even if you now begin treating me well, I still will keep my previous attitude. (3) It is very tiring to be treated nice. I would rather be relaxed, so please don't pay any attention to me. However, after this sentence became popular, people too easily show their true feelings.

古语：我，小人也。//《左传·襄公三十一年》
雅语：毋须客套
类语：我受不了这个

3.1.2>

不好意思
[I'm sorry!]

😊 对话 Conversation

① A：张医生，老给您添麻烦，真不好意思！
Doctor Zhang, I'm sorry to trouble you all the time.

　B：老朋友了，干吗那么客气。
We've been friends for a long time, you don't have to be so polite.

② A：抢了你的男朋友，不好意思！

I am sorry I took your boyfriend away from you!

B：做都做了，还有什么不好意思？

It's done now, so there is no point in being sorry.

 语境

　　这句话本来是"有点害羞"的意思，后来变成"道歉"的意思，和"对不起"差不多。是近年从香港、台湾流传过来的。如果给别人添了麻烦，要表示歉意与谢意，可以用，如在①中。再看②，那是故意做出伤害他人的事，仍然说出这句话，这显然是有意嘲笑对方，毫无道歉可言了。有些人不愿意说"对不起"，因为那里面有"我错了"的含义。可是说"不好意思"就方便多了，只是礼貌一下而已，该怎么做还怎么做。

 Context

　　This phrase originally meant to be "embarrassed", later, it shifted to "apologized" or being "sorry" for something. Recently introduced into China from Taiwan and Hong Kong, this phrase is used when someone gives others trouble and serves as an apology and expresses gratitude. This is the case in conversation (1). In conversation (2), A took B's boyfriend intentionally. She uses this phrase to ridicule B, not express remorse. Some people don't like to say they are "sorry" because they feel that it also admits, "I am wrong". It is much easier for them to be "embarrassed" or "sorry". It not only shows a certain social grace, but also lets you act the way you want to later.

古语：廉颇闻之,肉袒负荆,因宾客至蔺相如门谢罪//《史记·廉颇蔺相如列传》

雅语：抱歉

类语：对不起

不惜一切代价

[give it all you have]

对话 Conversation

① **A：老李啊，听说你要不惜一切代价跟你老婆离婚？**

Old Li, I heard that you planned to divorce your wife at all costs.

B：没错！不惜一切代价！

You are right! I'll give it all I had.

② **A：什么？抓一个逃犯竟然用了28个警察！**

What? The lives of twenty-eight policemen were sacrificed to catch one prison escapee.

B：有什么不对吗？说了"不惜一切代价"！

What's wrong with that? You said we should give it all we had.

语境

凡事都应该有代价。不计算代价的事，好像就不光是事而是有"面子问题"了。就算是"面子"，也要考虑代价。否则吃了天大的亏，还能算有面子吗？个人的事，划不来也就算了，如①。可是大家的事，就不可以"不惜一切代价"地去干了。因为你要代表大家的利益，既然是利益，那就得算！其实，喜欢那么干的人也不是没算，而是算了自己的小账，不算国家的大账。如果代价都由自己掏腰包，那才看得出谁"惜"谁不"惜"呢！

Context

You have to pay for everything one way or another. Not everything is calculated by money, sometimes you have to pay in other ways, such as "face". Even with such abstract concepts as "face", we have to think about cost. For example, if you failed at a lot of things, how can you still have your "face"? Conversation (1) is related to individual issue so you can let it go. But if the thing is more public, you have to give it all you have to get the thing done well. When you do something for everyone's benefit, you still have put your own life on the line. There are many people who only think to benefit themselves and not many of them put themselves on the line for the country. If someone can pay for others out of his own pocket, we can say this person "spares no expense"!

古语：项羽乃悉引兵渡河，皆沉船，破釜甑，烧庐舍，持三日
　　　粮，以示士卒必死，无一还心。//《史记·项羽本纪》
雅语：破釜沉舟
类语：无论如何也得赢

3.1.4>

丑话说在前头
[Let me make it clear at the beginning.]

对话 Conversation

① A：丑话说在前头，跟我在一起，你得永远过苦日子。
First let me make it clear, you will be always poor if you tie the knot with me.

B：只要你永远爱我，就足够了。
I don't care, as long as you will love me forever.

② **A：** 丑话说在前头，向我借钱，利息是200%。

Let me make it perfectly clear, if you borrow money from me you must return it with 200% interest.

B： 啊？可是……那少借点吧。

What? In that case...I will only borrow a little.

 ## 语境

骗人的人，总是把好话说在前面。在①中，为了说明不骗人，A先把最不好的情况告诉B，没想到，却更坚定了B的爱情。看来这种方法很有用。在②中，A知道B急用钱，就公开地敲诈。表面看，A对这事无所谓；实际上，A在话里看不起B。A的意思是：你很穷，借了也还不起，算了吧；如果你一定要借，那么以后别说我没讲清楚。用这种办法的，是最"酷"的坏人。

 ## Context

Someone who is trying to cheat you will always start with good words. In conversation (1), A doesn't want to deceive B so he begins with the worst possibility. He never thought that he would strengthen B's determination by doing so. So, this method can be quite functional. In conversation (2), A knows B needs money badly. A extorts B openly. In this case, you shouldn't take the surface behavior of A and think he doesn't care. In fact, A holds B in contempt and thinks that even if I lend you money, you will never have the money to repay me. Hence, if you still insist on borrowing money from me, I have to put my condition out in the beginning so you don't blame me later. Only a very cruel person treats others like this.

古语： 约法三章 // 《史记·高祖本纪》

雅语： 申明利害

类语： 亲兄弟明算账

3.1.5>

看花眼了

[I have no idea which one to choose.]

☺ 对话 Conversation

① A：小红，这么多衣服，你到底买哪一套啊？
Xiao Hong, there are so many clothes, which ones do you like?

B：哎呀，都不错，我都看花眼了。
All of them are nice, I'm overwhelmed.

② A：老李，这么多漂亮姑娘，你最喜欢哪个？
Old Li, there are so many pretty girls, which do you like the best?

B：哇！我都看花眼了，我都喜欢。
Wow, I have no idea which one, I like them all.

☞ 语境

　　小红和老李都掌握着主动挑选的权利，所以很有"面子"。但是，人们往往在众多的选择对象面前就失去了评估能力，问题都在本来就没有固定的标准。审美的不确定性，是个大问题。如果摆在你面前的东西都是美的，那么，等于一千枝花挡在你眼前，那时，谁也无法选择。所以，让人看花眼了的商场，不聪明。

☞ **Context**

Xiao Hong and Old Li both have the right to choose among many options, so they all have "face". But, people often lose their ability to pick things when they are faced with a lot of choices. The problem is that there is no fixed standard for aesthetics. If everything is beautiful and the choice is up to you, it would be equivalent to one thousand flowers in front of your eyes. There is no way to choose one from another. So, when any marketplace overwhelms your ability to make a good choice, it's not a smart way to do business.

古语：目好之五色 // 《荀子·劝学》
雅语：雾里看花
类语：眼睛不够使　看不过来了

3.1.6>

我是他的 "粉丝"
[I am a fan of his.]

☺ **对话 Conversation**

① A：你喜欢周杰伦吗？
　　Do you like Jay Zhou?

　 B：他是我的偶像，我是他的 "粉丝"。
　　Yes, he's my idol and I'm his fan.

② A：你为什么崇拜我？
　　Why do you adore me?

B：您的报告太精彩了！还没听完，我已经成了您的"粉丝"。
Your lecture was wonderful! I became a fan of yours before you even finished your lecture.

 语境

对于偶像的崇拜，似乎是原始宗教的遗存，其实是人类的基本需求之一。不同的时代有不同的追求，到了21世纪的今天，最吸引眼球的就是演艺界、体育界那些经常在媒体上露脸的明星了。明星是时尚人物，具有短暂性。从这个意思上讲，"粉丝"这个fans的音译词的词义还真的不错，因为粉丝是一种不能长久保存的食品。

 Context

Worshiping idols is a tradition that originated in primitive religion. It is one of human nature's fundamental desires. During different historical periods, people have pursued many different kinds of idols. In the 21st century, everyone's attention is toward movie stars and sports stars. Stars are fashionable people but only last as idols a short time. From this perspective, the Chinese pronunciation of "*fensi*" is a perfect translation of the English word "fans", because "*fensi*" is a food product and doesn't last very long.

古语：予未得为孔子徒也，予私淑诸人也//《孟子·离娄下》
雅语：私淑弟子
类语：追星族　拥趸　哈韩　哈日

无处下嘴
[I don't know where to start.]

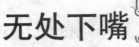 对话 Conversation

① A：这么大的肘子可怎么吃啊？根本无处下嘴！
This piece of pork is so big; I don't know where to start!

B：拿把刀来切着吃不就行了。
You'll have to cut it up with a knife first.

② A：这个课题当然要由我来主持，可是这么大的选题，我无处下嘴啊！
I'll take charge of this task. But this topic is huge; I don't know where to start.

B：没关系，多配几个助手就行了。
No problem, you should hire several assistants to help you.

语境

这句话在口语中一直使用，原意是对某种食物，不知道从哪开始吃。除①中的肘子外，还可以是其它较大、较圆、较硬或形状较奇怪的食品。但是这句话被当代作家王朔用过以后，转意为：对一件事情，一项工作来说，不知道从哪下手，如在②中。如果没有花时间了解情况，当然摸不着头脑。所以，"无处下嘴"的原因，大都是缺少事先的调查研究。

Context

This sentence has been used in verbal communication. It was originally used when people didn't know how to start to eat some food. Besides the pork leg in conversation (1), there are other foods that are strangely shaped or too big and tough to eat. But, the modern writer Wang Shuo used this sentence for another purpose. Here it means someone doesn't know how to start dealing with a job or a business, as seen in conversation (2). If you didn't spend the time to research the task facing to, you, of course, don't know where to start. So, you should get everything ready beforehand.

古语：刑罚不中，则民无所措手足 // 《论语·子路》
雅语：束手无策
类语：一点儿摸不着门儿

3 不给自己面子
Don't Give Face to Yourself

3.2
在均势中
Equal to Others

3.2.1>

不怎么样
[Same as always.]

😊 **对话 Conversation**

① **A：老李！好久不见，怎么样？**
Old Li, long time no see, how is everything?

B：老样子，不怎么样。
It's the same as always, not so good.

② **A：小红啊，你男朋友现在怎么样？**
Xiao Hong, how is your boyfriend doing?

B：不怎么样，他能怎么样！
Same as always, what can you expect of him?

👉 **语境**

"怎么样了"是对于情况变化的讯问，如果情况没有什么变化，就可以用这句话来回答。在①中，老李用了"老样子"，意思是：和过去一样。再用"不怎么样"，就又增加了一点"失望"的意思，因为他希望有好的变化，可是一直没有发生。在②中，小红的那句"他能怎么样"，意思是：他只能那样，不可能有好的发展。语气中表达了对男友的不满。

👉 **Context**

"How is everything going?" asks whether circumstances have changed. If nothing changed, you can respond with "same as always". In conversation (1), Old Li uses this phrase to show that there is no change. At the same time, he adds "not so good" to show his disappointment and say he has lost hope. In conversation (2), Xiao Hong adds "what can you expect?" This shows that her boyfriend can only be what he is and is unlikely to be better. Her response contains some discontent toward her boyfriend.

雅语：陈陈相因
类语：还那样

3.2.2>

烦着呢
[I'm in a bad mood.]

对话 Conversation

① **A：老李啊，你听我慢慢说嘛！**
Old Li, please listen while I explain.

B：烦着呢！别理我！
I'm in a bad mood, leave me alone.

② **A：老李，这个字怎么念？**
Old Li, how to pronounce this word?

B：烦着呢！呆会儿吧。
I'm in a bad mood! Ask me later.

 ## 语境

　　"烦着呢"这句形容北京男人心态的口语，出自生活，得自当代作家王朔笔下，曾经印在夏季"文化衫"背后，一直使用至今。每个人都有心情不好的时候，用一个"烦"字够了，变成"烦着呢"等于"正是最烦的时候"。可是，为什么那么烦呢？答案很简单：北京的男人们最要"面子"，做梦都想出大名、赚大钱，然后……！但是，他们没有本钱，没有项目，没有关系，没有办法，更不想一分钱一分钱地积累。于是，只剩下干着急。还有的不仅烦别人，也烦自己，最后所有人都特别烦。

 ## Context

This sentence describes the psychology of male population in Beijing and comes from real life. Writer Wang Shuo created this sentence and it was printed on the back of T-shirts for a while. Everyone can experience a bad mood sometimes. You can describe it as simply being "frustrated," but here it is used to confirm that the speaker is feeling bad right here and now. The reason the Beijing male is disgusted is simple. They all dream of being famous and rich, but they don't have money, business, connections, or any way to get these things. Moreover, they don't want to accumulate their capital penny by penny. So, all they can do is be anxious and helpless. Soon enough, they not only annoy other people, but also disgust themselves.

古语：病使人烦懑 //《史记·仓公传》
雅语：浮躁不安
类语：着急上火　气急败坏

3.2.3>

混得怎么样
[How are you getting on?]

☺ 对话 Conversation

① A：最近混得怎么样？
　　How are you getting on?

B：有点儿混不下去了。

I don't know where I am going next.

② **A：最近混得怎么样?**

How are you getting on recently?

B：还算混得下去。

I'm just managing to get by.

 ## 语境

"混"的意思是：比较随便的，不是认真的；比较消沉的，不是积极的；比较盲目的，没有固定追求目标的生活态度和生活方式。在①中，B的生活已经不能再继续下去。在②中，B对自己挺满意，话中还有点儿"谦虚"的味道。说实话，不少人是在"混日子"。他们缺少学历，缺少能力，缺少机会，更缺少奋起直追的心劲。所以，他们想来想去，只能"混"，"混"到哪儿算哪儿。当然，"混"自己，也就算了，严重的问题是：很多人在"混民族""混国家"。

 ## Context

This sentence is reserved for those people who are drifting along aimlessly day to day. They have a careless and depressed attitude toward life. In conversation (1), B doesn't even know how to take the next step. In conversation (2), B is kind of satisfied with himself and makes a modest response. Frankly speaking, there are many people who just fool-around in their life. They have no diploma, no skill, no opportunity, and, moreover, they have no energy to achieve these things. Their way of life not only damages them, but also harms our nation and country.

古语：存者且偷生 // 杜甫《石壕吏》
雅语：得过且过
类语：过一天算一天　做一天和尚撞一天钟

那我就不客气了

[I'll stop being so polite.]

😊 对话 Conversation

① A：老李，这些菜都是为你点的，怎么还不使劲吃啊！

Old Li, I order these dishes for you. Why don't you eat more?

B：哎，那我就不客气了！

Ok, I'll stop being so polite!

② A：战争期间，没有法律，不讲道德，想干什么干什么吧。

During war, there are no law and no morals, so people did what-ever they wanted to do.

B：说得对！那我就不客气了：金子、女子、车子、房子我全要！

You're right! So I'll stop being so polite: gold, women, cars, and a house, I want them all!

👉 语境

　　"客气"是有礼貌，一般人在初次见面时都比较礼貌，熟了也就无所谓了。当然，太客气了也受不了。如在①中，有人请老李吃饭。这种好机会，不大吃大喝还等什么？老李自然也想，于是用这句话结束了"客气"。②中的情况不同。不少人在干坏事的时候，会担心受到惩罚，但听到"绝对没事"的煽动后，就用这句话作为"施暴"的前奏。

Context

Politeness is good manners. People usually are comparatively polite when they meet for the first time. It doesn't matter as much after they become familiar with each other. Of course, people cannot bear if someone is excessively polite. In conversation (1), someone invited Old Li to have a meal. He should eat and drink to show he enjoys the food. So, Old Li uses this response to announce that he will stop being so polite. Conversation (2) is different. Many people are afraid of being punished when they do bad things. But when they hear an agitator's encouragement, they use this as an excuse to begin being violent.

古语：大行不顾细谨，大礼不辞小让。//《史记·项羽本纪》

雅语：不讲客套

类语：不管不顾

3.2.5>

舍不得
[I don't want to let any of that go.]

对话 Conversation

① A：把这些东西拿去扶贫救灾吧。

We should give all of these things to the poor and help people survive a natural disaster.

B：我有点儿舍不得。

I don't want to let any of these things go.

② A：你已经90岁了，还有什么放心不下的?

You're already 90 years old; why aren't you comfortable with this matter?

B：我舍不得财产、孙子和年轻妻子。

I hate to part with my possessions, grandson and young wife.

 语境

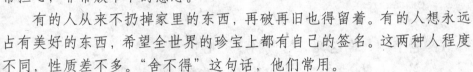

"舍"有"不要了""送人吧"的意思，"舍不得"就是还想保留。在①中，B是有些小气。在②中，"舍不得"是非常留恋、非常担心，非常放不下的意思。

有的人从来不扔掉家里的东西，再破再旧也得留着。有的人想永远占有美好的东西，希望全世界的珍宝上都有自己的签名。这两种人程度不同，性质差不多。"舍不得"这句话，他们常用。

 Context

This phrase means someone is reluctant to part with things or people. In conversation (1), B is a cheapskate. In conversation (2), B yearns for the past, and worries about the people who will live after him.

Some people never throw anything away, even when the things are broken or old. Some people want to own all the nice things and sign their name on all the world's treasures. These two kinds of people are similar in nature but at different extremes. They both use this phrase a lot.

古语：吾何爱一牛 // 《孟子·梁惠王上》
雅语：依依不舍
类语：放不下

添堵
[extra stress]

😊 对话 Conversation

① **A：** 前面塞车了，右拐绕过去吧。

There's a lot of traffic ahead, we should turn right and take a detour.

B： 啊？怎么右边塞车更厉害！真是添堵！

Wow, how can this road hold any more traffic? I don't need this extra stress!

② **A：** 老李啊，你这几天好像特不开心！

Old Li, you look very unhappy these days.

B： 是啊，前几天爱人下岗，正想办法呢，孩子又失学了！你说，这不是添堵吗！

You're right. My wife was laid off several days ago and I haven't found a way to recover from that yet. My children haven't been accepted to any school. I surely don't need any more stress.

 ## 语境

　　人，总会碰到不顺心的事。如果偶尔碰上一件，那也没办法。最怕的是刚刚碰上一件，还没解决呢，又碰上一件！同样难以解决。在这种情况下，人们不仅会烦，而且会觉得心里憋得慌，好像是一堵墙挡在了面前，这种感觉，就是"堵"。堵上加堵，就是"添堵"。如果你被"堵住"，最好找个朋友聊聊，然后静心等待，千万别干傻事！

Context

Sooner or later everyone experiences something unhappy. If you only have something unhappy happen once in a while, it would be okay. The worse situation is when you haven't had time to work out the first unhappy situation and a second one comes along. Under this stress, people will not only feel awful, they also find it hard to catch their breath. It feels like a wall is in the way and you cannot move around it. You feel stressed out. If you experience these kinds of circumstances, you'd better find a friend to talk to and then wait for good news. Please don't do anything stupid.

古语：心不快 //《史记·魏公子列传》
雅语：祸不单行
类语：添乱　裹乱

3.2.7>

万万想不到
[I can't believe it!]

对话 Conversation

① A：哎，电视说明天白天40度！那还不把人给热死！
Hey, the TV predicts it'll be 40 degrees tomorrow! That's deadly hot.

B：是吗？今年夏天这么热，真是万万想不到。
Really? I can't believe how hot it is this summer.

② A：哎，听说小红找了个工人。
Hey, I heard Xiao Hong has married a worker.

B：咦，万万想不到，瞧她平时那样，怎么还不得找个"款"哪！

I can't believe it. Based on her past behavior I thought that she would find someone with money.

语境

"想不到"就是"没往那儿想"。"万万"呢，就是即使想一亿次也不会想到那去。意思是根本不可能从那个角度去想。所以事情一旦发生，就觉得特别突然，简直无法接受。在①中，是想不到气温的高度。在②中，是想不到小红的归宿。其实，这两件事是"该想的"和"可以想出来的"吗？有的人经常使用这句话，说明他们想事的方式有问题。

Context

When you cannot believe something happened, it means you would never have imagined it even if you thought it over a million times. So, you should be very surprised and find it difficult to accept when it really comes to pass. In conversation (1), the weather is unexpectedly hot. In conversation (2), Xiao Hong acts out of character and unexpectedly decides to marry a worker. In fact, one cannot expect any certain results from these two circumstances. If someone uses this phrase too often, it only exposes a problem with their way of thinking.

古语：出人意表 // 苏轼《举何去非换文资状》
雅语：始料不及
类语：做梦也想不到　这怎么可能呢

这不是拱火吗

[Just trying to provoke me?]

😊 对话 Conversation

① **A：C 球队处处耍我们，这不是拱火吗？**
Team C is making fools out of us. Are they trying to provoke us?

B：千万别生气，找机会给他们点厉害！
Don't be angry. We'll find an opportunity to get back at them!

② **A：他先在公司骂我，又在街上用车挤我，他这不是拱火吗？**
He called me names in the office first, and then bumps against my car on the street. Is he trying to provoke me?

B：他是想和你打架，躲着他点吧。
He wants to fight with you and you'd better hide from him.

 语境

"拱火"，是想办法让对方生气，然后找机会打败对方的一种办法。在①中，C球队的水平高，但是不认真踢球，故意玩弄水平低的对手，这是不礼貌的。在②中，情况更复杂，"打架"里面，可能有很大的阴谋。不管怎样，当你发现有人"拱火"，千万别生气，要不然，就正好中了对方的计。

 Context

To provoke someone is to attempt to make them angry and create an opportunity to fight. In conversation (1), Team C is a better team, so they don't take the game seriously and intentionally play tricks on the other team. This is very impolite. In conversation (2), the situation is more complicated. When someone tries to provoke you into fighting them it may be a plot. You shouldn't let them make you angry, if you are angry, you just fall into their trap.

古语：欺人太甚 // 李贽《初潭集·卷三》
雅语：蓄意挑衅
类语：找茬打架

3.2.9>

这不是下套吗
[Is this a trap?]

☺ 对话 Conversation

① A：老李明知这事有假，还拉我去！
   Old Li already knew this thing was a fraud, but he still took me there!

   B：这不是下套吗？
   Was he setting a trap for you?

② A：这笔买卖好处太多了，我有点怀疑。
   There are too many benefits from this deal, it makes me suspicious.

B：会不会是有人"下套"？

Is someone setting a trap for us?

 ## 语境

　　"套"指"圈套"，原来是捕捉禽兽的方法，后来用在人的身上。意思是：设下圈套，让人上当。可叹的是，古今中外，每个人都被骗过，甚至自己钻进自己下的"套"。原因在哪儿？在人的欲望。危险在哪儿？在"套"里有你想要的东西。只要你有欲望，就早晚得被骗。如果你没有欲望，那不管什么"套"，就都没有用了。控制你的欲望！

 ## Context

Initially, a trap is what was used to catch animals, but lately it is used on human beings. Someone can set a trap and make others fall into it. Unfortunately, at one time or another, everywhere everyone has been cheated by someone. Some even walk into their own traps and cheat themselves. The reason for this is that people are filled with desires. Even though you know the dangers of walking into a trap, you can't control your desires and you take the risk. If you don't want to be cheated by others, you'd better control your desire.

古语：是网民也 // 《孟子·梁惠王上》
雅语：骗局　陷阱
类语：出老千儿　坑人

折了
[to lose]

😊 对话 Conversation

① **A：** 老李呀，这一段股市倍儿火，发财了吧！

Old Li, stock values have been going up; you must be rich by now.

B： 发昏吧！最近折了几十万。

Are you kidding? I've lost thousands recently.

② **A：** 老李，咱们上回谈那项目怎么样了？

Old Li, how's that project that we talked about?

B： 嗨，别提了！早折了。

Don't mention it! That project fell through a long time ago.

③ **A：** 哎，昨儿半夜那场球儿，咱们女足赢了吗？

Hey, did our women's soccer team win the game last night?

B： 唉，折了。

No, they lost.

👉 语境

　　"折"，原意是"断"，转意为"亏损"，引申为"终止"或"失败"。在①中，是炒股票赔进去很多钱。在②中，是一个项目的谈判已经停止。在③中，是比赛失利。在以上三个对话和当下的日常生活中，"折"都是一个不好的音，是丢了"面子"的意思。可是，中国有句古话叫宁折不弯，是说"折"比"弯"好。看来，"面子"也是会变的。

Context

This word originally meant to "break", and then to "lose money in business", later its meaning was extended to include "end" or "fail". In conversation (1), Old Li took a chance by buying stocks and lost a lot of money. In conversation (2), a proposed project has already failed in the negotiations. In conversation (3), the team lost the game. From these three dialogues and examples in daily life, this word implies a negative result and a loss of "face". Still, there is an old Chinese saying about it: it's better to break than bend. So, sometimes you may gain "face" even if you "lost" or "failed".

古语：赔了夫人又折兵 // 《三国演义·五十五回》
雅语：出师不利
类语：赔了　亏了　栽了

3 不给自己面子
Don't Give Face to Yourself

3.3
在弱势中
Weaker than Others

3.3.1>

不在状态
[to feel flat, unmotivated]

☺ 对话 Conversation

① A：还差三分钟就要比赛了，你怎么一点精神也没有？

   There are only three minutes left in the game, why aren't you excited?

   B：我，我紧张不起来，根本不在状态！

   I can't get motivated, I feel flat!

② A：今天大比分输给弱队，什么原因呢？

   We lost to a team that is not as good as us today, why?

   B：搞不清楚，可能不适应场地吧，反正大家都不在状态。

   I don't know, may be the venue didn't suit our team. In any event, we came out flat.

☞ 语境

本句中的"状态"专指"竞技状态"。即：有没有那种渴望决一死战的拼搏精神与体能准备。如果有，那就会将自己平时的水平发挥到极点；反之，就会稀里糊涂地败下阵去。有的人一比赛就失常，有的人一比赛就超常。其实，所谓"状态"主要是两个东西，一是心理平衡状态，一是身体兴奋状态。如果"心态"不好，"体能"也不好，那么各方面的水平和技巧就很难发挥出来了。

Context

This sentence refers specifically to athletic competition. It deals with

古语：心不在焉 //《礼记·大学》

雅语：心猿意马

类语：提不起精神

3.3.2>

差得太远了

[to lag behind]

☺ 对话 Conversation

① A：老李啊，你看看现在的大学生，又会英语，又会电脑，又会开车……什么都会！

　　Old Li, these college students now can speak English, use computers, and drive...!

　B：是啊，咱们差得太远了！只能等着下岗了。

　　Yes, our generation lags behind in these skills! We can only wait to be laid off.

② A：老李呀，你看看人家发达国家，"硬件"好，"软件"更好！

　　Old Li, the developed countries not only have better "hardware", they also have better "software"!

　B：是啊！咱们差得太远了！玩命追吧！

　　That's right! We lag behind them. We have to try very hard to catch up!

 语境

　　差距，总是有的。在①中，是中老年与年轻人的差距。在②中，是发展中国家与发达国家的差距。过去，我们不知道差距；现在，我们知道了。

 Context

There is always gap between people and things. In conversation (1), there is a gap between the skills of the older generation and the younger. In conversation (2), there is a gap between developing countries and developed countries. We were not sure about this gap between a developing country and a developed country before, but we know now.

古语：弗如远甚 //《战国策·齐策》
雅语：望尘莫及
类语：一辈子也追不上　没什么希望了

3.3.3>

 # 大锅饭

["Big-Pot" distribution system]

对话 Conversation

① A：这几年收入怎么样？

　　How is your income these days?

　B：嗨，"大锅饭"呗，能怎么样！

　　Hey, the same as always, in the "Big-Pot" system, everyone is the same.

② A：听说你下岗了？

　　I heard you were laid off?

B：是啊，连"大锅饭"也吃不上了！

Yes, I can't even eat in the canteen like everyone else.

③ **A：改革就是要打破"平均主义"，多劳多得。**

Economic reform will break up the "equalitarianism" system, from then on the more you work the more you earn.

B：说的对，可是多数人还得吃"大锅饭"。

You're right, but most people will still live in the "Big-Pot" distribution system.

 ## 语境

"大锅饭"原指一大家人在一个锅里吃饭，后来成了"平均主义"的同义词。其实，在一家人里，吃的多少也不一样，不是真正平均。不过，这种家庭吃饭的方式，变成社会分配方式以后，矛盾就出来了。改革开放二十多年来，想了很多办法去解决，但是不容易。

 ## Context

A "Big-Pot" system originally referred to family members eating from one pot. Later, it is used to refer to an "Iron Bowl" equalitarian distribution system. In fact, even in a family, some eat more and some less. There is no absolute equal. So, there are contradictions when we try to apply a family distribution system to a large social income distribution system. China has now been reformed and opened to the outside world for over 20 years. We have tried many ways to solve this problem. It is not an easy subject.

古语：盖均无贫 //《论语·季氏》
雅语：平均分配
类语：铁饭碗

倒霉
[bad luck]

😊 对话 Conversation

① A：今天真倒霉！干什么都不顺，刚才喝凉水都差点呛死！
I've got bad luck today, nothing is going right. It's so bad that I almost choked drinking some cold water just now.

B：老李呀！那就歇歇手，啥也别干，过两天就好了。
Old Li, you'd better take a break for a few days.

② A：小红！大家伙儿都在搬书，你怎么不动啊？
Xiao Hong, everyone is carrying books, why don't you help?

B：我倒霉了！
I have my period today!

 语境

"霉"指东西坏了，变质了。"倒霉"指撞上恶运。在①中，老李就因此而气恼。其实B当时的话是对的：人总有"顺"和"不顺"的时候；

如果连着几件事不顺，那就该停停手，不要硬顶。只要你能保持平和的心态，好运气不久就会转过来了。②中的用法比较特殊，是年轻女性的专用词，特指女性每个月来一次的那件麻烦事。

 # Context

　　This phrase means someone has bad luck. In conversation (1), Old Li is very angry about his bad luck. In fact, B is correct, anyone can experience lucky and unlucky times in their lives. When you continually run into bad luck, you'd better stop a while. If you can keep a gentle disposition, good luck will come to you soon. Conversation (2) is a special use of this phrase to describe a female's menstrual cycle.

古语： 时运不齐，命途多舛。// 王勃《滕王阁序》
雅语： 祸不单行　运气不佳
类语： 走背字　背时　不顺

3.3.5>

还真没看出来
[I didn't see (realize) that.]

😊 对话 Conversation

① A：老李，你睁开眼睛仔细看看，这块玉是清朝的！
　　Old Li, you should look at this more carefully, this piece of jade can be dated only to the Qing Dynasty!

　 B：我再看看……，哎呀！还真没看出来！我还以为是汉朝的呢！
　　Let me look again..., ah, I didn't see that! I thought it was from the Han Dynasty!

② A：老李啊，我这张画儿画了三个月呢！

　　Old Li, I've spent three months painting this picture!

　B：噢？还真没看出来！

　　I couldn't tell!

语境

　　这句话大概有两种用法，一是把破东西看成了好东西。如在①中，老李差点让卖旧货的给骗了。这是很丢"面子"的事情，所以老李在用这句话为自己解嘲。二是在据说不错的东西里，并没有看出什么意思来。如在②中，老李的话是暗含讽刺。意思是说：像这种画还用画三个月呀！三小时都多。

Context

This sentence can probably be used in two ways. One way is when you mistake some invaluable thing for something valuable. In conversation (1), Old Li was almost tricked by the salesman at the second-hand shop so he is very embarrassed. He uses this sentence to excuse himself. The second way is when you cannot recognize some valuable things. In conversation (2), Old Li uses this to ridicule A's painting. He is implying that the painting is not good enough to be worth three months work, not even three hours.

古语：胜不敢复相士 // 《史记·平原君列传》

雅语：大跌眼镜

类语：走眼了　打眼

3.3.6>

就等着那一天吧

[Just you wait, the day will come.]

☺ 对话 Conversation

① A：老李呀，听说你要攒钱买辆奔驰？

　　Old Li, I heard you are saving money to buy a Mercedes Benz?

　B：比较遥远是不是？没问题，就等着那一天吧。

　　Some day I will. No problem, just wait, the day will come.

② A：孩子他爸，你什么时候能给我们娘儿俩买幢别墅住住？

　　Child's father, when will you buy a villa for us to live?

　B：有希望，啥时咱也能贷上款，不就齐了吗！就等着那一天吧。

　　There's hope. When we can get the loan, we'll buy it. We have to be patient, the day will come!

 语境

　　很多上了点年纪的人，喜欢说这句话。因为，在这句话里，流露着太多的挣扎，太多的无奈，太多的希望，太多的疲乏。如在①和②中，一辆中高档轿车，一幢郊外的别墅，对于一个普通的中国男人来说，确实是必须付出一生的心血，才有可能实现的梦想。放弃这个梦，身上就一点劲也提不起来，追求这个梦，又觉得太累，比较渺茫。不少大男人们的生命，就流失在这坚韧的磨砺之中。

☞ **Context**

Many older people like to use this phrase because they have experienced many struggles, periods of powerlessness, unfulfilled desires, and exhaustion in their life. In both conversations (1) and (2), a normal Chinese man has to make a lifetime of effort to pay for a-middle-to-high grade car or a suburban house. If they give up that dream, they will loose their will to live. But in their pursuit of this dream, they feel very tired and uncertain. Many a man's life is drained away by these kinds of hardships and anxieties.

古语：心向往之 // 《史记·孔子世家》
雅语：翘首以望
类语：慢慢熬吧　活着的人都看得见

3.3.7>

来不及了
[It's too late.]

☺ **对话 Conversation**

① **A：老李快走！电影还差 10 分钟就开演了！**
　　Old Li, quickly! There are only 10 minutes before the movie starts.

　B：来不及了！我的自行车还得打气呢！
　　That's not enough time! My bicycle tires still need air.

② **A：小红啊，你应该和你男友谈谈，一起去美国发展。**
　　Xiao Hong, you ought to talk to your boyfriend and go to USA together.

B：来不及了，他昨天已经飞了。

It's too late, he left yesterday.

 ## 语境

"来不及了"，大概有两种情况。一是具体的意思：还有一点时间，但是肯定不够用。如在①中，等老李出了门，打完气，电影早就开演了。二是抽象的意思：时机已经错过，再说也没用了。如在②中，想去美国，早就该谈啊，干吗等人家在那边都下了飞机了，你在这边才动心思呢？不管是看电影还是去美国，我们最好在事先有比较充分的准备。一个成熟的人，应该不用"来不及了"这句话。

 ## Context

This phrase can be used in two different cases. One case is to describe actual time: there is a little time left, but not enough. In conversation (1), if they wait for Old Li to pump up his bicycle tires, the movie would have already started. The second case is to draw a conclusion from objective facts: someone has missed the opportunity; there is no point in talking about it anymore. In conversation (2), if you wanted to go to the USA with your boyfriend, you should have talked about this earlier and it isn't useful to mention after he left. No matter of watching movie or going to the Unite States, we had better have adequate preparation. As a mature person, you shouldn't use this phrase much at all.

古语：岂可及哉 // 《说苑·建本》
雅语：错过时机
类语：赶不上了　晚了

3.3.8>

脸都丢尽了

[to lose face]

☺ 对话 Conversation

① A：哎，听说你老婆昨天到公司来骂了一天？

Didn't I hear that your wife nagged you all day?

B：嗨，别提了，我的脸都丢尽了。

I'm so embarrassed; I have lost all my face.

② A：哎，这件事要是让亲戚朋友们知道了怎么办？

What will we do if all of our relatives and friends know about this?

B：是啊，我怕的就是这个，那咱们的脸就都丢尽了！

You're right; I'm also worried about this. We'll lose all our face if they find out.

☞ 语境

"脸"，就是"面子"。我们碰到的各种麻烦，都和"面子"有关。人，活的就是个"面子"。不同的时代，不同的地区，不同的人群，有不同的"面子"。可是，"面子"到底在哪儿呢？对一般人来说，它就在①中的同事，②中的亲戚和朋友们的嘴上。对于一个国家、一个民族来说，它的"面子"就在舆论界的嘴上。所以，说来可笑，人们实际上都是为他人的看法在活着，我们最怕的，是那些看不见的嘴。

Context

People care about their dignity, their "face", and there is always a close relationship between a person's "face" and the troubles and difficulties they run into. There are varying degrees of "face" in different areas and among different groups. But, it is hard to say where the concern for one's "face" ends. In conversation (1), the "face" in question is between colleagues. In conversation (2), the "face" in question concerns relatives and friends. In general, "face" depends on what is said in the media and press when we talk about a country and a nation. It is ridiculous to admit that people live their lives in fear of other's opinions. We are most afraid of other people's mouths.

古语：我何面目见之 // 《史记·项羽本纪》
雅语：无地自容
类语：没脸见人　栽面儿

3.3.9>

全都红了眼

[green with envy]

😊 对话 **Conversation**

① A：领导啊，一车间每人发了 1000 块钱奖金！咱们的人全都红了眼！

Boss, everyone in the first workshop got 1000 *yuan* bonuses. Our people are all green with envy!

B：老李呀，咱们车间情况不同，100 块也发不出来呀！

Old Li, the situation with our workshop is different, we even can't even offer 100 *yuan* bonuses.

② A：书记，邻村生产搞得好，小伙子们全娶了媳妇！

Secretary, the next village has boosted their production and all their young fellows can find girls to marry.

B：咱们村的光棍全都红了眼是不是？那就玩命干活吧！还等什么？

The single men in our village must be jealous, aren't they? They should work harder! What are they waiting for?

 语境

　　外国有很多社会学家，谈到人生的种种需要，讲得比较复杂。孟子说得挺直接，认为基本上就是"食"和"色"。今天的人更简单，只剩下一个"钱"字。似乎有了钱就有了一切。如果钱真是万能的，那么人看

209

到钱以后，眼睛因为充血而发"红"，也就不奇怪了。用劳动去换钱吧，那才是真正的"面子"；用眼睛去看别人的钱，只会给自己添堵。

 ## Context

Many foreign sociologists talk about human needs in a very complicated way. But, Mencius treated the topic in a simple and straightforward way. He divided human needs into two categories: food and companionship. Today, people see their need primarily through one term: money. It seems if you have money, you will have everything. If money really can do everything, it would be understandable that people's eyes would turn green from jealousy. But, the only way to get rich is through hard work. If you look at other people's money, it will increase your unhappiness.

古语：垂涎闪舌兮 // 柳宗元《招海贾文》
雅语：垂涎三尺
类语：见钱眼开

3.3.10>

让您见笑了

[Please excuse me.]

对话 Conversation

① A：老李呀，你这文章里语法错误不少啊！
　　Old Li, there are a lot of grammar mistakes in your article!

　 B：是，是，让您见笑了，我的语法真的不灵！
　　Oh, yes, yes, my grammar is not good at all, please forgive me!

② A：老李呀，你昨天给我家送那些礼物干吗？

Old Li, why did you give me all those gifts yesterday?

　　B：哎呀，什么礼物？都是老家的土产，让您见笑了！

They're not gifts. Please excuse me; those are only local products from my hometown!

 ## 语境

很多人都喜欢争"面子"，摆"架子"，但是，那也得看是谁。当面对上级或师长的时候，这句很谦虚的话就有用了。假如尊长们提出了一些意见，那么大多数人在找借口的同时，还是会点头称是的。例如很多人会用这句话，但是很少有人说"我错了"。所以，这句客气话里，有一点虚假的味道。

 ## Context

Many people struggle to gain "face" and put on airs. But, they change their attitude completely when they talk to their supervisor or leaders. Then, they usually use this phrase. If the leaders suggest changes, most of these people will make some excuse and agree with the leaders' opinion. By using this phrase they demonstrate their politeness and avoid admitting any mistake.

古语：吾长见笑于大方之家 //《庄子·秋水》

雅语：污人耳目

类语：不好意思　拿不出手

我哪儿会啊
[How can I know how to do that?]

☺ 对话 Conversation

① **A：想进我的公司？好，老李呀，你会英语、电脑吗？**
You want to work at my company? Okay, Old Li, can you speak English and use a computer?

B：这些新玩艺儿，我哪儿会啊！
How can I know these new skills?

② **A：老李呀，结婚以后，买菜、做饭、带孩子什么的都归你。**
Old Li, you will have to cook, do the shopping, and take care of a child after you are married.

B：啊？这些事，我哪儿会啊！
What? How will I know how to do that?

👉 语境

　　"会"，有面子；"不会"，没面子。谁不愿意说"我会"呀？可是，社会发展太快，越来越多的人，只会过去的东西，如果你问他新知识、新技能，他肯定非常气愤地说："我哪儿会啊！"在①中，老李是过时的人，不可能会，也补不上了。在②中，老李却必须回到传统女人的角色，去干那些本来不该男人做的事。所以，老李在②中的意思是："我不应该会呀！"

Context

If you know how to do everything, you gain a lot of face. So everyone likes to say "yes, I can do it." But, society is developing so fast, most people can't keep up with it. If you ask them about new knowledge and new technology, they become very angry and say: how am I supposed to know? In conversation (1), Old Li's knowledge and skills are out-of-date, and it is impossible for him to learn fast enough. In conversation (2), Old Li has to do the jobs that are traditionally female work. So, he emphasizes this by saying that he did not expect to have to know these things.

古语：我不能 //《孟子·梁惠王上》
雅语：掌握不了
类语：我什么也不会

3.3.12>

我哪说得上话啊
[I have no Influence.]

😊 对话 Conversation

① **A：** 这件事我麻烦大了！老李呀，你帮我跟领导说说情儿。

Old Li, I am in a lot of troubles, could you plead my case to the leader?

B： 我倒是想帮你，可是我也没什么份量，哪说得上话啊！

I would like to help you, but my word doesn't carry any weight with the leader. I have no influence.

② **A：老李呀，我老婆跟我分居八年了！你帮我说和说和吧！**

Old Li, I have been separated from my wife for eight years, could you help patch things up between us?

B：可以是可以，但我从来没见过你老婆，我哪说得上话啊！

Okay, but I haven't even met your wife, why would she listen to me?

 ## 语境

这句话大概有两种情况。一是推辞。在①中，A的麻烦很大，谁也不想帮，老李在这用了"自贬"的方法，意思是：我没有资格去和领导谈这件事。二是关系太远。如在②中，老李不识A妻，当然无法在两边进行沟通。总之，此话的意思是：无论从哪个角度都没办法进行谈话。

 ## Context

This sentence is generally used in two situations. One situation is to refuse something. In conversation (1), A is in a lot of trouble and nobody wants to get involved to help him. Old Li refuses to help by stressing that his word has no value with the leader. The second situation is also a refusal and relies on the fact that there can be no influence if there is no relationship. In conversation (2), Old Li doesn't know A's wife, so of course he cannot nego-tiate their relationship because there is no way to begin a conversation to change someone's mind.

古语：人微言轻 // 苏轼《上执政乞度牒赈济因修廨宇书》
雅语：不容置喙
类语：我说话没用

我是看蹭票的
[I never buy a ticket.]

😊 对话 Conversation

① A：哎，后天的芭蕾舞你买着票了吗？
Hey, have you bought a ticket for the Ballet the day after tomorrow?

B：买什么票啊，我是看蹭票的！
Why should I buy a ticket, I can get in for free.

② A：哎，老李什么演出都能混进去，有窍门吗？
Hey, Old Li seems to have a free-pass for all the shows, what's his secret?

B：嗨，他是蹭票的专家，什么招儿都有！
He's an expert at getting free tickets; he knows a lot of tricks.

☞ 语境

"蹭"，本意是"摩擦"。在流行语里，专指不花钱却能达到目的的方式。比如："蹭吃""蹭车"什么的。在①和②里说的都是"蹭票"，就是不买票，白看演出。方法大概有：找赠票，等退票，跟演员交朋友，认识检票员等等。出现这种死不买票的人，是因为票价太贵呢？还是因为"白看"很有面子呢？这只能请"老李"来回答了。

☞ Context

This sentence originally means to rub, but in popular use it means a way to reach your goal without spending any money. Two examples of this are a party crasher and someone who steals a ride on the bus by not buying a ticket. In conversation (1), B never buys tickets for shows because he either finds a free ticket, waits for a ticket that someone else cannot use, makes a friend of someone in the show, or knows the ticket-taker so he can sneak in. We should ask Old Li whether these kinds of people don't have enough money or think they gain "face" by getting in a show for free.

古语： 你又赶了来撤茶吃 // 《红楼梦·四十一回》
雅语： 蒙混过关
类语： 找张票呗　　混进去得了　　搭顺风车呗

3.3.14>

下台阶
[to give excuse]

😊 对话 Conversation

① **A：** 我说过要打败他，却打成了平手！怎么下台阶呢？
　　I said that I would beat him, but we played to a draw. What can I use as an excuse?

　 B： 就说昨儿晚没睡好。
　　You should say that you didn't sleep well the night before the game.

② **A：** 三年前我离开了家，现在又想回去，怎么下台阶呢？
　　I have left my home three years ago and now I'd like to go back. What reason can I give?

　 B： 是啊，得找个体面的理由。
　　You're right, you need to find a decent excuse for returning.

语境

在①中，A 说大话，说了以后，不能实现。这时，需要找点借口来解释一下。不然，A 就丢了"面子"。在②中，A 犯了错误，家里人不原谅。这时，需要找一个家里人能接受的理由；不然，就无法沟通。总之，A 都是在丢了"面子"的时候说这话的。

Context

In conversation (1), A bragged but couldn't back it up. So he needs to find an excuse to explain why he fell short. If he doesn't, he will lose a lot of "face". In conversation (2), A made a mistake and his family can't forgive him. He needs to find a reason his family can accept. Then, they can restore the relationship. In short, A uses this sentence because he has lost "face" in front of his family.

古语：君子疾夫舍曰"欲之"而必为之辞 //《论语·季氏》
雅语：寻找借口
类语：有个说法　怎么收场

3.3.15>

现了大眼了
[to be shamed]

☺ 对话 Conversation

① A：咱们儿子的学习成绩一直全校第一，可是这次没考上大学！
Our son's study has always scored at the top of his school, but he wasn't admitted to university!

B： 唉，明天亲戚朋友同事什么的就都传开了，咱们可现了大眼了!

Sigh, all our relatives and friends will find this out tomorrow. We'll be so embarrassed.

② **A：** 你的儿子昨天被警察抓走了!

Your son was taken away by the police yesterday!

B： 咳! 警笛在楼下叫了10多分钟，全楼的人都瞧见了，这回我可现了大眼了!

Sigh, the police siren sounded for over ten minutes, everyone in the building saw it. What a disgrace!

③ **A：** 听说你昨天误入女厕所了?

I heard that you went into a women's bathroom by mistake yesterday.

B： 嗨，没带眼镜，看不清牌子，我这次可现了大眼了!

Sigh, I didn't have my glasses on so I couldn't read the sign. I am so ashamed!

 语境

"现眼"这个词的份量，比"没面子"重。意思是：正当最没面子的时候，被很多熟人看见、知道和议论。在①中，是儿子没考上大学。在②中，是儿子被警察抓走。可是这两个例子中有一个问题：真正"现眼"的人——儿子的态度并不知道，觉得特别"现眼"的，反到是亲近的人。所以，造成"现眼"和觉得"现眼"，有时不是一回事。在③中，是自己做的事，自己"现眼"。

Context

This phrase implies something more serious than losing one's "face". It means that all of one's friends and acquaintances know something happened that spoils one's reputation. In conversation (1), everyone will know that the son didn't do well enough on his exams to go to university. In conversation

(2), everyone saw the police taking the son away. There is a problem with these two examples: we don't know how the sons felt about these incidents — we only know the shame their family felt. Doing something that causes shame and feeling shame about it are two different things. In conversation (3), the person who made the mistake is also the person who felt embarrassed by it.

古语：且籍与江东子弟八千人渡江而西，今无一人还，纵江东父兄怜而王我，我何面目见之？//《史记·项羽本纪》

雅语：无地自容

类语：丢人　丢脸　出丑

3.3.16>

一点儿小意思

[This is just a small token.]

☺ 对话 Conversation

① A：太客气了吧，送这么多礼物！

You are being too polite by giving me so many gifts!

B：哪里，一点儿小意思，不承敬意。

Not at all, these are only small tokens of my respect and are hardly worth noticing.

② A：一点儿小意思，不值一提。

These are only small gifts, don't mention them.

B：哎呀！这么重的礼，我怎么敢收呢！

My god, we wouldn't dare accept such large gifts!

语境

我们知道很多人习惯了吹牛。可是，为什么在送礼的时候，一定要那么客气呢？因为，送礼的目的，是要给人家添麻烦。这份礼物和那个麻烦相比，再大也还是小。所以，"一点儿小意思"就成了送礼的专用语。

 Context

We know that many people like to brag. But, why are they so polite when they give gifts? Because they know when they give gifts, they will later ask the person receiving the gift for a favor. So, no matter how big the gift is, it will be smaller than the trouble it causes for the person receiving it. Hence, this phrase has taken on a special meaning for gift giving.

古语： 不腆蔽器，不足辞也 // 《左传·文公十二年》
雅语： 区区薄礼
类语： 算什么呀　不算什么

3.3.17>

这回栽大了

[Lost it all.]

 对话 Conversation

① A：老李呀！你做买卖这么多年，从没败得这么惨吧？
Old Li, you've been in business for so many years, have you ever failed so badly?

B：是啊，这回栽大了！老本全赔进去不说，还欠着银行不少！
You're right, I lost it all! I not only lost my own money, but also owe the bank a lot of money!

② **A：老李呀！你搞政治这么多年，从没跌得这么狠吧？**
Old Li, you've been in politics for years. Have you ever lost this badly?

B：唉！这回栽大了，一撸到底！党籍、公职全没了！
Sigh, I lost it all this time! I lost my party membership and all my positions!

 ## 语境

"栽"有摔倒的意思，口语中用来比喻各种严重的失败。在①中，是生意做赔了。在②中，是犯了大错误。"栽"也可以用在其他地方，比如炒股票、谈恋爱什么的。但是，用"栽"的含意，主要不在承认指失败，而在"不过摔了个跟头，我爬起来还能继续干"。所以，很多人喜欢说"栽了"，不愿意讲"败了"或是"完了"。其实，"不服输"是对的，不认输是不对的。

 ## Context

This phrase means something is waning. It describes all kinds of hard failures. In conversation (1), Old Li lost money in business. In conversation (2), Old Li made a big mistake. This phrase can be also used in other situations, for example, when speculating on stocks or being in love. This phrase doesn't mean that someone admits failure, but expresses that the failure is nothing to him and that he can stand up and continue going. Thus, many people use this phrase when they make mistakes striving to reach their goals. In fact, it's right not to give up easily, but it's wrong not to admit one's mistakes.

古语：一败涂地 //《史记·高祖本纪》
雅语：满盘皆输
类语：惨了　折了　完蛋了

这下完了
[We're finished now.]

😊 对话 Conversation

① A：刚才上边来人把账全封了！
The inspectors just sealed our books!

B：这下完了！我们是经不住检查的！
We're finished this time! We'll never pass their audit!

② A：听说明天考语法。
I heard we'll have a grammar test tomorrow.

B：这下完了！我还没准备呢！
I'm done for now! I'm not ready yet!

③ A：你妻子刚才来电话，我说你回家了。
Your wife just called, I told her that you had gone home.

B：这下完了！我和她说我出差半个月呢！
I'm in trouble this time; I told her I would be away on business for half a month.

 语境

　　在①中，B在工作上有犯罪心理。在②中，B在学习上有懒汉心理。在③中，B在夫妻关系上有侥幸心理。这些人总是把事情朝有利于自己的方面想，一旦出现漏洞，就责怪他人。其实，只有老老实实地做人，才是最聪明的，也是最从容的。

☞ Context

In conversation (1), the book keepers have a guilty conscience. In conversation (2), B has been too lazy to keep up with his studies. In conversation (3), B took a chance that his wife would not find out, but she did. These people always think they can take advantage of the situation. If something unexpected happens, however, they blame the situation rather than themselves. In fact, the smartest way to do things is to be truthful about what you do.

古语：祸至无日矣 // 《资治通鉴 · 六十五卷》
雅语：大祸临头
类语：这回糟了　这下麻烦了

3.3.19>

真够糟心的
[This is too much.]

☺ 对话 Conversation

① A：老李呀，什么事这么不开心？脸都黑了！
　　Old Li, what made you so unhappy? You look upset!

　 B：唉！孩子待业，老婆得癌，我这又快下岗了！你说这有一件好事吗？真够糟心的！
　　Sigh, after graduation my child hasn't found a job. My Wife's illness was just diagnosed as cancer and I'll be laid off soon. Can you see any good in this? I'm extremely upset!

② A：小红！什么时候结婚哪？

Xiao Hong, when will you get married?

B：可别提结婚了，我妈死活看不上我男朋友，真够糟心的！

Don't say anything about marriage. My mother doesn't like my boyfriend. I'm really upset!

 ## 语境

"糟心"的意思是：因为事情太复杂，没有好办法，所以造成心情上的极度烦乱。在①中，该来的不来——孩子的工作。不该来的都来了——老婆的病和下岗的事。这三件事谁碰上也受不了。在②中，丈母娘看不上姑爷，这很少见，所以更不好办，只好慢慢来啦。没有一个人愿意糟心，可是又没有一个人没糟过心。这就是人的最大的玩笑。

 ## Context

This phrase is used when things are very complicated and there's no way to make them better. So people feel troubled and upset. In conversation (1), the child's lack of work, the wife's illness and an immanent lay off, are all things that would make someone upset. When these things all come together, it is enough to make one extremely upset. In conversation (2), it is unusual for the mother-in-law not to like a possible son-in-law. It's hard to deal with this situation, so Xiao Hong has to handle it very slowly. Nobody likes to be upset, but everybody is upset about something at one time or another. This is a part of life.

古语：心烦意乱，不知所从 // 《楚辞·卜居》

雅语：心乱如麻

类语：烦死了

指不上

[can't count on anyone]

😊 对话 Conversation

① A：这东西我们搬不动，还是请邻居帮帮忙吧。

We can't carry this by ourselves, why don't we ask the neighbors to help?

B：邻居，指不上吧。

Neighbors, we can't count on them for help.

② A：你有三个儿子，为什么不让他们来照顾你呢？

You have three sons, why don't you ask them to look after you?

B：嗨，一个也指不上！

Sigh, I can't count on any of them!

语境

毛泽东有句名言：自力更生。可是一般人有了困难，总是希望得到亲戚朋友们的帮助。这种希望，在口语中叫"指望"。"指不上"的意思就是：别指望他们会来帮忙。在①中，"指不上"是因为邻居一直是陌生人。在②中，是因为三个儿子住得都很远，工作都很忙，抽不出时间来照顾老人。没有可指望的人，是最没"面子"的人了。

Context

One of Chairman Mao's well-known sayings is: one should rely on one's own efforts. In real life, however, when people come across difficulties, they always hope for help from their relatives and friends. This phrase reminds us that one can't count on others to help. In conversation (1), one can't count on neighbors because they are often strangers. In conversation (2), you can't count on your sons if they live far away and are busy with their jobs. They don't have time to look after their parents. If someone doesn't have anybody to help him, he would be most embarrassed.

古语：不可冀也 // 《左传·僖公三十二年》
雅语：指望不上
类语：没的靠

3.3.21>

走一步看一步
[step by step]

☺ 对话 Conversation

① A：咱们的发展速度是不是太慢了？
Aren't we growing too slowly?

B：太快了不行！走一步看一步。
It can't go too fast! We have to take it step by step.

② A：老李，你考虑过 20 年以后的生活吗？

Old Li, have you ever thought of what your life would like twenty years from now?

B：想那么远干吗？走一步看一步。

Why should I think so far ahead? I just take it day by day.

☞ **语境**

邓小平搞改革，提出："摸着石头过河"。意思就是①中的"走一步看一步"。实践证明：中国富强了。在②中，这话有缺少计划的意思。但是，当代社会变化太快，越来越多的人开始同意：走一步看一步。

☞ **Context**

Deng Xiaoping called for economic reform and used an analogy of crossing a river, where one should test the depth of the water with each step to describe it. Conversation (1) reminds us that the guiding practice of step by step is a good policy for China's economic growth. In conversation (2), Old Li is not planning for his future. But, as society is developing so rapidly, more and more people agree that they have to plan step by step to adjust to the changes.

古语：欲速则不达 // 《论语·子路》
雅语：稳扎稳打
类语：摸着石头过河　边走边看

露了一怯
[I made a fool of myself.]

😊 对话 Conversation

① A：听说昨儿的会上你露了一怯？
I heard that you made a fool of yourself in public yesterday.

B：也没什么，就是把"赤裸裸"念成"赤果果"了。
It wasn't serious, just a slip of the tongue.

② A：老李呀，你会吃西餐吗？
Old Li, do you know how to use western utensils to eat?

B：还说呢，昨儿就把叉子掉到地上，露了一怯。
Don't ask me anything about Western food. I made a fool of my-self by dropping my fork yesterday.

 ## 语境

　　这话专指当众发生小的失误。关于中国人"没面子"的程度，大概有三级：一是"露怯"，二是"丢面子"，三是"现大眼"，份量是越来越重。当然，每个人都有"露怯"的时候，在①中是"失音"，在②中是"失手"。这本来都是难免的。重要的是："露怯"以后，要真心感谢指出你的错误的人。可惜，有些不但不感谢，反而心中怨恨，这样下去，你就会接着"丢面子"，最后"现大眼"！

 # Context

 This sentence is used when someone makes a small mistake in public. According to the Chinese conception of "face", there are roughly three degrees of embarrassment: a small mistake in public, to lose "face", and to be shamed. Each degree is worse than previous one. Of course, everyone makes a mistake or two. In conversation (1), B just mispronounced a word. In conversation (2), B accidentally drops a fork. These kinds of things can't be avoided. You should be thankful to the people who point out your mistakes, not hateful to them. Denying your mistakes leads to making even bigger mistakes until one is completely shamed.

古语：我虽不能，只得勉强出丑。// 《红楼梦·三十七回》
雅语：偶有闪失
类语：跌份

4 不给别人面子
Don't Give Other People Face

4.1
在强势中
Stronger than Others

不必了

[Don't bother.]

😊 对话 Conversation

① A：小红啊，你最近气色不好，我帮你找个大夫看看吧。
Xiao Hong, you don't look well, I can find a doctor for you.

B：不必了！你上次给我找那电脑专家就是假的。
Don't bother! Last time you found someone for me, it was that computer specialist who was a fraud.

② A：院长啊，我想针对咱们学院的问题再写几份个案调查。
President! I would like to write several investigative reports about our institute's problems.

B：不必了！你上次写那两个全"捅了马蜂窝"。
Don't bother! The reports you wrote last time stirred up enough trouble.

👉 语境

　　对拒绝某种动议来说，这句话是最简洁也最有效的。在①中，老李"献殷勤"的方式比较奇怪，小红只好坚决拒绝。在②中，老李虽然是一腔热血，忧国忧民，可是不讲策略地乱讲，很可能会影响到安定团结的大局；所以也遭到了领导的断然拒绝。不知为什么，现在死缠烂打的人比较多，对待他们的执着欲望，只能多说几句"不必了"！

 Context

This is the most simple and effective response when rejecting a proposal or suggestion. In conversation (1), Old Li pays excessive attention to Xiao Hong and she has to be firm in refusing his recent offer of help. In conversation (2), although Old Li is concerned about his institution, he doesn't know how to do things diplomatically. His reports may, once again, disturb the overall political stability and unity of the institution. So the leader absolutely rejects his suggestion. It is hard to explain why so many people's aspirations have grown greater than before. In response to these kinds of people, we have to use this phrase more and more.

古语：吴王曰："将军罢休就舍，寡人不愿下观。" //《史记·
　　　孙子吴起列传》
雅语：不劳大驾
类语：算了吧　省点吧你

4.1.2>

不管怎么说
[Whether you like it or not.]

对话 Conversation

① A：我们对工作安排有意见！
　　We have different opinions about the job assignment.

B：不管怎么说，上边决定的事，照办吧。
　　The upper office made this decision, you have to accept it whether you like it or not.

② A：我想上这所大学，可是不喜欢这个专业！

I'd like to go to this university, but I don't like their specialty!

B：不管怎么说，这是我和你妈反复考虑过的，就这样吧。

Whether you like it or not, this is what your mother and I have decided. You'll study this subject.

 语境

这句话，具有命令的口吻，给人不讲理的感觉。如果有人要说话，那就让他说呗！要是大家不能取得共识，在工作中就难免出毛病。当然，B的意见有时也是对的。在①中，人多，意见更多，都说，三天也说不完；民主，也得有点分寸，不能没完没了。在②中呢，父母们一般来说总还是比孩子们考虑的全面些。所以，这句话有时是用得着的。

Context

This sentence sounds like an order that could be unreasonable. One should let other people talk and listen to opposing ideas and suggestions. If you are unable to reach a consensus up front, it's hard to avoid mistakes later when you try to work together. But, B's opinion is also right in conversation (1), everyone has opinions and the leader can't pay attention to all of them. There is a limitation even in a democracy. In conversation (2), parents usually examine issues more thoroughly than children. So, this phrase is sometimes necessary in dealing with children.

古语：善哉！虽然，公输盘为我为云梯，必取宋。//《墨子·公输》

雅语：无论如何

类语：随你怎么说

4.1.3>

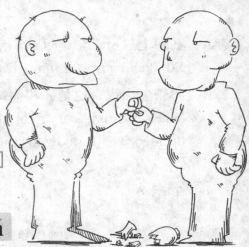

都怪你
[All your fault.]

对话 Conversation

① A：哎呀！花瓶掉地下了！

My god! The flower vase fell off the table!

B：都怪你！老和我聊天！

It's all your fault! You're always talking to me!

② A：唉，忘了拿歌剧票了！

Hey, I forgot to take our tickets for the opera!

B：都怪你！那怎么办啊！

It's your fault! What can we do now?

 ## 语境

"都怪你"这句话，是女人对男人的专用语。在①中是妻子对丈夫，在②中是女友对男友。不管女人结婚与否，反正只要是发生麻烦，她们之中的99%都会把全部责任推到男人身上，而且还要继续生气，直到男人想出让她们开心的好办法。男人呢，在听到这句话时，一定不说话，理由是：懒得吵架。

Context

This sentence is used by a woman speaking to a man. In conversation (1), a wife talks to her husband. In conversation (2), a girlfriend talks to her boyfriend. Whether the woman is married or not, whenever any problem happens, men are responsible ninety-nine percent of the time. Moreover, women are usually angry about it until the man finds a way to make them happy again. When a man hears this sentence, they usually don't answer. The reason is that they don't want to quarrel over every little thing all the time.

古语：维子之故 // 《诗经·郑风·狡童》
雅语：都是你的错
类语：都是你　真是的　你怎么搞的

4.1.4>

多新鲜呢
[Why not?]

☺ 对话 Conversation

① A：你为什么用这么贵的东西洗碗？
   Why do you use something so expensive to wash dishes?

   B：多新鲜呢！这是最去油的。
   Why not? This is the best for cutting the grease.

② A：天气这么热，你还关着窗户！
   The weather is so hot, but you still keep all the windows closed!

   B：多新鲜呢？这样热气进不来。
   Why not? It is the only way to stop the heat from coming in.

语境

　　"多新鲜呢"，不是"很新鲜"的意思，而是"当然应该这样"。因为，"新鲜"有"奇怪"的意思。所以，"这不新鲜"等于"这不奇怪"。"多新鲜呢"是反话，是"这有什么新鲜的"，说这句话，有看不起提问者，并且懒得解释的用意。

Context

　　This phrase means that there is nothing new or strange about something and things are just as they should be. When one uses this phrase, he usually shows some disdain for whoever questions and is too lazy to explain the situation to them.

古语：不亦异乎 // 《孟子·离娄下》
雅语：自有道理
类语：这有什么可奇怪的　　有没有搞错

4.1.5>

废话
[Of Course! / meaningless]

😊 对话 Conversation

① A：哎，下雨了，我把衣服收了吧？

　　Hey, it's raining. Should I bring in the washing?

　 B：废话！赶紧！

　　Of course! Hurry up!

② A：哎，不少同事下岗了，我也该做思想准备了吧？

Sigh, many of my colleagues have already been laid off. Should I prepare for it to happen to me?

B：废什么话！你该去活动活动！干吗干等着呀！

Of course! You should do something about it! Why just wait for it to happen!

③ A：我那篇5000字的文章，你看了吗？

Did you read my 5000-word article?

B：嗯，能用的就500字，其余的全是废话。

Well, only 500 words of it are on topic, the rest of it is meaningless.

 语境

"废话"是"没有用"的话，大概分成三种。在①中，A讲的"废话"是对的，只是不用说，去做就是了。在②中，A讲的不仅是"废话"，而且是错话！是不能那样想那样做的。所以B让他去找找关系，托托熟人，别只是等着失业。在前两种情况中，用"废话"表现出来的是不客气的，缺乏耐心。③中的现象更多，很多文章又臭又长，只是为了骗点稿费。

Context

This phrase means something is obvious or meaningless. It can be used in three situations. In conversation (1), what A says is right, but he doesn't need to have a discussion about it, he just needs to do it. In conversation (2), A's talk is not only nonsense, but also wrong. He can't just wait for the company to lay him off, so B suggests that he finds some help from his relatives, friends or connections. In the first two cases, it is used to show the speaker's impatience and distain. There are many cases like the one in conversation (3), because articles today are too long and not on topic and are simply written to squeeze more money from the publishers.

古语：而委心逐辞，异端丛至，骈赘必多 // 刘勰《文心雕龙·
　　　熔裁》

雅语：无庸赘言

类语：扯淡　屁话

4.1.6>

废物
[useless]

☺ 对话 Conversation

① A：你怎么那么废物，连自行车都不会修！

How could you be so useless, you don't even know how to repair a bike!

　B：嗨，我这方面是不行。

Hey, I'm not good with this kind of stuff.

② A：让老李去当门卫行吗？

Can we ask Old Li to be a guard?

　B：那个老废物，连男的女的都看不清了。

He's absolutely useless in his old age, he can't even distinguish men from women anymore.

☞ 语境

　　"废物"的本意是"没有什么用的东西"和"用过的东西"。后来多指没有能力的人，如在①中，丧失了能力的人，如在②中。这种不礼貌的话，一般不是当面讲的。而且，对正常人来说：第一，是各有专长。第二，谁最后都是"废物"。因此，这句话还是忘记的好。

 # Context

This phrase originally meant some useless material or used material.
Later, it became more and more to be used to describe someone who is good-
for-nothing and like waste material. But it is very impolite to say this phrase
to a person's face, even if they're a close friend. Normally, everyone has
their special skills and nobody knows how to do everything. Sooner or later
we all will be old and unable to do much at all. So, we shouldn't say this
phrase to anyone.

古语：朽木不可雕也//《论语・公冶长》
雅语：苗而不秀　银样蜡枪头
类语：没用的东西　蠢才　笨蛋

4.1.7>

该怎么办怎么办
[Do what you are supposed to do.]

😊 对话 Conversation

① A：校长啊，那个违反纪律的人是不是要开除？
　　Dean, should we expel the students who broke the rules?

　 B：不是有规章制度嘛，该怎么办怎么办！
　　The school's rules are published, so you should do what you're
　　supposed to do.

② A：老板，明天银行的人来检查营业情况之后，要不要招待一下？

Boss, should we entertain the people from the bank after they check our operations?

　B：当然，该怎么办怎么办！

Of course! We're supposed to do that!

 ## 语境

　　这句话在现代汉语里的意思是怎么办合理恰当，就怎么办！在流行口语中变成了一句上级对下级说的话。在①中，领导指示有关部门依法办事，不要讲人情。这是符合原意的。在②中，老板认为请银行的人吃饭是应该的，不仅要吃，而且要吃好！因此根本不该有此一问，这就不合理而是腐败了。

 ## Context

In modern Chinese, this sentence means that we should do whatever is reasonable and suitable. But in popular spoken Chinese, this sentence is used by superiors to talk to those under them. In conversation (1), a leader instructs the officer to operate by the rules and ignore relationships. This use complies with the original meaning of the phrase. In conversation (2), the boss thinks they should have a meal with the people from the bank, not just to eat, but eat well! The boss thinks that it is not necessary to even ask this question. This suggests that something is not necessarily reasonable, but could be corrupt.

古语：法者，天子所与天下公共也。今法如此，而更重之，
　　　是法不信于民也。// 《史记·张释之冯唐列传》
雅语：公事公办
类语：照老黄历办

够黄的
[It's lewd.]

😊 对话 Conversation

① **A：老李！你怎么看这种片子？够黄的！**
Old Li, how could you watch this sort of film? It's lewd!

B：啊……，不是，是别人非借我看的！
Well... No, someone insisted on lending it to me.

② **A：老李！你怎么看这种小说？够黄的！**
Old Li, how could you read this kind of novel? It's lewd!

B：噢……，一开始不知道，是、是很没意思！
Eh..., I didn't know at first. Yes, you are right, it's not interesting!

👉 语境

　　"黄色"在中国大陆特指色情。在①中是黄色电影。在②中是黄色小说。有趣的是，同指色情，英语国家用"蓝色"；法国、韩国、意大利、西班牙用"红色"；日本用"粉色"；阿拉伯为"紫色"；中国的港台则称之为"桃色"等等。其实，全世界原本都用"红色"来指代。"红灯区"并非外国首创，我国唐代都市就设"红灯区"（绛纱灯）。无产阶级革命后，"红色"成为革命的象征，而代表革命对象——封建皇权与资本货币的"黄色"便被赋予了新的涵义。显然，"红""黄"的词义演变是受到了政治生活的影响。

　　至于中国大陆，大约从 1966 年开始，"黄色"指色情才逐渐流行起来，1990年代起，语意已定。现在，各级政府都设"扫黄打非办公室"，专门清除那些淫秽的东西。

Context

This phrase refers specifically to pornography in mainland China. Conversation (1) concerns a pornographic movie and conversation (2) refers to a pornographic novel. It is interesting to know that while China calls pornographic subjects "Yellow," England refers to them as "Blue", the French, South Koreans, Italians and the Spanish refer to them as "Red", the Japanese as "Pink", Arabs as "Purple", and people from Hong Kong and Taiwan refer to them as "Leach", etc. In fact, the entire world uses "Red" to identify the region around a city area that contains pornographic or lewd material and activity. We can find this in Tang Dynasty documents in China. But since the proletarian revolution, "Red" has come to symbolize the revolution, and "Yellow" feudalism, imperial authority, and capital currency which have become symbols targeted by the revolution. This is clearly designed to fit the political background. In China, "Yellow" began to refer to pornographic subjects in 1966 and was firmly established by the 1990s. Now, the office for "Wiping out Pornography" has been set up at all levels of the Chinese government. Its specific job is getting rid of lewd stuff.

古语：今纳夏姬，贪其色也，贪色为淫。//《左传·成公二年》
雅语：淫秽不堪
类语：少儿不宜　带色儿的　三级片

惯的
[spoiled]

☺ 对话 Conversation

① **A：哎，你瞧那孩子，除了吃什么都不会！**
Look at that child; he doesn't know how to do anything except eat.

　B：嗨，都是她爹妈给惯的。
Sigh, that's all because her parents spoil her.

② **A：你说这伙人可怎么管理呀？一去厕所就半个小时，打一个电话又是半个小时！**
How can I manage these fellows? They take 30 minutes to go to bathroom and another 30 minutes to make phone calls during work hours.

　B：惯的！明天开始计件工资，看谁还耗点！
They are in the habit of moving slowly! We should begin to pay them by the piece, and then we'll see who'll still be dawdling around!

  语境

　　"惯"这个词，这种现象，可以解释很多社会问题：孩子的毛病是家长惯的，学生的毛病是老师惯的，女友的毛病是男友惯的，丈夫的毛病是妻子惯的，前辈的毛病是晚辈惯的，工人的毛病是老板惯的，群众的毛病是领导惯的，反之亦然。单方的纵容与双方的迁就，惯出了谁也无法纠正的老毛病。更有意思的是，看到别人在"惯"，一定开口批评；可一到自己身上照旧还是"惯"。

 # Context

This word is often used and becomes a phenomenon. It describes a lot of social problems. Children's bad habits are created when they are spoiled by their parents. Student's bad behaviors come from their teachers spoiling them. A girlfriend's bad temper continues because she is spoiled by her boyfriend. A husband's errors are not corrected because he is spoiled by his wife. The older generation's shortcomings spoil the younger generation. Workers are spoiled by their bosses. The masses' are spoiled by their leaders. This situation goes both ways. Either one side acts in connivance with the other side or the two sides agree to an excessively accommodating relationship. All of this leads to a lot of bad habits that never get corrected. The amusing thing is that people usually can see and criticize others, but don't want anything to change when they are involved.

古语：今媪尊长安君之位，而封之以膏腴之地，多予之重器，而不及今有功于国，一旦山陵崩，长安君何以自托于赵？// 《战国策·赵策》

雅语：娇生惯养

类语：宠的

另类

[What a character.]

☺ 对话 Conversation

① A：哎，你看他那德性，言行穿戴，
发型颜色都和别人不一样！

Hey, look at that guy, his speech, actions, hair style and hair color are very different!

B：这就叫另类。

He's something else, what a character.

② A：哎，哲学系那小伙子篇篇论文都有创意，表达上也很有特点，
真让人妒忌！

Hey, every paper written by that student from the Department of Philosophy is creative and unique. He really makes me jealous!

B：有什么了不起，不过是哗众取宠的另类罢了。

He's nothing extraordinary, he's just a character who talks big to impress people.

 ## 语境

　　每一个时代的年轻人都有自己的亮点和新的称号，像"××族""××代"什么的层出不穷。他们的基本倾向可以表述为要做另外一类人，即：另类。另类的主要特点是：脱离主流，疏远传统，崇尚个性，不拘小节。当然，这可能只是青春期的冲动，但这总比一潭死水有意思。虽然大多数人还不欣赏另类，虽然这个称号暂时还不算很有面子，可是从

趋同到求异，这是进步。

 # Context

The young people of each era all have their own special interests and jargons. For example, they present themselves as belonging to "xx class" or "xx generation" etc., to express the existence of this new character. Their main characteristics are: separating themselves from the main stream, drifting away from tradition, advocating individual character, and ignoring minor rules about behavior. Certainly, it is possible that this is because they are adolescences and act on impulse. But their action stirs things up and is better than a pond of stagnant water. Although most people can't accept such characteristics and they don't gain any "face" by acting weird, it is a form of progress from every-one acting the same to the idea that everyone should search for diversity.

古语：其特立独行，有如此者。//《礼记·儒行》
雅语：与众不同
类语：新潮　怪异　各色

4.1.11>

没感觉
[uninspiring]

☺ 对话 Conversation

① A：你为什么不喜欢那个漂亮姑娘？
Why don't you like that pretty girl?

B：漂亮是漂亮，就是没感觉。
She is pretty all right, but she doesn't inspire me.

② A：这首歌怎么样？
How is this song?

B：没感觉。
It doesn't inspire me.

③ A：那个 10 号真玩命，满场跑！
That #10 player is really playing hard; he is covering the entire field!

B：瞎跑，在门前一点感觉都没有。
He is aimless and uninspired in front of goal.

 ## 语境

过去，绝大多数人不说这句话，也不把"感觉"作为一个标准。因为，在很长的时间里，只有统一的"对"或者"错"。所谓"感觉"，仅仅是极少数艺术家的偶然。现在，几乎每个城里人和相当比例的农民，都会有针对性地谈点"感觉"。还有一首流行歌曲就叫"跟着感觉走"。这当然是进步。可是，如果人太多，"个人感觉"太多，又不能理解和尊重他人的"感觉"，那就很难有"共识"。所以，总的"感觉"是比较乱。

 ## Context

In the past, most people didn't use this phrase or use "inspiring" as a standard to judge things or people. There were only two ways to think of things, "right" or "wrong", for a long period of time, and what is now called "feeling" or "inspiring" was used by a few artists. Right now, almost everyone from the city and even a big percentage of peasants, all express their opinions on this topic. There is even a popular song called "Walk with Feeling". This way of expressing ourselves is certainly succeeding. But if every one of us only cares about our feeling rather than trying to understand and respect other people's feeling, it will be hard to form a "common view". So, it all easily feels confused.

古语：味如嚼蜡 //《楞严经·八》
雅语：兴味索然
类语：没意思　没味道　白开水　温吞水

4.1.12>

你成吗
[Can you handle it?]

😊 对话 Conversation

① A：老李呀，有人推荐你当总经理，你成吗？

Old Li, someone recommended you for the General Manager position. Can you handle it?

B：总经理也是人干的，我为什么不成？

If other people can be the General Manager, why can't I?

② A：老李呀，我要给你介绍的这个女人很凶，还带着四个孩子……这副重担，你成吗？

Old Li, the women that I am going to introduce to you is very tough and she has four children...do you think you can handle it?

B："凶"是有味道，孩子多更热闹！我什么时候去见面？

A tough woman must be interesting and the more children around the more lively things are! When will I meet her?

 ## 语境

　中国古代有一句非常有名的话，叫做："遣将不如激将"。大意是：

如果你想派一个人去做一件事情,可以采用怀疑的态度去激励他,那样,这个人会用200%的努力去做好这件事。在①中,总经理的位置当然很有"面子",但老李的水平显然不够;所以,老板用了"激将法"。在②中,再婚的条件比较差,介绍人怕老李不要,也用了"激将法";老李是要"面子"的人,果然就上当了。注意:有的人,可以"激",一"激"就出成绩;有的人,"激"也没用,因为"激不活"。

👉 Context

There was a well-known saying in ancient China that said: If you want to send someone off to accomplish one thing, you could motivate him by telling him you doubt his ability. This way this person will use two hundred percent of his strength to finish this thing well. In conversation (1), without a doubt the General Manager's position is an elevated position; Old Li obviously doesn't have enough ability. So his boss uses this phrase to prod him into action. In conversation (2), A is going to introduce someone whose situation is only average for a second marriage. The matchmaker is afraid that Old Li won't want to meet her so he uses this phrase to challenge him. Old Li has fallen into the trap because he cares too much about his "face". Please pay attention here, this phrase can only work on those people who can motivate to do well. But, there are others who have no enthusiasm for anything anymore.

古语:可以小试勒兵乎? // 《史记·孙子吴起列传》
雅语:疾锋而试
类语:你行吗　你有把握吗

你太抬举我了
[You flatter me too much.]

☺ 对话 Conversation

① **A：** 我觉得你的剧本比《哈姆雷特》还好！

I think your drama is even better than *Hamlet*!

B： 你太抬举我了，我怎么能和莎士比亚比呢！

You flatter me too much. How can I compare with Shakespeare?

② **A：** 你将来肯定比比尔·盖茨还有钱！

You're sure to become richer than Bill Gates!

B： 你太抬举我了，那怎么可能呢！

You flatter me too much. It's impossible!

 语境

有的人喜欢吹捧别人。当然，那是有目的的。但是，如果吹得太过分，被吹的人就不舒服了，就会怀疑：吹捧者是故意用这种方法害人。因为每个人都知道，抬得越高，摔得越重。而且，被吹捧者明明知道，即使自己有最好的运气，也绝不可能达到那种高度。这种情况，在汉语里叫：牛皮吹漏了。

 Context

Some like to flatter others, of course, they have some mysterious purpose. But, if you puff up someone too much, it will make them feel uncomfortable and raise some doubts. The flatterer purposely uses this method to attain their goal and harm others. Because, as we all know, the higher you lift someone up, the harder they will fall. And the listeners undoubtedly know that even if they have the best luck, they still can't achieve the height that the flatterer describes. We call this situation "blowing up the cattle's hide until it pops" in Chinese.

古语：好面誉人者，亦好背而毁之。//《庄子·盗跖》
雅语：誉过其实
类语：太肉麻了

4.1.14>

你也来了
[You are here too!]

😊 对话 Conversation

① A：小红！我都等半天了，快坐下。咦！老李？你也来了！
Xiao Hong, I've been waiting for you for hours. Please take a seat. Hey, Old Li? You've come too!

B：噢，不是，我是在饭店门口碰上小红的，顺便进来瞧一眼就走。
Oh, no, I happened to meet Xiao Hong at the entrance of the hotel. I just dropped by and will leave right away.

② A：今天的会很重要，都是各部门的第一把手。咦！老李？你也来了？
Today's meeting is very important. The participants are all heads of each department. Oh, Old Li, you're here too?

B：噢，我不是开会，我是来找我们头儿签个字就走。

Oh, I won't stay for the meeting. I only came for my boss's signature.

 ## 语境

　　"也"，有很多用法和作用。但它在口语交际中表现出来的"不应该的""不合时宜的"意思，是字典里没有的。在①中，A先生请小红吃饭，多半是私人感情的事，当然需要"二人世界"。老李非要看看是谁和小红约会，这太俗气了。在②中，领导们要开重要会议，老李应该等散了会再去签字，干吗挤进会场去添乱呢？真不知进退。所以，A先生在两个地方都用了"也"字，含蓄地表达了"不欢迎"的意思。

 ## Context

　　The word "too" has many meanings and functions in practice. And some of the uses that you can't find in the dictionary are, for example, "shouldn't" and "inappropriate" in spoken communication. In conversation (1), A invited Xiao Hong for a meal most likely because he likes her and wants to talk with her alone. Old Li wants to find out who is dating Xiao Hong. This is too mischievous. In conversation (2), the leaders are going to have a meeting and Old Li could certainly wait to get the signature later. He doesn't have to be there as the meeting is going on. He has no sense of propriety. Hence, A used "too" in both conversations as an implicated criticism of an unwelcome intrusion.

古语：有不速之客三人来 //《周易·需》

雅语：不请自来

类语：你怎么来了

瞧你那德行

[Look at you!]

🙂 对话 Conversation

① A：爸，咱们上王府井吧！

Daddy, shall we go to Wangfujing market?

B：瞧你那德行，我怎么领你出门啊！快去洗洗脸，换身衣服。

Look at you! How can I take you anywhere! Hurry up to wash your face and change your clothes.

② A （一个男职员哭着跑进办公室）：老板不好了！警察把咱们公司的大门给封了！

(A male staff runs in with tears in his eyes): Oh boss, something bad happened. The police sealed our company's gate!

B：瞧你那德行，好像死了人似的！没什么大不了的。

Look at you! You'd think somebody just died! It's not that bad!

③ A （队员比赛失败后，垂头丧气，一言不发）：……

(Team members have just lost a game and are in low spirits, nobody talks) ...

B （教练）：瞧你那德行，不就是输场球吗？真不像条汉子。

(Coach): Look at you! That's just one game. You don't act like real men!

253

语境

　　这句话大多是强势者辱骂弱势者时用,有时好朋友间开玩笑也用。比如:在看到别人吃东西的样子不好看,衣服穿得不合适,言行举止不礼貌,事情做得不漂亮的时候,都可以用;但应注意要笑着说,否则,很容易引起对方强烈的反感。

Context

This sentence is used when powerful people insult their inferiors. Sometimes it's also used between good friends joking with each other. For example, you can use this phrase when you see somebody who has poor table manners, wears inappropriate clothes, uses impolite words and manners, and makes a lot of mistakes. But you should say it with smile; if not, it would be easy for them to be very angry.

古语:固不堪入目矣 //《镜花缘·二十三回》
雅语:太不像样
类语:看你那样

4.1.16>

让我怎么说你呢
[I don't know what to say about you!]

☺ 对话 Conversation

① A:妈妈,我的作业本在哪儿呢?
　　Mom, where is my homework booklet?

B：我的宝贝女儿，让我怎么说你呢？

My baby daughter, I don't know what to say about you!

② A：老板，一会儿签合同的时候，咱们是甲方还是乙方？

Oh boss, are we Party A or Party B when we sign the contract later?

B：让我怎么说你呢！你还是去做"中方"吧。

I don't know what to say about you! You'd better be the middle man.

 ## 语境

喜欢批评他人，指导他人的人，都是很会说话的人，可是他们也会遇到说不出话来的情况，那就是碰到了那些料想不到的"低级错误"。在①中，是学生找不到作业本。在②中是业务员不明白责任关系。在这种气得说不出话来的时候，这句话可以表达出内心的愤怒和失望。

 ## Context

Some people like to criticize and give advice to other people. These people are usually very skillful with words. But when they meet someone who makes the simplest mistakes, they don't know what to say to them. In conversation (1), a student can't even find the homework booklet. In conversation (2), a business man doesn't understand the basic liability relationships when he signs the contract. This phrase could be used to express irritation and disappointment when someone is too angry and does not want to talk.

古语：宰予昼寝。子曰："朽木不可雕也，粪土之墙不可圬也，于予与何诛？"//《论语·公冶长》

雅语：不可理喻

类语：我简直没法说你

是人就会
[Anyone can do it!]

☺ 对话 Conversation

① A：老李呀，管儿灯坏了，你会修吗？

　　Old Li, the fluorescent light doesn't work. Can you fix it?

　B：不就是管儿灯吗，是人就会！

　　It's just a fluorescent light, anyone can do it!

② A：老李呀，你刚才说是人就会，可这灯还是没亮啊！

　　Old Li, just now you said that anyone could repair the light. But it still doesn't work!

　B：话不能这么说，这……，这是零件坏了嘛……

　　Oh, that's not the same; this... some parts must be broken.

☞ 语境

　　"是人就会"的意思是：只要你是人，就一定会。含意是：这件事极容易。等于：每个人都会。换成反话是：如果你不会，你就不是人。这话里有自吹的感觉，更有认为"不会的人"太笨的评价。当然，对讲这句话的人来说，"会"是绝无问题的。在①中，老李让人相信他会。可是在②中，老李修了半天的灯仍然不亮。虽然老李照例会找到借口，但是，根据这句话的用法，老李——不能算人了。

Context

"Anyone can do it" means that if you're a human being, you should know how to do it. It is excessively easy. It could also be taken as: if you can't do it, you are not a human being. When people use this sentence, they must feel good about themselves and think that those people who can't handle it are stupid. In general, the person who uses this sentence should know how to do whatever they are talking about. In conversation (1), Old Li leads others to believe that he can fix it. But in conversation (2) we see he couldn't repair the light. Although, as usual, Old Li can find some excuse — by the logic of this sentence — Old Li isn't a human being.

古语：变所欲为，易于反掌，安于泰山。// 枚乘《上书谏吴
　　　王》
雅语：轻而易举
类语：小菜一碟

4.1.18>

太不像话了
[This is outrageous!]

😊 对话 Conversation

① A：是谁把痰吐在地毯上的？是谁！
　　 Who spat on the carpet? Who?

　 B：太不像话了！吐痰也不找个地方！
　　 That's outrageous! Why don't they find a proper place to spit!

② A：错了就认错，又吵又闹的，太不像话了！

You'd better admit you made a mistake. It's no use quarrelling and making a terrible scene. This is outrageous!

  B：谁错了？谁又吵又闹了？请您搞清楚了再批评人！

Who made a mistake? Who's quarrelling? You should think about things before criticizing anyone!

 ## 语境

　　传统道德是依靠话语存在的，通过言语表达的。当小孩们改正了自己的错误时，大人们常说："这才像话。"所以，"不像话"的意思就是：不合理的，错误的，因为坏事一般是不用"话"说出来的。在①中，随地吐痰是通病。如果吐在墙角或土地上，那也就算了。可是把痰吐在地毯上，确实是"太不像话了"！简直不像是人干的事！在②中，"不像话"已经超出个人坏习惯的范围，达到扰乱办公秩序的程度，而且居然不听劝阻，顶撞领导，这种"不像话"的人，应该考虑他的下岗问题了。

 ## Context

Traditional moral sense depends on the right phrase to express right and wrong. When adults correct the mistakes of little children they usually say: "This way will make better sense." So, if something is outrageous and doesn't make any sense, it must be unreasonable and wrong. In conversation (1), people have a bad habit of spitting everywhere. If one spits at the corner of a wall or on the dirt, we can forget it. But if one spits on the carpet, it surely is disgusting. It's simply not civilized human behavior! In conversation (2), B has gone too far and disturbed the work environment of the office. B even went so far as to argue with the leader. The boss should consider dismissing this kind of unreasonable employee.

古语：言非礼义，谓之自暴也。//《孟子·离娄上》
雅语：不成体统
类语：不成话　太过分了

太过分了
[go too far]

😊 对话 Conversation

① **A：** 那家伙一天之内三次把脏水泼在我家门口！

That guy has thrown his swill in front of my gate three times today!

B： 这也太过分了吧！

He's gone too far.

② **A：** 他骂我几句也就算了，他骂我妈！

It wouldn't have been too bad if he had only cursed me. But he cursed my mother!

B： 那太过分了！

He's gone too far.

  **语境**

中国传统中一直有"退让"的说法，认为不要因为一件事情就和人家吵架，怕的是影响了关系，将来还是麻烦。可是如果对方继续欺负你，那怎么办？那时就该说这句话了。它第一是表明：实在忍耐不下去了。第二是预报：反击马上开始。因此，如果你在欺负人，希望你马上打住。如果你在被人欺负，那就请你再忍耐一次。

☞ **Context**

There is general understanding in Chinese tradition when people have a disagreement; at least one side should make a concession. People shouldn't bicker over something unimportant. If people quarrel too often, it affects their relationships and is always there to cause some potential trouble. But, if the other person continues to take advantage of you, what can you do? Then, you should use this phrase. First, you express that you can no longer be tolerant of their behavior. Second, you announce that you are going to strike back immediately. So, if you are taking advantage of someone, you should stop it. If you are suffering because another is taking advantage of you, you should be patient once more.

古语：殊甚 //《史记·廉颇蔺相如列传》
雅语：欺人太甚
类语：太没分寸　不像话

4.1.20>

闲的
[Don't you have anything to do?]

☺ **对话 Conversation**

① A：我的儿子，你没事儿看点书好不好，整天就知道玩电脑，闲的！
My dear son! If you have nothing to do, you should read a book. You can't play at the computer every day! Don't you have anything to do?

B：我的爹地，你应该知道我是在电脑上学习呢，忙得很！

Dad! I'm studying on the computer, I'm very busy!

② A （老板）：上班时间不准聊天，闲的！每个人的定额都提高20%！

(Boss): It's against the rules to engage in idle conversation during work hours. Don't you have anything to do? Let's increase everyone's production quota twenty percent!

B （众职工互相对视）：……（开始工作）。

(Every worker looks at each other) ... (Starts working).

语境

不知为什么，很多领导人不能看到年轻人或下级处于无事可做的状态，他们希望每一个人都很忙碌，不要浪费宝贵的时间。这种心情是好的，但是每一个人都是需要休闲的，过于紧张的学习与工作节奏，效果不一定好，健康反而会受到影响。

Context

For some reason, many leaders can't stand to see young people or their employees sit there doing nothing nowadays. They hope everyone stays busy and doesn't fritter away their time. We understand their feeling, but everyone needs to take a break. If everyone works excessively or studies all the time, the results won't be very effective and it won't be good for the health either.

古语：其人之为诗者，亦必闲散放荡，岩居川观，无所事事
　　　而后可。// 清·黄宗羲《万贞一诗序》
雅语：无事可做
类语：没事儿干

要不然说你年轻呢
[You haven't been around long enough!]

对话 Conversation

① A：老板真英明，您估计的情况全都出现了，一开始我还不信呢！
Boss, you're brilliant. I didn't believe you in the beginning, but all the things you said would happen did happen!

B：嘿，要不然说你年轻呢，我早就都算到了。
Hey, I thought all of this through. You haven't been around long enough!

② A：老李呀，我看人怎么老看不准呢？
Old Li, why can't I judge anyone appropriately?

B：是啊，要不然说你年轻呢！还得多历练啊。
Oh well, you haven't been around long enough! You still need experience and toughening.

语境

　　说这句话的人，一般是年纪比较大，又自以为比较有经验的。说这句话的环境，一般是年轻人客气地向上级或师长汇报工作或请教问题的时候。听这句话的年轻人，一般要一边听，一边频频点头，表现出特后悔、特自责、特服气的表情，把"面子"全给说这话的人。于是，在以后的日子里，你会得到较好的评价与进一步帮助。

Context

The people who use this phrase usually consider themselves senior and more experienced. They use it when young people report on their work to them, or ask them for advice. The listeners usually listen carefully and nod their heads again and again. They express their regret and self-criticism and are influenced by the older people's wisdom. By this, they give "face" to the senior colleague. Therefore, these youngsters will receive a better evaluation and get more help later.

古语: 少，未知可否？ // 《左传·襄公三十一年》
雅语: 还欠火候
类语: 嫩点儿不是

4.1.22>

有这事儿吗

[Really?]

😊 对话 Conversation

① A: 老李，你听说了吗？老赵有个私生子，都二十多岁了，昨天找上门去了！
   Old Li, have you heard that Lao Zhao has an illegitimate child who's over 20 years old? He visited Lao Zhao yesterday!

   B: 有这事儿吗？你亲眼看见了吗？
   Really? Did you see it?

② A: 哎，听说昨晚上 UFO 光临市中心广场，省电视台都播了！
   Hey, I heard that a UFO appeared in the Central Square last night. It was on the provincial television broadcast!

   B: 有这事儿吗？我一直不太相信有飞碟。
   Really? I've never believed in UFOs.

语境

很多人喜欢用听说和据说来保护消息来源，可是还是这些人，当他们听到别人的消息时，又往往要用"有这事儿吗"这句话来显示自己的鉴别能力。在①中，B是半信半疑；在②中，B是基本否定。当然，有些信息是难以证实也不需证实的。人家那么一说，你那么一听，也就完了。

Context

Many people like to use "heard" and "it is said" to protect the source of their information. But the same people still like to respond with "really" to demonstrate their ability to differentiate between true and false news. In conversation (1), B is uncertain of what to believe. In conversation (2), B basically denies it. Of course, some news is difficult to verify or doesn't require proof. Others talk like that and you just listen like that.

古语：有诸？//《孟子·梁惠王上》
雅语：空口说白话
类语：不太可能吧

4.1.23>

再怎么说也不行
[No matter what you say!]

☺ 对话 Conversation

① A：校长，就让孩子入学吧，我和孩子他妈给您跪下了。
　　Principal, please permit my child to go to your school. His mother and I are on our knees begging you.

B：入学是有分数线的，她没上线，再怎么说也不行。

Everyone has to score a certain number of points to enroll in this school. No matter what you say, if he doesn't have enough points, he can't get in.

② **A：老李呀，你帮我在领导那儿多美言几句行不行?**

Old Li, could you please put in a good word for me with my leader?

B：嗨，上次你把他弄得太没"面子"，我再怎么说也不行了呀！

Sigh, that doesn't work anymore, not since you made him lose so much "face" last time.

③ **A：小红，你再跟你妈说说，咱们一起去蹦迪吧！**

Xiao Hong, please talk to your mother one more time so she will let us go to the disco.

B：没戏，我妈说死了也不让我去，再怎么说也不行。

There's no hope. No matter what I say, my mother would rather die than let me go to the disco.

 **语境**

　　求人不容易，总要三番五次地说，甚至下跪，如①。拒绝人也很难，一定要翻来覆去地解释，还不能让对方死心。如①。如果再和②③的情况联系起来看，那么这句话不管是谁跟谁说，都有"无论再说什么也是没有用的"，即："别再说了"的意思。所以，如果你听到这句话，就别再继续废话了。

Context

　　It is not easy to plead for help. One usually has to beg three to five times, and even kneel down, just as in conversation (1). It is not easy to refuse people either. One usually has to explain the reasons from different perspectives so people don't lose their hope forever. This can be seen in conversation (1). If we combine this with the other two conversations, then, the phrase "no matter what" is used to respond to people who beg for help or who refuse to help, it all means the same thing: "It is not useful to say anything, please don't talk anymore." Hence, when you hear this phrase, you'd better stop the nonsense.

古语：寡人不之疑矣 //《商君书·更法》
雅语：白费唇舌
类语：死活不同意

4.1.24>

真是的
[What!]

😊 对话 Conversation

① A：哎，刚才有电话找你，我说你不在。

Hey, there was a phone call for you just now; I told him that you weren't here.

B：真是的！就上个厕所的功夫，我正等那电话呢！你就不会喊喊我？

What! I went to the washroom. I have been waiting for that phone call, why didn't you call me?

② A：哎，今儿晚上吃什么呀？

Hey, what should we eat tonight?

B：真是的！都这会儿了！做什么也来不及了。

What! It's already too late, there's no time to cook anything.

 ## 语境

"真是的!"这句话是当代年轻女性的专用语,专门用在对男人们不满意的时候。在①中,只错过了一个电话,女同事就生气了。在②中,A没有及时请示并落实晚饭,又被老婆批评了一顿。在生活中,女人们往往只用"真是的"三个字表示生气,并不具体再说什么。那时男人都会关心地问:"亲爱的,怎么了?"反正女人们随时可用这句话来显示自己的高雅、脱俗和正确,男人们却只能受着。

Context

"What!" is often used by young women when they are dissatisfied with a man. In conversation (1), A didn't find B when she had a phone call and that made her very unhappy. In conversation (2), A didn't ask for instructions in time and get the dinner ready, so his wife criticizes him. In real life, women usually use this phrase to show their anger without providing any further explanation, and then, men will ask "my dear, are you okay?" Anyway, women use this phrase to show how elegant, sophisticated and correct they are, but guys can only put up with so much of such behavior.

古语:维子之故 //《诗经·郑风·狡童》
雅语:都是你的错
类语:你看你　都怪你

4 不给别人面子
Don't Give Other People Face

4.2
在均势中
Equal to Others

八成是不行了

[It doesn't look good!]

☺ 对话 Conversation

① **A：大夫大夫，刚进去那车祸的病人怎么样了？**

Doctor, doctor, how is the patient from the car accident you just treated?

B：八成是不行了。

It doesn't look good!

② **A：小红的婚事拖了这么久了，怎么回事啊？**

What's happening, why is Xiao Hong's wedding on hold for this long?

B：喷，八成是不行了。

Things don't look good!

 ## 语境

"八成"，是80%的意思。在①中，病人伤得太重，救过来的希望太小，所以医生用了这句话。在②中，小红的婚事困难重重，大家认为不太可能举行了，所以也用了这句话。由此，当一件坏事情即将发生，用什么办法也不可能阻止的时候，就该用这句话跟有关的人打打招呼了。

☞ Context

The speaker of this phrase assumes the result is at least eighty percent assured. In conversation (1), the patient is critically injured and there's not much hope for survival. So, the doctor uses this phrase to acknowledge the patient's slim chances. In conversation (2), people use this phrase because they think that Xiao Hong has so many problems and she will cancel the wedding. Thus, this phrase is used to let others know that a deteriorating situation is very likely to lead to a disappointing result.

> **古语**：日薄西山，气息奄奄，人命危浅，朝不虑夕。// 李密
> 　　　《陈情表》
> **雅语**：行将就木
> **类语**：没戏了　吹台了

4.2.2>

扯淡
[talk nonsense]

😊 对话 Conversation

① A：行了，别扯淡了，快讨论正题吧！
　　All right, no need to talk nonsense. We should get back to the topic at hand now!

　 B：是吗？我说的可都是正经事。
　　What? All I've been talking about is business.

② A：老李真能说呀，一开口就得一个小时以上。
　　Old Li, you are really talkative. Every time you open your mouth it takes about an hour for you to finish.

　 B：可惜说不到点上，全是扯淡话。
　　Unfortunately, none of it is relevant to the subject. It's all nonsense.

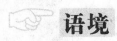 语境

　　"扯"，有"聊天""谈话"的意思。例如：有时间咱们扯扯。"淡"，是"没味儿""没意义"的意思。两个字放在一起，就是"说没有用的话"的意思，这话往往用来批评那些喜欢表现自己，说话没有内容，白白耽误听者好多时间的人。

 Context

　　One word in this phrase means to "chat" or "talk", and the other means "tasteless" or "meaningless". When these two words are put together, the phrase means to "talk nonsense." This phrase is usually used to criticize people who like to show off and end up talking a lot of nonsense and wasting other people's time.

古语：予尝为女妄言之，女以妄听之。// 《庄子·齐物论》
雅语：言之无物
类语：胡说　神聊　瞎侃

打耙
[Change plans at the last minute.]

☺ 对话 Conversation

① A：原来说得好好的，怎么变了！
　　We'd already made a decision about this, how could you change it?

　B：嗨，老李就是喜欢打耙。
　　Sigh, Old Li is always changing plans at the last minute.

4 / 不给别人面子 / Don't Give Other People Face
4.2 / 在均势中 / Equal to Others

② A：这回可说定了，绝不能再打耙。

We'd settled on the time, you can't just change it.

B：我说话算话。

I'll keep my word.

语境

　　"打耙"的故事出自《西游记》中的猪八戒，他经常在逃跑时"倒打一耙"，吓人一跳。后来用来比喻：临时改变决定，并把责任推到对方身上的事。是"反悔"和"无赖"的意思。其实，谁都知道"信用"的宝贵。喜欢"打耙"的人，大概也是因为"不得已"吧。

Context

　　This phrase comes from the novel *Journey to the West*. One of the characters on the pilgrimage often "wields a big rake (weapon) toward the back" to frighten people. Later, the phrase came to be used to describe people who change plans at the last minute and then shift the blame for it onto others. It also refers to people who "go back on their word" and "act shamelessly". In fact, everybody knows the value of their "reputation". People who can't keep their promises may not "have an alternative".

古语：朝令而暮改 //《汉书·食货志》

雅语：出尔反尔

类语：说话不算话　　不讲信用

跌份
[lose face]

😊 对话 Conversation

① **A：**哎，听说老李昨天在讲台上摔了一跤！
Hey, I heard that Old Li had a fall on the podium yesterday.

B：唉，不服老不是？真跌份！
Hey, he must think he's still young! What a shame!

② **A：**哎，听说小红考英语四级"烤煳了"！
Hey, I was told that Xiao Hong failed in her level-four English test!

B：是吗？本来她想长一份，没想反倒跌了一份。
Really? She wanted to be the winner, but instead she's lost "face"!

👉 语境

"跌"有"下落"的意思。"份"是身份的"份"，原指社会地位，在口语中作为"面子"的别称。"跌份"，也就是发生了使人很丢"面子"的事。在①中，是当众出了丑。在②中，是考试没通过。"跌份"的原因呢？一是身体不好了，一是没准备好。因此，要"长份"，就需要健康和实力；要不，你就别去竞争，否则你只能是不断地"跌份"。

👉 Context

A direct translation of this phrase is that someone's "social position has fallen". In oral conversation, its alternative meaning is someone has "lost face".

In conversation (1), Old Li is shamed because he fell on the podium. In conversation (2), Xiao Hong didn't pass the exam. What's the reason for these "falls"? One is caused by a health problem and the other comes from not being ready for something. So if you want to be the winner, you'd better have good health and be fully prepared. If not, you'd better not enter the competition. Otherwise you will continually "lose face".

古语：若俯首贴耳，摇尾而乞怜者，非我之志也！//唐·韩
愈《应科目时与人书》
雅语：有失身份
类语：掉价儿　现眼

4.2.5>

多事
[troublemaker]

对话 Conversation

① A：哎，昨儿我帮着人家介绍老伴儿来着，可好玩了！
　　Hey, I introduced an older lady to an old guy so they can share some companionship. It was really fun!

　 B：哎呀，你真多事，老伴儿最难说成了！
　　My god, you are too noisy, being a match maker for old couples is hard.

② A：前天我听老张说了老刘很多坏话，昨天我都告诉老刘了。
　　I heard Lao Zhang saying something bad about Lao Liu two days ago, so I told Lao Liu the whole story yesterday.

B：你也太多事了！你等着吵罗圈架儿吧！
You're really a troublemaker! Their quarrel will turn into a big fight now!

③ **A：喂，菜里别放大蒜啊，我讨厌那种味儿！**
Hey, don't put any garlic in the dish. I hate the smell!

B：哎，你怎么那么多事啊，大蒜是美容的！
Sigh, everything is problem for you. Garlic can make you more beautiful!

 ## 语境

中国有句俗语"多一事不如少一事"，大意是：事情多没有事情少好。从有这种说法起，"多事"就成了很多种毛病的代称。在①中，是做了一般人懒得管的"麻烦事"。在②中，是管了不该管的"闲事"。在③中，是坚持了给别人添麻烦的"个人习惯"。总之，三个对话中的A都够"事儿的"。其实，"事儿"不等于"热心"。人们需要的是"热心人"，不是"多事之人"。

 ## Context

An old Chinese saying states that: "It would be better to have one thing less than one thing more." The general idea here is that too many things to do are not as good as nothing to do. Saying it this way, this phrase can be alternatively explained as "too many problems". In conversation (1), A has done something that nobody cares to do. In conversation (2), A pokes his nose into other people's business. In conversation (3), A makes trouble for others because of her own habits. In conclusion, all three As are troublemakers and show no compassion for other people.

古语：庖人虽不治庖，尸祝不越樽俎而代之矣。//《庄子·
　　　逍遥游》
雅语：多管闲事
类语：事儿妈

4.2.6>

跟着哄
[following the crowd]

☺ 对话 Conversation

① A：最近买 VCD 的人挺多，听说老李也买了。

So many people purchased VCDs recently. I heard that Old Li also bought one.

B：唉！他连电视都没有，纯粹是跟着哄！

Sigh! He doesn't even own a television. He's just following the crowd.

② A：到底是谁有意见，站出来说！

If anyone has any complaints, please speak up!

B：就是嘛，公司一直很照顾大家，不要跟着哄嘛。

Precisely, the company has taken care of everyone, so don't blindly echo what others say!

语境

　　"跟着哄"是很常见的"从众心理"，也叫"头羊现象"。一般分为两类：一是流行类，如在①中。但是与广告的关系不大，因为中国古代有太多的故事，比如学步态的、学病态的等等。二是闹事类的，如在②中，本来问题不大，但总有少数人制造麻烦，又往往有些人"跟着哄"，结果气氛就紧张了。为什么去提意见要人多点呢？传统上有句话叫"法不责众"，所以……

Context

　　"Following the crowd" is common because everyone has a psychological predisposition to copy or follow the people around them. This phenomenon is also called "following a bellwether". It can be divided into two categories: one is to follow a popular trend, as in conversation (1). But this is different from its commercial use because there are many old stories not related to ads, such as copying someone's walking style or the look and motion of someone who has a certain illness. The second category concerns making trouble, just as we see in conversation (2). The situation might be nothing much in the beginning, but when a few people make trouble, more often than not, other people start to follow the crowd and the result is a very uneasy social environment. Why do people like to be part of a group despite holding differing opinions? Because, as the traditional saying goes, "the law doesn't punish the masses."

古语：楚灵王好细腰，而国中多饿人。//《韩非子·二柄》
雅语：邯郸学步
类语：赶时髦　随大流

4.2.7>

还知道姓什么吗

[Remember who you are.]

☺ 对话 Conversation

① A：哎，我儿子考上耶鲁大学了！

　　Hey, my son enrolled at Yale University!

　B：哼，还知道姓什么吗？准备学费吧你！

　　Hey, remember who you are. You still have to find a way to pay his tuition, you know!

② A：告诉你！我评上副教授啦！

　　Let me tell you. I am now an associate professor!

　B：嘿，还知道姓什么吗？你的同学早都是正教授了！

　　Oh, don't be so proud of yourself. Your classmates are all already full professors!

 语境

　　有的人，情绪太容易波动。一点坏事，就觉得天已经塌了下来；一点好事，又乐得合不上嘴。在①中，上耶鲁当然是有"面子"的事，可是学费也绝对够A一呛。在②中，A好不容易评上副教授，可是，如今的职称用处大吗？再过几年，教书的全是教授，搞技术的都是高工了。所以，对A这种太容易高兴的人，很需要B来泼泼冷水。

☞ **Context**

Some people cannot control their emotions. On the one hand, if a small bad thing happens, they feel that the sky has fallen. If a little good thing happens, on the other hand, they will laugh so hard that they can't close their mouth. In conversation (1), A gains a lot of "face" when his son enrolls at Yale University. But he needs to think about whether he can pay all the expenses involved. In conversation (2), it's not easy for A to become an associate professor, but the title isn't of much use nowadays. In several years, all teachers become professors and all technicians become engineers. So, it's necessary for B to throw a little cold water on A's conceit.

古语：魏其者，沾沾自喜耳。//《史记·魏其武安侯列传》
雅语：得意忘形
类语：找不着北

4.2.8>

好是好
[It's good, but...]

☺ 对话 Conversation

① A：老李呀，对小红的建议，你有什么看法？
　　Old Li, what do you think of Xiao Hong's suggestions?

　B：她的建议好是好，就是不太完善，补充一下就更好了。
　　They're good, but they're not perfect and need to be fleshed out.

② A：小红啊，你的男朋友对你好不好？

　　Xiao Hong, is your boyfriend nice to you?

　B：嗯，怎么说呢？好是好，可他太穷了！不能给我买好衣服！

　　He's nice all right, but he's too poor. He can't afford to buy any nice clothes for me.

 ## 语境

　　听到"好是好"的时候，一般人都会注意听后边的话。因为，前边的这个"好"，只是个礼貌，后边的话才是重点。这句话在使用中大概有两种情况。在①中，是虽然比较好，但是还差一点的意思，所以老李说要补充一下。在②中，就变成了"不好"的意思。因为小红觉得男友很难把"好"表示出来，那当然就等于"不太好"了。

 ## Context

　　When anyone hears this phrase, he usually pays attention to what follows, because after the word "good", which is used to be polite, comes the second part that goes to the heart of the sentence. This phrase should probably be used in two situations. In conversation (1), although Xiao Hong's suggestion is good, it's still not perfect so Old Li wants to add some further points. In conversation (2), the second part turns the sentence into something that is "not good" because it shows Xiao Hong feels her boyfriend is too poor to qualify as a "good" boyfriend.

古语：巧则巧矣，未尽善也 // 《傅子·附录》

雅语：美中不足

类语：成是成　　行是行　　可以是可以

4.2.9>

话可得讲清楚

[Let me clear about it.]

😊 对话 Conversation

① **A：我说，话可得讲清楚！你管生产，我管销售，谁也别瞎掺和！**
Let me clear about this! You're in charge of production and I'm in charge of sales. Neither of us should interfere in the other's business!

B：没错，工作责任当然要分清楚。
That's for sure, we should be clear about our responsibilities.

② **A：哎，这笔生意做成了，你拿三成，我拿七成，行吗？**
Hey, if this deal goes through, how about you taking 30% of the profit, and I'll take 70%?

B：那哪成啊？话可得讲清楚，咱们对半分才对！
No way! Let me make this clear, each of us gets 50%!

 语境

在谈到双边利害关系的时候，这句话很有用。因为很多人在事先没把话讲清楚，或是故意不想把话讲清楚，所以事后经常会吵架。在①中，工作责任分不清，同事之间闹矛盾事小，给国家造成损失，事可就大了。在②中，朋友之间的分账最麻烦。往往是赚了钱会翻脸，赔了钱更要翻脸，甚至连亲兄弟也变成仇人。所以，事先把话讲清楚并签订合同，才是认真合作的态度。

☞ **Context**

This phrase is very useful when discussing common interests. Because many people don't make things clear, or are intentionally vague beforehand, they often have arguments afterwards. In conversation (1), when individual responsibility at work is not clear, conflicts between colleagues will result, and beyond that, it could lead to a great loss to the country. In conversation (2) we see that it is very difficult to be clear in business between friends. As often happens, whether the deal makes money or not, they will have a disagreement. Even blood brothers become enemies. So, making the deal clear and signing a contract in advance is the most conscientious and cooperative attitude for doing business.

古语：言之凿凿，确可信据 // 蒲松龄《聊斋志异·段氏》
雅语：有言在先
类语：话可得说明白　这事不能含糊

4.2.10>

活该
[It serves him/her right!]

☺ **对话 Conversation**

① A：哎，听说了吗？老李昨天出车祸了！

　　Hey, did you hear that Old Li was involved in a car accident yesterday?

B：活该！那个人人恨的老东西！

　　It serves him right! He's a horrible old guy!

② A：哎，听说了吗？张小姐大肚子了！

Hey, have you heard that Miss Zhang is pregnant?

B：活该！她浪漫得也可以了！

It serves her right! She's just too romantic!

③ A：哎，听说了吗？那个独裁者终于被抓起来了！

Hey, have you heard that the dictator has been arrested?

B：是吗？活该！老天爷总算睁开眼睛了！

Really? It serves him right! There's divine justice after all!

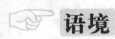 ## 语境

看到别人碰到麻烦，自己心里却挺高兴。这是因为什么呢？可能是仇恨，如在①中。可能是嫉妒，如在②中，也可能是别的原因。但是不管怎样，B都觉得现在发生的事情，是早就应该发生的。所以，B的长久愿望得到了满足，心理也得到了平衡。③中的情况，不是个人恩怨。B的开心，代表了广大人民的喜悦，是对天意的感谢。

Context

Why are people happy to see others suffer? It could be because of bitter hated, as in conversation (1). It could be because of jealousy, as in conversation (2). Or there may be other reasons but, in any event, B's long standing wish has at last come true. She can feel there is some balance in the world. The case in conversation (3) is not a personal. B's feelings represent everyone's joy and thanks for divine retribution.

古语：合该 //《聊斋志异·席方平》

雅语：理应如此

类语：该他倒霉了　该轮到他了

叫板
[challenge]

😊 对话 Conversation

① A：我这么说，他非那么说！

He contradicts everything I say!

B：是啊，这不是叫板吗？

So I see, is he just challenging you?

② A：你在麦当劳对面开了一家中式快餐？

Did you open a Chinese fast food restaurant opposite McDonald's?

B：对，我就是要跟它叫板！

Yes, I'm going to go head to head with them at their own game.

☞ 语境

"叫板"原来是戏曲专用词。指演员出场时用力发声，作用是：引起注意、试音、连接正式唱段。后来，有时用在人际关系上，意思是：故意作对。有时用在经济关系中，意思是：开始竞争。

☞ Context

This phrase originally comes from traditional Chinese opera. In order to get everyone's attention when beginning the performance, test their voice, and make an impressive opening, the actor or actress comes on to the stage accompanied by a powerful sound. Later, this phrase was occasionally used for personnel relations, when people challenge each other. Sometimes it is used for economic relations, when people begin competing against each other.

古语：秦数挑战 //《史记·廉颇蔺相如列传》
雅语：对台戏
类语：对着干　　叫阵

4.2.12>

就会耍嘴皮子
[mere empty talk]

😊 对话 Conversation

① A：老李那个人怎么样？
What do you think about Old Li?

B：他呀，就会耍嘴皮子！
He's a slick talker.

② A：老李就会耍嘴皮子。
Moan, Old Li is a slick talker.

B：是吗？让他去做推销员吧。
Is he? Then he could be a salesman.

 语境

　　喜欢说话也会说话的人，一般称为"耍嘴皮子的"。按照传统的看法，这种人是有点问题的，因为"言多必诈"。所以从古到今一直认为：说话多的人，会少做事情。如在①中。但是，随着市场经济的扩大，爱说、会说的人又有用了。在买卖上、交际中，不会说话怎么行呢？如在②中。其实，会不会说话，除了语言问题，还有思维逻辑问题，最重要的是良心问题。如果你是诚实的人，那么话多话少又有什么关系呢？

 ## Context

We usually call those people who like to talk and are good at it "slick talkers." From a traditional perspective, these people have some problem because they use all their time to talk rather than work. And there must be some cheating or tricks with their use of words, as suggested in conversation (1). These people are quite useful in marketing products today. They can be mix well in social situations, and use their skill to do business, just as in conversation (2). In fact, the skill at conversation depends on more than one's mouth, but also on a person's ability to think and his conscience. For an honest person, it doesn't matter much if a person speaks more or less.

古语：徒以口舌为劳 // 《史记·廉颇蔺相如列传》
雅语：善于言辞
类语：侃大山

4.2.13>

看上去很美
[look beautiful]

☺ 对话 Conversation

① A：哎，你见过咱们老板的夫人吗？
　　Hey, have you seen our Boss's wife?

B：远远地碰到过一次，看上去很美。

I saw her once, but only from a distance. She looks beautiful.

② **A：哎，你去过云岭吗？都说那儿是环境最好的旅游点。**

Hey, have you been to Yunling? People say that it's the best tourist environment.

B：没去过，可是我有一些风景照，看上去很美！

I haven't, but I have some pictures of it. It looks beautiful!

 ## 语境

这句话，是当代作家王朔的小说的名字，本来好像没什么特别的意思，但是大家纷纷使用以后，马上就串味儿了。例如：《北京青年报》1999年8月1号头版，刊出美国杀人狂巴顿一家四口的照片，在左上角就用了这句话。因为照片中的感觉与凶杀事件的距离太大，所以现在只能说"看上去很美"了。由此，不论是在①中还是在②中，不论是王朔的小说还是别的东西，今后人们只要听到或看到这句话，它都已经变成了相反的暗示。

 ## Context

This phrase is the title of a novel by Wang Shuo. The phrase didn't attain any special meaning until more and more people used it and begin to apply it to other situations. For example, there was the text, "Look Pretty" next to the photo of killer Mark Barton with his second wife and two children on the front page of the Beijing Youth Daily newspaper, August 1, 1999. The editor used this phrase as a bit of irony, because this phrase is far from what people would feel after reading the story of Barton's killing. Thus, from now on, whether in conversation (1) and (2), or in Wang Shuo's novel, this phrase is usually used with some hint or implication that just the opposite meaning is implied.

4.2.14>

了不起呀

[What's so special about it?]

对话 Conversation

① A：昨儿我和外国朋友吃饭来着！

I had dinner with my foreign friends yesterday!

B：和外国人吃饭了不起呀？

What's so special about having dinner with foreigners?

② A：我已经出了好几本书了！

I've written and published several books!

B：出几本书了不起呀？

What's so great about publishing a few books?

 语境

　　"了不起"是夸赞人的词。可是"了不起呀"就变成了"并没有什么了不起嘛"的意思。有的人，喜欢把自己"有面子"的事告诉别人，希望得到"了不起"的评语。但是，也有人不喜欢听别人的好事。于是就有了这句语气很硬，不给人"面子"的话。

☞ **Context**

This phrase means that there is nothing unusual about what is being said or offered. Some people like to show off with the hope of earning the "admiration" of others. But some people dislike this kind of behavior, so they use this phrase to refuse to give the speaker any extra "face".

古语：何足置之齿牙间 // 《史记·刘敬书叔孙通列传》
雅语：不过如此
类语：很有面子吗　算什么呀

4.2.15>

乱了套了
[It is a mess.]

☺ **对话 Conversation**

① A：快叫电工，四边的红绿灯都坏了！

Call the electrician quickly. The traffic lights in all four directions have gone wrong!

B：啊？那不乱了套了吗！

What? That'll be a mess!

② A：课堂里怎么那么乱啊？

Why is the classroom in such disorder?

B：老师没来，当然就乱了套了。

The teacher hasn't come yet, so of course the students are wild.

289

③ A：一个国家没人管行吗?

　　Can a country run without a government?

　B：那哪行啊！那还不乱了套喽！

　　Of course not, it would be a mess!

 ## 语境

　　这句话，本来是说马车出了麻烦，是马身上的"套"乱了。后果：马会受伤，车会翻倒。后来，比喻各种对规矩的"出轨"。在①中是交通秩序，在②中是课堂秩序，在③中是社会秩序。有意思的是，同一个人，对"乱套"的态度会变：当他在下层，就喜欢乱；当他在上层，就不喜欢了。

 ## Context

This sentence originally meant that a carriage had a problem because the harness for the horses was messed up. This would injure the horses and result in the carriage turning over. Later, this sentence was used to compare things that overstep the bounds. In conversation (1), it is used for traffic regulations. In conversation (2), it is used for class rules. In conversation (3), it is used for public order. The interesting point is that one can change their attitude toward a "mess" as a result of changes in their social position. When they are in the lower strata, they favor chaos. But when they are in upper strata, they are afraid of such messes.

古语：齐师败绩 //《左传·成公二年》

雅语：失去控制

类语：一锅粥

4.2.16>

没见过你这种人
[I've never seen anybody like you.]

😊 **对话 Conversation**

① A：喂，你怎么踩了人家的脚，连句"对不起"都不说呀？没见过你这种人！

Hey, you stepped on my toe, and didn't even say "sorry"! I've never seen anybody like you!

B：咦？车这么挤，又不是故意的，踩了就踩了呗，我也没见过你这种人！

Why should I? The bus is crowded, and anyway I didn't do it on purpose, and it isn't that big a deal, I've never seen anybody like you either!

② A：老李呀，怄点气也是难免的，你怎么能一气就八年不回家呢？没见过你这种人。

Old Li, anyone can have a bad temper sometimes, but how can you be so angry as to leave home for eight years? I've never seen anyone like you.

B：嗨，你不知道，这里面事多了，说不清楚。

Sigh, it's too complicated to explain.

语境

老说这句话的人，似乎是什么人"都"见过，其实不是，这个"都"，只是符合传统习惯的人和事。一旦遇到"出轨"的情况，这种人就会说"没见过"了。当然，这句话是不礼貌的。它的含意是：因为没有……所以没见过……。等于：你不是人。所以，第一是最好别用这句话，免得吵架。第二是如果别人对你讲这句话，你最好当做没听见，省得生气。如果你一定要回嘴，那么也可以这样说："今天就让你见见！"

Context

People who often use this phrase haven't really seen all kinds of people or things. They have seen only those kinds of people and things that occur in their normal routines. Once people or things are outside of that expected norm, they will say that they've never seen such thing. Of course, this sentence is rude. It means: because one didn't...so whatever it is isn't right.... It is equivalent to acting as if someone or something wasn't human. Hence, it would first be better not to use this sentence at all if you don't want to argue. Second, if anyone says this sentence to you, you'd better act like you didn't hear it in order to avoid being angry. If you decide that you want to respond, you could say: "Okay, I'm just broadening your horizon today!"

古语：鲜矣 // 《论语·学而》
雅语：罕见
类语：真少见　什么人哪

没劲
[It's boring.]

😊 对话 Conversation

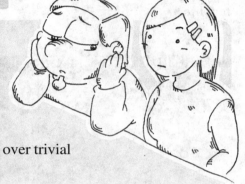

① A：你的女朋友可爱吗？
   Is your girlfriend a nice person?

B：除了生闲气，她什么都不会！没劲。
   All she does is get angry, even over trivial things! It's boring.

② A：当了三年大学生，感觉怎么样？
   How do you feel about having been a university student the past three years?

B：不能说没学东西，可是骗局和陷阱太多，真没劲！
   I can't say that I didn't learn anything, but there are too many traps and cheats, it's been boring!

👉 语境

　　表示否定的话很多，如果想学一句万能的，那就是"没劲"。评论一个人，可以，如在①中；评价一种生活，可以，如在②中。只要你对某人、某事、某物不感兴趣甚至丧失兴趣，都可以说"没劲"。当然，随便说"没劲"，是不礼貌的，也是不负责任的。但是，谁又能经常碰到"没劲"的反面——"有劲"呢？

☞ **Context**

There are many sentences that can be used to express something negative. But if you want to learn one sentence that serves as an all-purpose response, this is the one. You can use it to comment on a person, as in conversation (1). You could also use it to discuss a life-style, as we see in conversation (2). This sentence can be used when you've lost interest in some people, some things, or just about anything. But, it is very impolite and irresponsible if you use this sentence too freely. Anyway, it is rare to meet anything that is so interesting in real life.

古语：荒山甚无趣 // 杜甫《送高司直寻封阆州》
雅语：味同嚼蜡
类语：没意思

4.2.18>

那还用说

[by all means; certainly]

☺ **对话 Conversation**

① A：老李呀，饭后安排余兴节目了吗？
　　Old Li, will there be any entertainment after dinner?

　B：那还用说，包您尽兴！
　　Certainly, just leave it all to me!

② A：你说你的心里只有我，没有他是吗？
　　You said that I'm the only one in your heart. Are you sure?

B：那还用说。

Certainly!

 语境

"那"，指的是对方所说的话，"还用说"是不用说，合起来就是非常肯定，根本不需要担心的意思。此话的用意是要让对方相信，我已经考虑得很周到，安排得很妥帖，绝无发生意外的可能。此话的言外之意是：你这样不放心，实在是小看我、怀疑我，我对你这种态度有点反感。当然，对这句经常顺嘴讲出来的话，我们还是不能全信，因为那很可能是敷衍之辞。所以，该过问的还得过问，该核查的必须核查。否则，真到"用说"的时候就晚了。

 Context

This phrase emphasizes an affirmative answer and assures the listener that they don't have anything to worry about. It should make the listener believe that everything has been very thoughtfully and carefully worked out. There will be no mistakes. What is actually meant, however, is that someone worries too much and is criticizing or doubting. I dislike such attitudes. Of course, since people use this phrase so casually, you shouldn't always believe it when you hear it. So, if you feel that you need to know all the details, you should take up the matter personally. Otherwise, it'll be too late to do anything when you finally discover the problem.

古语：子孙弃者无论焉 // 袁枚《黄生借书说》
雅语：无须赘言
类语：这是常识　废什么话呀

4.2.19>

那哪行啊

[No way./ That won't do!]

☺ 对话 Conversation

① A：老李，今晚我去你家住吧。

Old Li, may I stay at your place tonight?

B：那哪行啊！我们家没地儿！

No way, we don't have any spare room!

② A：这笔生意虽然有风险，咱们也得咬牙做了！

Although there are some risks involved in this deal, we'll just have to put up with them!

B：那哪行啊！我们不能拿国家的钱开玩笑！

That won't do! We can't take any chances with the country's money!

 语境

　　这句话，是坚决反对的意思。在①中，A先生的要求比较过分，这在今天的城市里是很难被接受的，所以老李一口回绝了他。在②中，A先生在没有把握的情况下，要拿国家的钱去冒险。这一是不负责任，一是其中很可能有个人私利；B不怕得罪人，坚决不同意，这才是国家主人应有的态度。

 Context

This phrase means to be firmly against something. In conversation (1),

Mr. A's request represents an excessive imposition for people living in the city. No one would allow someone to stay in his home unless they were a very close friend. So Li flatly rejects him. In conversation (2), Mr. A is going to use government money to make a risky business deal. He is not only irresponsible, but is also likely seeking some personal gain. B isn't afraid of offending anyone about this and resolutely opposes it. B is a good guardian of the country's resources.

古语：未可 // 《左传·庄公十年》
雅语：绝对不行
类语：那可不成

4.2.20>

你累不累啊

[Aren't you fed up?]

☺ 对话 Conversation

① A： 我每天都忙到晚上10点多才回家。
　　　 I have to work until ten every night before I can go home.

　 B： 你累不累啊？ 一分钱也不多挣。
　　　 Aren't you fed up? They don't even give you any extra pay for it.

② A： 为了孩子的教育问题，我操碎了心。
　　　 I have gone to a lot of trouble to see to the education of the children.

　 B： 你又不懂教育！ 你累不累啊？
　　　 You don't know anything about education yourself! Aren't you fed up with it?

③ **A：我白天也想她，晚上也想她。**

I miss her day and night.

B：这是爱情？你累不累啊！

Is that love? If it is, aren't you tired of it?

 ## 语境

很多人怕"累"，也有人找"累"。在①中，A是为了工作，可是B认为毫无意义。在②中，家长在孩子身上花了太多的精力，B却认为，起不了好作用。在③里，A在相思中煎熬，B认为这种爱情太沉重了，女人应该使男人轻松才对。其实，每一个都有自己的"累"。100%的轻松——更累！怎么才能不累呢？如果心不累，那就哪儿都不累了。

 ## Context

Some people are afraid of being "fed up", but others are looking forward to being "fed up". In conversation (1), A feels that he's given his all for his work, but B thinks that what he's doing is pointless. In conversation (2), parents dedicate too much of their energy toward their children's education, but B thinks that all the parents' efforts didn't have much of an effect on the children's study. In conversation (3), A suffers a lot from love, but B thinks this kind of love is too tense and that a woman should make their boyfriend feel more relaxed.

古语：使敌疲于奔命//《后汉书·袁绍传》
雅语：如牛负重
类语：有这个必要吗　你图个什么呀

你以为你是谁呀

[Who do you think you are]

☺ 对话 Conversation

① A：老张啊！有关的事儿你都安排一下，别忘了把茶沏上。

Old Zhang! Please take care of the arrangements, and don't forget to make some tea.

B：老李呀！你以为你是谁呀？我们是同级！

Old Li! Who do you think you are? We're colleagues!

② A：这饭店条件太差了！你知道我一天要洗三次澡，这不，又没热水了！

This hotel is not up to my standards! You know that I have to take a shower three times a day, and there's no hot water again!

B：你以为你是谁呀？麦当娜啊！凑合点儿吧。

Who do you think you are? Madonna! You've got to put up with these things. You'll get used to it in a few days.

👉 语境

说来奇怪，很多一般的人，却有一些"不一般"的心理。他们一遇机会，突然就露出很大的口气，摆出很大的架子，好像天老大，他老二，别人都是老三似的。在①中，老李让同事为自己服务。在②中，A女士认为出门跟在家一样方便。当然，两个人都受到了"教育"。

☞ **Context**

It may be strange; but many ordinary people develop some "unusual" feelings toward different things. If an opportunity presents itself, they can suddenly take a high tone and put on airs. They can also begin to act like they're the boss. In conversation (1), Old Li asks another colleague to serve him. In conversation (2), A thinks that a business trip should have the same conveniences as she has at home. Of course, both of these people are given some education about their attitudes in the responses of their colleagues.

古语：肉食者谋之，又何间焉？ // 《左传·庄公十年》
雅语：自不量力
类语：你还知道自己姓什么吗

4.2.22>

你怎么这么不知趣啊
[How can you be so naive?]

☺ **对话 Conversation**

① A：老李呀，你怎么这么不知趣啊！小红已经有对象了，你还瞎掺和什么？

　　Old Li, how can you be so naive? Xiao Hong already has a boyfriend. Why are you still messing around with her?

　B：我怎么知道她有了？再说，不是可以公平竞争吗？

　　How do I know she has boyfriend, anyway, why can't I chase after her too?

② A：老李呀，你怎么这么不知趣啊！院长和书记正谈事儿呢！你闯进去干吗？

Old Li, how can you be so careless? The President and Party Secretary are talking. What do you mean rushing into the room like that?

B：不是提倡"集体办公"吗？何况我确实有事！

Oh, don't they advocate "teamwork"? Besides, I really have something that I need to talk to them about.

 ## 语境

"不知趣"的意思是：在人际关系上不知进退，在公共场合中没有分寸。在①里，老李忘记了自己的年龄，想当"第三者"，A 提醒他，他还狡辩，简直是没有大脑。在②中，两位领导在谈话，当然应该回避，可老李觉得没关系。对于这种人，也真没有什么办法。

 ## Context

"Naive" means that one has no sense of propriety regarding interpersonal relationships or public occasions. In conversation (1), Old Li forgets his age and wants to be "the third person" in another person's relationship. A reminds him of this but he still thinks he's right. He doesn't have a clue about the reality of the situation and is naive. In conversation (2), when two leaders have a meeting, Old Li should, of course, avoid interrupting their discussion. But Li thinks that it's not a problem rushing into their meeting like that. We have no way of dealing with these kinds of people.

古语：为国以礼，其言不让，是故哂之。//《论语·先进》

雅语：不知进退

类语：不识相　没眼力价　二百五　13点

你怎么知道的
[How do you know?]

☺ 对话 Conversation

① A：哎，院长和书记昨天吵架了！

Hey, the President and the Party Secretary had a quarrel yesterday!

B：你又不在场，你怎么知道的？

You weren't there, how do you know?

② A：据说老李在外边还有一所房子。

I've heard that Old Li has another house somewhere.

B：不会吧，你怎么知道的？

That can't be true, how do you know?

③ A：快买点油吧！又要涨价啦！

Go and buy some gas quickly! The price is going to rise!

B：你怎么知道的？别瞎说！

How can you know that? Don't talk rubbish!

☞ 语境

很多人喜欢问"你怎么知道的"。表面看，这句话的意思是希望得到消息来源，以便证实。但在不同场合，也有别的意思。在①中，B用反问句表示怀疑，是不相信的意思。在②中，B用否定句表示反感，是反对管闲事的意思。在③中，B是批语的语气，意在制止A造谣。

Context

Some people like to respond to other people's assertions with "how do you know?" On the surface, the words sound like they just want to know the source of the information in order to confirm it. But there are other meanings. In conversation (1), B responds to A with a question that casts doubts on A's statement. In conversation (2), B responds negatively and shows disdain for A's behavior. B thinks people should mind their own business. In conversation (3), B criticizes A, and wants to put a stop to the rumor.

古语：何以知之 //《史记·廉颇蔺相如列传》
雅语：从何得知
类语：从哪儿听说的

4.2.24>

墙里开花墙外香

[The blooming flower within the wall exudes its fragrance beyond.]

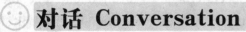

对话 Conversation

① A：只看见小红每天写东西，原来她在外边很有面子！
We see Xiao Hong writing every day, but it turns out she has a good reputation among the general public!

B：没想到吧，墙里开花墙外香！

You didn't suspect that, did you? She's like the blooming flower within the wall that exudes its fragrance beyond!

② **A：老李为什么非要出国讲学呢？**

Why must Old Li lecture abroad?

B：这你就不懂了，墙里开花墙外香嘛。

You don't understand it, it's like the adage: the blooming flower within the wall exudes its fragrance beyond.

 ## 语境

这句话在古代的意思，是对领导有意见，说领导只盯着外边的人才，却不重用身边的人。在现代的意思呢，是指出一种现象，距离太近就不容易被发现和重视，如在①和②中。其实这种毛病人人都有，就像80%的男人都说街上的女孩子漂亮一样。但是最近又听到一句话，说"交流就是力量"。于是忽然想到：你在外人眼中，不也是外人吗？你的"香味儿"又在哪儿呢！

 ## Context

In past times this sentence implied a grievance against the leader in regards to their assessment of talent, especially against hiring talented people from outside the organization rather than paying any attention to the skillful people next to them. Currently, this meaning has expanded to include more. It now refers to a larger social phenomenon. If something is too close to you, you can't fully appreciate or understand it, just as seen in conversation (1) and (2). Another example would be the fact that eighty percent of men think the girls they see in the street are more beautiful than the girl they have at home. Recently, however, there is a new saying: "Exchanging experiences creates strength." From this perspective the situation suddenly makes some sense: everyone is an outsider for others, if flowers bloom, we can smell the fragrance from inside as well as outside of the wall.

古语：臣闻吏议逐客，窃以为过矣。// 李斯《谏逐客书》

雅语：舍近求远

类语：隔墙吹喇叭　外来的和尚好念经

4.2.25>

且得耗着呢

[We'll be waiting for a long time.]

☺ 对话 Conversation

① A：几点开机拍戏？

When do we start filming?

B：嗨，那边还没化妆呢，且得耗着呢！

Hey, they haven't even made up yet. They'll take forever!

② A：咱们的报告什么时候批下来？

When will our report be approved?

B：领导出国了，且得耗着呢！

The department head has gone abroad. We'll be waiting for that for a long time.

☞ 语境

　　"且"是"长时间"，"得"是"必须"，"耗"是"使人着急的等待过程"。这三种感觉都是很烦人的，如果都碰到一起，当然就更受不了了。虽然，这种状况是大家经常都要遇到的。这里面，有管理水平的问题，有工作效率的问题，也有官僚主义的问题等等。反正急性子的人早晚会被磨成慢性子。要不然，你就走。

4 / 不给别人面子 / Don't Give Other People Face

4.2 / 在均势中 / Equal to Others

 Context

This sentence describes the three stages of the waiting process: "have to wait", "wasting time", and "waiting for a long time." Any one of these stages is very annoying, let alone when all three of them come together. No one can put up with it. Although we often experience this kind of situation and discover the problems in management, efficiency and bureaucracy in our workplace, we have no way to change them. In the end, an impetuous person will be worn down into a slowpoke. If not, you will have to leave the job.

古语：吾子其少安 // 《左传·襄公七年》
雅语：假以时日
类语：且呢　早着呢　等着吧　熬着吧

4.2.26>

水货
[smuggled merchandise; faked goods]

☺ 对话 Conversation

① A：你买的 VCD 机怎么这么便宜？
Why was the VCD you bought so cheap?

B：嗨，水货呗。
Sigh, it was smuggled, that's why.

② A：你怎么不看那个电视连续剧了？
Why did you stop watching that TV series?

B：前两集还可以，后面就水了！

The first two parts weren't bad. But the rest was not worth watching at all.

③ **A：你经常去批发市场吗？**

Do you often go to the wholesale market?

B：不，那儿的东西全是水货！

No, the goods there are all fake!

 ## 语境

在①中，"水货"指走私商品。也可只用一个"水"，如在②中，指水平低，节奏慢的文艺作品。在③中，指各种假冒伪劣的商品。当代社会，什么都进了市场。在市场里，什么样的商品都有。让人遗憾的是，"水货"越来越多，精品越来越少。

 ## Context

In conversation (1), this phrase means "smuggled merchandise". In conversation (2), this phrase means the TV program moves too slowly, and is not that good. In conversation (3), it means all kinds of phony products. In contemporary markets, there are all kinds of goods. Unfortunately, more and more of them are fake goods; only a few of them are the real thing.

古语：金玉其外，败絮其中 // 刘基《卖柑者言》
雅语：赝品
类语：假的　冒充的　差的　骗人的

谁也甭说谁

[If I'm to blame, then everybody is; The pot shouldn't call the kettle black.]

对话 Conversation

① A：老李呀，你经常陪客户出去吃饭吧？

Old Li, you go out to dinner with clients often, don't you?

B：啧，咱们谁也甭说谁，不就是公款吃喝嘛！

If I'm guilty of eating at the state's expense, then everybody else is too!

② A：老李呀，你怎么老是盯着漂亮姑娘看哪？

Old Li, why are you always looking at beautiful girls?

B：哎呀，你从来没看过吗？咱俩谁也甭说谁！

Don't you ever look at them? The pot shouldn't call the kettle black!

 语境

有的人，喜欢指出别人的毛病。可是，他们总是忘记自己也有同样的问题。这个时候，就用得着这句话了。在①中，经常把国家的钱，吃到自己肚子里的人，不少。可是A的眼睛却总盯着老李，大概是想和他比比，谁吃得更过瘾吧。在②中，喜欢看美女是男人的权力，更是佳丽们的"面子"。这本来没什么可说的，但是A却认为老李"好色"，那就难怪老李也要揭他的短，堵他的嘴了。

☞ **Context**

Some people like to pick up on other people's faults. They often forget, however, that they have the same shortcomings themselves. This phrase can be used in these types of conditions. In conversation (1), many people use state money to pay for what they eat and drink. But A only picks on Old Li. A probably wants to compete with Old Li, to see who can spend more of the state's money on food. In conversation (2), there is nothing special here as all guys like to look at good-looking girls. But A believes Old Li loves women too much, no wonder Old Li gets back to him and stops his nonsense.

古语：如一丘之貉 // 《汉书·杨恽传》
雅语：彼此彼此
类语：咱俩一个德性　你比我好不了多少

4.2.28>

说句不好听的
[to speak bluntly]

☺ **对话 Conversation**

① A：老李呀，说句不好听的，这么多年我对你一直有看法。
　　Old Li, I'm going to speak bluntly, I have been annoyed with you for many years.

　B：好啊，说来听听，提意见不算"不好听"。
　　That's all right. Just tell me. There's no harm in speaking out.

② A：小红呀，说句不好听的，从根儿上我就没想和你结婚。

Xiao Hong, to be honest, I never intended to marry you in the first place.

B：老李呀，我也说句不好听的，你这老家伙根本不是人！

Old Li, I'll be blunt too, I think you're despicable!

 ## 语境

这句话，是个不礼貌的前奏，是向听者打个招呼，后边的话一般就是相当直率、让人不舒服的、实质性的意见。在①中，A先生要发表重要意见，当然要用这句话来强调一下。其中暗含着使老李不能生气的用意。在②中，老李要坦白自己的态度，他怕小红受不了，希望以这句话来使小红做好思想准备。可惜，小红还是太传统了。对于这种过于浪漫的剖白，除了受到精神伤害以外，似乎没有别的可能。

 ## Context

This phrase is used as a preface and lets the listener know the real substance of the remark is coming next. Of course, the real stuff is often straightforward and makes the listener very uncomfortable. In conversation (1), A is going to make comments against Old Li and uses this phrase to warn Li not to get too excited or angry. In conversation (2), Old Li wants to make a confession to Xiao Hong and uses this phrase to prepare her to accept what he wants to say. Unfortunately, Xiao Hong is very traditional and resents Li's confession, so she can only feel hurt by his comments.

古语：开诚心，布公道。//《三国志·诸葛亮传评》
雅语：忠言逆耳
类语：恕我直言

死活看不上眼
[take a complete dislike to]

☺ 对话 Conversation

① A：老李呀，你的儿子学习怎么样？
   Old Li, how are your son's studies going?

   B：他很聪明，也很努力，可是老师死活看不上眼！
   He's clever and works hard too. But the teacher seems to have taken a complete dislike to him.

② A：唉，为什么大家都不喜欢小红呢？
   Hey, why doesn't anybody like Xiao Hong?

   B：也没什么，就是她的化妆太恐怖，所以大家死活看不上眼。
   It's nothing much, only that her make-up is too strange, so no one likes her.

 语境

　　中国古代有一位名人，用"白眼"看不喜欢的人，用"青眼"看喜欢的人。现在的"靓"字，就是从他那来的。今天的人们更过分，不仅是不用"正眼"看人，而且是"死活"——无论如何都看不起一个人。有这种毛病的人，肯定是以前经受过这种锻炼。如果你正在被领导或老师"死活看不上眼"，那该怎么办呢？努力，努力，再努力！用最好的成绩，让所有的人死活都看得上眼！

Context

A famous person in Chinese history once said: look at the people that you dislike with "white eyes"; look at the people that you like with "black eyes". So, today we have the word " 靓(liàng)", which means "pretty" from this. Now, people go one step further, they not only use "white eyes" to look at people they dislike, but use "dead eyes". If they dislike someone, they use every possible means not to change their view. What can you do if you are the one who is "completely disliked" by the leader or teacher? The only way is working harder and harder to show your ability until they change their opinions of you.

古语：无以先入之语为主 // 《汉书·息夫躬传》
雅语：心怀成见
类语：就是不喜欢　横竖不待见

4.2.30>

下课
[let a person go; give someone the sack]

对话 Conversation

① A：这个姓李的哪儿配当国家队的教练啊!
This Li doesn't deserve to be the coach of the national team!

B：是啊，你没听体育场里八万人一齐让他"下课"吗?
You're right, didn't you hear 80 thousand people in the stadium shouting "fire him"?

② A：哎，电视里那些球迷喊的是什么呀，听了半天也没听明白！

Hey, what were the football fans shouting on TV? I couldn't make it out even after listening for a long time.

B：嗨，是用四川话喊的"下课"！就是"别干了，回家去吧"的意思。

Oh, they were shouting in the Sichuan dialect: "Class is over!" meaning "Give him the sack! Send him home!"

语境

"下课"这个词，本来是老师和学生们上完了一节课，该休息了的时候用的。可是从中国足球实行俱乐部制起，这个词就变成了一句有新意的话，从四川球场，流入全国。这句话，主要是球迷针对足球教练说的。因为有人觉得：中国球员虽然有自己的毛病，但是主要问题还是在教练身上，是教练的无能，才导致了比赛的失败。其实，问题是复杂的，把责任都推给教练，有点冤。

Context

This phrase was originally used for school schedules and for the time teachers and students break in between classes. Since China soccer teams use the Club system, this phrase has taken on a new meaning that started in Sichuan and spread across the entire country. It's mainly used by soccer fans yelling at the coaches. People think that Chinese soccer players have some problems, but the main reason that China's soccer play is so awful is the coach's fault. It's because the coaches are not able to train the players, so they lose games all the time. In fact, there are more complicated reasons for this than just the coaching. It's wrong to blame the coach alone for the failure.

古语：有罪得以黜出，有能得以赏。// 柳宗元《封建论》

雅语：左迁　撤职

类语：下岗　炒鱿鱼　走路　回家去吧

现在可好
[But now...]

😊 对话 Conversation

① A：老李呀，你这辈子最开心是在什么时候？

Old Li, what was the happiest time of your life?

B：那当然是小时候了，吃饱了就玩，什么都不愁。现在可好，一天到晚的糟心事！

When I was little, of course I just ate and played, and never worried about anything. But now, I'm irritated from morning till night.

② A：老李呀，你能说一下几十年来物价的变动吗？

Old Li, can you tell us about the change in prices over the past few decades?

B：噢，我记事儿那会儿，猪肉八毛一斤，西红柿一毛一筐！现在可好，10 倍都不止了！

I remember when I was a little boy, back then people could buy one *jin* of pork for eighty cents and a basket of tomatoes for ten cents. But now, they are at least ten times that much!

 ## 语境

　　这是一句反话。就跟"好热呀""好贵呀"一样，是"好"得让人受不了的意思。"怀旧"，是中老年人都有的毛病，其实他们也不是非说过去好，而是借"怀旧"在回忆自己年轻时的某些感觉，就像年轻人活在美梦里，中年人活在奢望里一样。但是，各种"脱节"的心理都是有害的，我们都应该活在今天，这不是讲今天最好，而是说今天是最真实的。

 ## Context

This is a fine irony. It's like "too hot", "too expensive", and means too much of something to bear. Older people like to remember the good old days. In fact, they don't mean that the old times were so good, but they are just trying to recall the feelings they had when they were young. It's just like young people living in a dream and middle age people living in extravagant hope. But all of these thoughts are not much to us unless we face up to today. Today may not be the best day, but it's the only day we have.

古语：江河日下 // 宗山《词学集成》
雅语：今不如昔
类语：还是那会儿好

4.2.32>

想什么呢你
[Are you dreaming?]

对话 Conversation

① A：我要是有了钱，一买别墅，二买大奔，三买全套意大利家具和日本电器，还要服务小姐……
   If only I had money, first I would buy a villa, then a Mercedes, then a set of Italian furniture and Japanese electric appliances, and then a maid...

B：**想什么呢你！**

Are you dreaming?

② A：**现在世道多好！我要是赶上这年月，先考个博士，再出国转转，找个洋妞，然后住到瑞士的小城市去……**

What a good time we have now! If only I had had this when I was young, first I'd get a Ph. D., then go abroad and find a foreign girl, and I would live in a small town in Switzerland...

B：**想什么呢你！**

Are you dreaming?

 ## 语境

　　每个人都难免做点梦，但是，有的人得梦做得太过分了。在①中，还算是一般人的梦，梦境仍在国内。在②中，是个有知识的人的梦，梦境已经覆盖了全世界，就差上外星了。

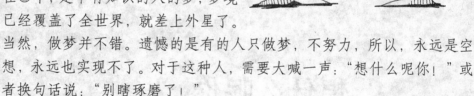

当然，做梦并不错。遗憾的是有的人只做梦，不努力，所以，永远是空想，永远也实现不了。对于这种人，需要大喊一声："想什么呢你！"或者换句话说："别瞎琢磨了！"

 ## Context

People can't help but dream about things. But some people's dreams are excessive. In conversation (1), the dream might be closer to possible because it still takes place in China. Conversation (2), is a scholar's dream. This dream covers the entire world. Of course, there is nothing wrong with dreaming. Unfortunately, some people only dream and don't work hard at all. They are always living in a dream and don't face reality. We should use this phrase to wake these kinds of people up and help them escape their confusion.

古语：只知紫绶三公贵，不觉黄梁一梦游。// 苏轼《被命
　　　南迁途中寄定武同僚》
雅语：异想天开
类语：白日梦　大白天说梦话

4.2.33>

一锤子买卖

[a one-time deal]

☺ 对话 Conversation

① A：老李呀，你是赞成"薄利多销"，还是喜欢"一锤子买卖"？
Old Li, do you favor a small profit with a quick turnover or a one-time deal?

B：前者太麻烦，要几十年才能赚钱；后者可能一笔就发了！
The former is too troublesome and the profit is too slow in coming. The later can make you a fortune in just one deal.

② A：老板，别"一锤子买卖"嘛，我以后还会来的。
Boss, don't make it "a once-and-for-all deal". I'll come again in the future.

B：别说那个，全国十几亿人，一人来一次我就发了，根本不用第二次。
Stop that. There were 1.2 billion people in China. Even if each came only once, I'd be rich. There would be no need to come a second time.

语境

在①中出现的两种做生意的办法，是很值得研究的。如果每位商人都能坚持"薄利多销"的方法，那对大家多合适啊！同时对市场的促进更大。可惜，很多老板的想法都和②中的 B 一样，经常做着全国、全省或者全市每个人都来让他骗一次的美梦，很少在服务的质量和态度上下功夫，很少全力去提高"回头客"的比例。而且，一旦碰上大买卖，总希望"一锤子"就大大地赚一笔！就算翻脸也没关系。可是，还是好好地想一想吧，信用——才是经营之本。如果你骗了一位顾客，那实际上也就等于骗了所有的顾客。

 Context

The two methods of doing business in conversation (1) warrant careful consideration. If every businessman were all in favor of small profit but quick turnover, people would really appreciate them! This way would also provide an impetus to the markets. Unfortunately, many businessman are just like B in conversation (2), they dream that they have an opportunity to eventually cheat everyone in the country and all the provinces. They do not care much about quality of service or their attitude, or increasing the number of "returning customers". Moreover, if they have a chance to make a one-time deal and make a lot of money, they don't care about falling out with their partners. But, these people should think again, the principle for management is building credit. If you cheat one customer, in reality, you've cheated all customers.

古语：竭泽而渔，岂不获得，而明年无鱼 //《吕氏春秋·义赏》

雅语：急功近利

类语：一刀宰　一遭够

一根筋

[stubborn; sticking to one way]

☺ 对话 Conversation

① A：老李明知错了，就是不改！

Old Li knows he's wrong, but he won't correct it!

  B：那人，一根筋。

That guy is simply too stubborn.

② A：既然这条路走不通，就别一根筋了，换个研究课题吧。

Since we are making no progress this way, we shouldn't stick with this subject. Let's change to another one.

  B：不行！我非得把它完成了不可！

No way! I've got to stick with it until I finish it!

☞ 语境

"一根筋"也叫"少根筋"，通常指那种脑筋不大灵活，坚持原来想法的人。其实，这种人最少有两类：在①中，是知道错了，还坚持错误，那是没有用的。在②中就不同，很多科学研究的成功者，都是"一根筋"。因为，要做好一件困难的事情，总是少不了"坚持阶段"的。

☞ Context

This phrase also refers to being "lacking in intelligence". It is often used to describe a person who is not quick witted and has a narrow way of thinking rather than a flexible approach to problems. In fact, we can divide this kind of people into two types: in conversation (1), Old Li knows he is wrong but obstinately persists in his errors. That is not a useful way to do things at all. The case in conversation (2) is different; many successful scientific researchers are "stubborn". If they want to break through the difficult challenges in their research, they can't succeed without a "period of persistence".

古语：汝心之固，固不可彻 //《列子·汤问》
雅语：固执己见
类语：认死理　叫真儿

4.2.35>

有病了
[She/He's sick!]

☺ 对话 Conversation

① A：我的腰怎么直不起来了？
  Why does my back hurt so much when I stand up?

  B：有病了。
  There must be some problem with it.

② A：小红昨天捡了1万块钱，上交派出所了。
  Xiao Hong found ten thousand *yuan* in the street yesterday. She turned it over to the local police station.

  B：有病了。
  She's sick.

③ A：老李每个休息日都加班。

Old Li worked extra hours every weekend.

B：有病了！

He has some problem!

 语境

很多人以为"有病"仅仅指生理上发生的不正常状态，如①。其实，因为心理上的原因造成的不正常状态，也属于"有病"的范围，如②。但是在②中真正有病的不是A，而是B。如今的世界很无奈，越来越多的事情失去了公认的是非标准，越来越多的人找不到正常的心理状态。这大概就是所谓的"现代综合症"吧。在③中，指某人在心智方面有点奇怪，他所做的事情，违背了一般人的道理和规矩。

 Context

Many people imagine that "sick" applies only to some abnormal physical condition, such as illnesses, as seen in conversation (1). In fact, if the abnormal condition is caused by psychological reasons, the person suffering it can also be referred to as being "sick", as seen in conversation (2). The sick person in conversation (2) is not A, but B. However, more and more things have slipped away from any universal standard of right and wrong in today's world. The result is that more and more people can't determine just what a normal psychological state is. This is probably what is called a "Complex of Modern Times". Conversation (3) describes someone who acts strange and whatever this person does runs contrary to the principles and rules used by normal people.

古语：知不知，尚矣；不知知，病也。//《老子·第七十一》

雅语：神经病

类语：有毛病　少根筋

4.2.36>

有点找不着北

[doesn't know north from south; be confused and lose one's bearings]

😊 对话 Conversation

① A：咦！这是什么地方？好像从来没来过！

Hey! Where is this place? I don't think I've ever been here before.

B：是啊，北京的变化太大了！连我这个老北京也有点找不着北。

Yes, Beijing has changed a lot! Even old residents of Beijing like me can get confused and lost.

② A：喂，你的文章到底什么意思呀？我怎么有点找不着北啊！

Hey, what on earth does your article mean? I haven't got a clue!

B：是，这是现在流行的写法，不说谁对谁错。

Well, this is a popular style of writing; it's not supposed to make clear who's right and who's wrong.

 语境

　　"北"，在汉语里有指示目标的意思，"找不着北"，就是失去了方向。在①中，迷路的情况反映出上世纪九十年代的北京，出现了太多的高楼大厦与新街道，北京人自己也经常要问路了。在②中，看不懂一篇文章的现象，反映出当代文艺理论的一个问题，就是怎么说都可以，都有道理，结果是看了比没看更糊涂。这大概就是所谓的"多元化"吧。

☞ **Context**

The Chinese language uses "north" to indicate a direction that can be used to find one's way, and this phrase means that one has lost their direction and become confused. In conversation (1), A and B both are lost because there are so many big buildings and new streets in Beijing since the 1990's, that even people who've grown up in Beijing have to ask for directions. In conversation (2), B can't understand an article. This mirrors a current problem in the theory of literature and art. This theory claims that whatever you write can have as many explanations as there are readers, so people are more confused than before after they read an article. This should probably be called "multi-variate" writing.

古语：性好道术，能作五里雾。// 《后汉书·张楷传》
雅语：如堕烟海
类语：晕头了　转向了

4.2.37>

有没有搞错
[Are you joking?]

☺ **对话 Conversation**

① A：哎，昨天我看见你和一位姑娘在一起散步。
　　Hey, I saw you strolling with a girl yesterday!

　B：啊？有没有搞错，我做梦都想那样呢！
　　What, are you joking? I've done that only in my dreams!

② A：小姐，你不可以穿拖鞋进阅览室。

Miss, you are not allowed to enter the library in slippers.

B：哎！你有没有搞错？这是新式凉鞋！

What! Are you kidding me? These are new-style sandals!

 ## 语境

这句话，在上世纪八十年代初期，从广东传入北京。表面上的意思是：你是不是误会了？实际上的意思是：你错了！这句话在语气上有两种用法。一种较轻，如在①中，虽然是反驳，但仍在调侃，并没有生气。一种较重，如在②中，是已经发了脾气，是斥责对方的意思。

 ## Context

This phrase came into Beijing from Guangzhuo at the beginning of 1980's. The literal meaning is "have you misunderstood?" The real meaning is that "You are mistaken about this!" This phrase can be spoken in two different tones. One of them is light, as in conversation (1). B refutes the assertion, but still makes a joke about it and is not angry. The other tone is more serious, as seen in conversation (2). B is annoyed and severely reprimands A.

古语：然，非与？ // 《论语·卫灵公》
雅语：似是而非
类语：是吗　不对吧

再说我跟你急

[If you keep saying things like that, I'll be angry with you.]

😊 对话 Conversation

① A: 小红啊，你平时说话、化妆
都多注点意，要不然……
Xiao Hong, you should be
more cautious when you speak
and put on makeup. Otherwise....

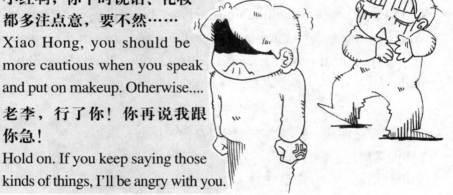

B: 老李，行了你！你再说我跟
你急！
Hold on. If you keep saying those
kinds of things, I'll be angry with you.

② A: 小红啊，找男朋友主要看思想政治水平，什么酷啦、车啦、房
啦等等，全是次要的！
Xiao Hong, the most important thing in a boyfriend is his politics.
Other things like whether he has a car or a house, or what he
looks like are less important.

B: 老李呀，你跟我废什么话！再说我跟你急！
Old Li, what kind of nonsense is that! If you keep talking like that
I'll be angry with you.

 ## 语境

说出这句话，往往是对对方的说法已经不能再听下去的时候。但是，

还得给对方稍微留一点"面子",所以是"再说"才"急";如果不说了,也就算了。在①和②中,老李以"假道学"的面孔出现,唠唠叨叨地给年轻人上课。可是今天的年轻人什么不懂啊!谁还愿意听这种空洞的说教啊!总算老李上了点年纪,小红才没跟他当场翻脸。

 ## Context

This phrase is used to stop comments from people who lecture others about their actions, but still leaves them some "face". The message here is that if the other party continues to say these types of things, the other will be angry. If he stops, the other will let it go. In conversation (1) and (2), Old Li acts like a "sanctimonious person" lecturing young people. But the young people today understand everything and none of them welcomes his empty speech! It is only because he is older that Xiao Hong didn't fall out with him.

古语:一之谓甚,其可再乎! //《左传·僖公五年》
雅语:勿谓言之不预也
类语:别说了　有完没完

4.2.39>

怎么说话呢
[How can you say that?]

🙂 对话 Conversation

① A:你的腿怎么那么弯哪?
What, you are bowlegged?

B：……！你怎么说话呢？
How dare you say such a thing?

② **A：听说你离了六次婚，真棒！**
I heard that you've been divorced six times, that's wonderful!

B：怎么说话呢？我离几次婚和你有什么关系?!
How can you say that? It's none of your business!

 ## 语境

　　言语交际中的礼貌，是个大问题，在①中，A说的应该是事实，但是构成人身攻击。在②中，A说的也可能是真的，但是侵犯了B的个人隐私权。在①和②中，B都可以请律师了。当然，有的人不是故意伤人，而是没受到好的教育。用"怎么说话呢"来反问，可以使那些人冷静一点。

 ## Context

Staying polite during conversation is a big issue. In conversation (1), although what A said is true, it becomes an insult. In conversation (2), what A said is also true, but intrudes upon details of the other person's private life. In conversations (1) and (2), B might have grounds to take the case to a lawyer. Of course, some people do not hurt other people intentionally, but simply lack the education (or sophistication) to converse politely. You can use this phrase to respond to impolite people and push them into rethinking their behavior.

古语：此之谓不知类也//《孟子·告子上》
雅语：不知轻重
类语：你会说话不会

这不是拆台吗
[Isn't that deliberate sabotage?]

☺ 对话 Conversation

① A：我正在讲话，他把人叫走了一半！

I was making the speech, when he took half the audience away.

B：这不是拆台吗？

Isn't that deliberate sabotage?

② A：咱们球队的三大主力，被人家挖走了两个！

Two of the three top players on our team have been lured away by other teams.

B：这不是拆台吗！

That's deliberate sabotage!

☞ 语境

"台"是唱戏的地方，拆了台，戏就不能唱了。"拆台"的意思，就是破坏别人的事情。"拆台"与"对台戏"有什么不同呢？"对台戏"是公开竞争，"拆台"是暗中破坏。"拆台"的特点，是利用一个借口，让对方说不出什么。在①中可以是上级有任务。在②中可以是"转会"。如果双方之间有了"拆台"的事情，那就永远是敌人了。

☞ Context

The literal meaning of this phrase is to pull down a stage, so that actors can no longer act on it. Its real meaning is to destroy other people or things. What is the difference between "destroying a show" and "a show of rivalry"? The later one is a public competition with others and the former is a kind of clandestine damaging of others. When someone wants to damage someone or something, they have to find an excuse to do so that the other party can't criticize it even if they are harmed. In conversation (1), this act can take the form of assigning a new task. In conversation (2), it can be the leaders who give these players away to other teams. If two parties destroy each other, they will always remain enemies.

古语：权谋倾覆幽险而亡矣 // 《荀子·天论》
雅语：阴谋诡计
类语：撤火　挖墙角

4.2.41>

至于吗
[Is it that serious?]

😊 对话 Conversation

① A：她的走，使我终生愁苦！
I've been miserable ever since she left.

B：至于吗？
Is it that serious?

② A：你不听我的话，死都不知道怎么死的！
If you don't listen to me, you'll be dead before you know it.

B：至于吗？
Can it be that serious?

③ A：民族问题会引起第三次世界大战！

National conflicts will bring about the Third World War!

B：至于吗？

Is the situation that serious?

④ A：昨天考试差点得100分，太可惜了！

I almost got 100% on yesterday's exam. What a pity!

B：至于吗？

It's not that bad!

 ## 语境

"至于"在这里指"程度"，加个"吗"字，意思是：到不了那种程度吧？在①中，B认为A反应过度。在②中，B吓了一跳，他怎么也想不到有生命危险。在③中，B怀疑大战的可能性。在④中，B认为A对"分"看得太重了，有点瞧不起的意思。很多人对别人的事，不太重视，对别人的感受，也不能理解。可是，如果事情发生在自己身上，那就什么都"至于"了。

 ## Context

This phrase means that one can "go so far as to" get something done. It's used as a question, but implies that the situation isn't that serious. In conversation (1), B thinks A is overreacting. In conversation (2), B is stunned because he never imagined that his life was in danger. In conversation (3), B doubts that there will be a world war. In conversation (4), B thinks A cares too much about scores and looks down on A. Many people don't pay any attention to other people's situations and don't understand other people's feelings. But, if these things happened to them, they would think all of it was "serious".

古语：何苦来 // 《红楼梦·三十一回》
雅语：不至于
类语：没那么严重吧　不会吧

4.2.42>

走后门
[going through the back door]

😊 对话 Conversation

① A：咱们的孩子不能进幼儿园，这可怎么办？
Our child can't get into this kindergarten. What can we do?

B：走走后门呗。
Let's try a back door.

② A：天天说堵后门，为什么总堵不住？
People talk about closing the back door all the time, why isn't it ever closed?

B：有的事情，不走后门不行。
Because there are some things that can only be done in this way.

👉 语境

　　"走后门"这话和那些托人情趋关系的现象，上世纪五十年代没有，大概是上世纪六十年代经济困难时期出现的。从上世纪七十年代到上世纪九十年代，又有一个从商品方面向人事方面的转移。过去的"后门"，主要在商店和医院；现在的"后门"，主要在学校和政府。有趣的是，听见别人走后门，大家都生气；可是如果自己有"后门"可走，反倒觉得很有"面子"。为什么"后门"总是可以走？因为，对"门外的人"来说，在"前门"办事太困难；对"门里的人"来说，如果没人走后门，也就失去了大笔的收入。

 ## Context

    This phrase refers to the phenomenon of asking an influential person to help arrange something and establishing personal contacts to get something. These social mechanisms all began during the 1960's when China was undergoing a difficult financial situation. Later in the 1990's the phrase shifted from just being about things to include personal matters. In the earlier period, the back door mainly referred to department stores and hospitals. Now back doors are focused on schools and governments. The interesting thing is that people get very angry when they hear that other people are going through a back door. But if they can find a back door, instead of being angry, they feel they gain a lot of "face". Why is there always a back door? It exists simply because it is too hard to get things done if you go through the regular channels. It also helps the people inside the door, they lose a lot of extra income if no one asks for their help with a back door solution to their problems.

古语：商鞅因景监见，赵良寒心 // 司马迁《报任安书》
雅语：疏通一下
类语：托人情　趋关系　打招呼

不给别人面子
Don't Give Other People Face 4

4.3
在弱势中
Weaker than Others

4.3.1>

报应
[retribution]

😊 对话 Conversation

① **A：老李做了那么多坏事，日子却越过越好！**
Old Li has done so many wicked things; still, his life is getting more and more comfortable!

B：别着急呀，他会有报应的！
Just be patient, one day he'll get what's coming to him!

② **A：老李得肠癌了。**
Old Li has intestinal cancer.

B：这是报应，谁叫他那么爱整人，一肚子坏水！
That's retribution. He thought he had authorization to persecute others all the time, but he only had a stomach full of bad water!

③ **A：你害死了一千多人，不怕报应吗？**
You murdered over a thousand people. Aren't you afraid of retribution?

B：我已经八十多岁了，还怕什么？
I'm over 80 years old, what's there to be afraid of?

👉 语境

　　这句话，来自佛教。意思是做好事有好结果，做坏事有坏结果，现在只指后者。在很多人的心里，这句话的力量，比法律大得多。不少人不敢做坏事，不是怕警察，而是怕报应。在①中，人们等待天去惩罚坏人。在②中，B接受自己的恶运。两者仍然是部分当代人的心理。可惜，③中B的想法，现在越来越多了。所以，相信报应，有好处；要不然，社会会越来越乱。

Context

This phrase comes from Buddhist philosophy. It means that if one does good things, the outcome will be good, and vise versa. In many people's hearts, this phrase is more powerful than the law. Many people are afraid of doing bad things, not because they are afraid of the police, but of retribution. In conversation (1), it means that people are waiting for God to punish bad people. In conversation (2), B thinks that Old Li should accept his misfortune because he has done so many miserable things in his life. Unfortunately, more and more people think like B in conversation (3). Therefore, it is a good thing if people believe in retribution. Otherwise, in the future, society will suffer still more chaos.

古语：天网恢恢　疏而不失 // 《老子·七十三章》
雅语：天理昭彰
类语：现世报　来世报

4.3.2>

不服不行
[You have to admit that.]

对话 Conversation

① A：听说老李评上教授了！
I was told that Old Li has been made a professor!

B：连他也评上了！真是不服不行啊。

Even Old Li! Well, I suppose we have to give him some recognition.

② A：哎！老李已经升到副部级啦！

Hey! I heard that Old Li has been promoted to the level of a vice-minister!

B：他呀，是会做官，不服也不行。

Well, he really knows how to be a bureaucrat. You have to admit that!

 ## 语境

"服"有佩服、信服的意思。口语说"服了"是承认自己不如对方，是承认失败。这种承认很难，所以就有了"心服"和"口服"的不同。"心服"是心里真的服了。"口服"是嘴上服了，心里并没有服。"不服不行"呢，又麻烦了一层，是虽然心也服了，口也服了，但是一点都不佩服。也就是：事实虽然如此，但是，我仍然看不起……。造成这种"死也不服"的原因，有的是志向不同，有的是妒嫉心；另外也有一些"领导说了算"和"走后门"的情况。

 ## Context

This phrase means both to admire, and to be convinced of something. When used in oral conversation, it means to admit that that person is better than the speaker and admits the speaker's failure to recognize it before. It is not easy to convince people, and there is a difference between being "convinced from the heart" and merely saying one is "convinced from the mouth". We can easily see that being convinced from the heart is more authentic than one that comes only from the mouth. The phrase "you have to admit that" means that even though one is convinced from both heart and mouth, one doesn't necessarily admire the person at all. It says basically that: although it's done, it's still not respected.... The causes of this attitude by an "acknowledged enemy" are jealousy and the fact that two people hold different ambitions. Other reasons might include unjust behavior, as when "one leader has the final say" or "goes through the back door".

古语：罔不宾服 // 《史记·秦始皇本纪》
雅语：无可奈何
类语：不服又怎么样

4.3.3>

吃什么醋啊
[Why are you so jealous?]

☺ 对话 Conversation

① A：他和那个女人在谈工作，你吃什么醋啊？
　　He's just discussing business with her. Why are you so jealous?

　 B：我也知道，可是心里就是不舒服！
　　I know that, I just feel very uncomfortable about it!

② A：他能干的我也能干，老板为什么不用我？
　　I'm as capable as him, why doesn't the boss let me do it?

　 B：老板就是愿意用他，你吃什么醋啊！
　　The boss likes to use him. Why should you be so jealous?

语境

　　"吃醋"的故事出自唐代，一个将军的妻子不能生孩子，又不让将军再找女人。皇帝也为这事着急，就把刚刚研制出来的一碗"醋"放在她面前，说："这是毒药，如果你不让将军再找女人，那就喝下去！"没想到，将军的妻子很坚决，端起来一口气就给喝了。从此，就把对于男女关系中"第三者"的感觉，叫：吃醋。后来，又把上级重用别人，冷谈自己的感觉，也叫吃醋。

Context

The legend behind "jealous" comes from the Tang Dynasty. A General's wife couldn't become pregnant, and she wouldn't permit the General to find another woman to bear his children either. The King became very concerned about this and placed a bowl of "vinegar" in front of this woman saying: "This is a bowl of poison. If you don't permit the General to find other woman, you had better drink this." He never imagined that woman was so determined. She finished the vinegar in one gulp. From then on, we call someone who is jealous of couple the one who "drinks vinegar". Later, we came to use the same phrase to describe the feeling when a leader only pays attention to certain persons and ignores others.

古语：蛾眉不肯让人 // 骆宾王《为徐敬业讨武曌檄》
雅语：嫉妒
类语：争风　酸溜溜的

4.3.4>

哪儿跟哪儿啊这是
[What's the comparison?]

对话 Conversation

① A：我小时候被猫抓过，所以我也怕狗！
When I was young, a cat scratched me with its claws, so now I'm also afraid of dogs!

B：猫跟狗有什么关系？哪儿跟哪儿啊这是！
What's the relationship between cats and dogs? What's the comparison, these are two different animals!

② A：你刚才说头疼，现在又说肚子疼，哪儿跟哪儿啊这是！
You just said that you had a headache, now you say your tummy hurts. What's the real problem?

B：你没听说过肠胃型感冒吗？
Haven't you heard of flu called intestinal and stomach influenza?

 语境

　　事物之间有各种关系，如因果关系、逻辑关系。前者比较紧密，后者比较严谨。还有一些比较松散或相当遥远的关系，那就不大容易被理解了。就像猫和狗虽然都是宠物，都是四条腿，但是除了①中A的类比性联想以外，一般人是不会在核心记忆中掺入其他形象的。在②中，我们不能对自己不了解的关系做出轻易的判断，表面上是笑话对方，不给对方面子，实际上是自己很没面子。

Context

There are many kinds of relationships between different things, such as, the cause and effect relation or a logical relation. The two examples above have rather close and compact relationships. There are other relationships that are more loose or distant, and those are harder to understand. Take the relationship between cats and dogs, both are animals kept as pets with four legs. But A in conversation (1) makes a kind of connection between them that people would not normally make and combines these two kinds of animals for other reasons. In conversation (2), we can't conclude there is any relationship if we don't fully understand the situation. This example gives the impression that A is laughing at B and not giving B any "face". In fact, A makes himself look ridiculous by asking something like that.

古语：唯是风马牛不相及也 // 《左传·僖公四年》
雅语：毫不相干
类语：不搭界

4.3.5>

PK 就 PK
["Player Killing" is nothing!]

☺ 对话 Conversation

① A：明天去卡拉 OK，你敢跟我 PK 吗？
　　We are going to Karaoke tomorrow; do you have the nerve to play "Player Killing" with me?

　 B：PK 就 PK！谁怕谁啊？
　　Okay! Do you think I'm afraid of you?

② A：现在到处都动不动就PK，我好怕哟！

Everybody is playing PK now, I'm really afraid of it!

B：PK就PK，怕什么！淘汰了再上别处去。

"Player Killing" is nothing, don't be afraid! If we're eliminated in one place, we can go to another place.

 ## 语境

PK，是英语 Player Killing 的缩写。这种用法始于电脑游戏，所以有个"玩"，因为电脑中多有暴力场面，所以又有一层"杀死对方"的意思。这个电玩词汇刚一在湖南卫视的"超级女生"中出现，就立刻被大众接受，进入流行口语。其实，这种竞争性游戏古已有之，那就是秦、汉时期流行的"角抵"。它的玩法是，两个人把牛角戴在头上，互相顶着玩。后来就泛指各种淘汰性的文体活动。在古罗马的竞技场上，不也有大批的角斗士吗？只不过那是真的将对方杀死！与我们所说的在比赛中战胜对手完全不同。应该讲，无论是"角抵"还是"PK"，都对提高大家的竞争意识有帮助。所以，很希望有更多的新PK出现！

 ## Context

PK is an abbreviation for "Player Killing". Because this phrase originated from computer games, the word "player" remains in the phrase. In addition, as there are so many violent scenes in computer games, there is another meaning included, which is "murdering the opposing side". Since it first appeared in the TV program "Super Schoolgirl" on Hunan TV, this phrase was accepted by the public immediately. In fact, there was a similar kind of game long time ago in China. That game was popularly referred to as "Horn Butt" in the Qin and Han dynasties. It's played by two people wearing horns on their heads and butting each other. Later, people extended the use of this phrase to cover all kinds of "knockout matches". Weren't there numerous wrestlers fighting in the arenas of ancient Rome? The only difference is that those wrestlers were really killing each other, and what we are talking about is merely knocking out the other side of the competition. Whether it's called "Horn Butt" or "PK", all these games add to the competitive mindset of the Chinese people. So we hope to see more products like PK on the market!

古语：头戴牛角而相抵 // 梁·任昉《述异记》

雅语：较量

类语：比一比　谁怕谁

4.3.6>

瞧把她美的

[Look how pleased she is with herself!]

☺ 对话 Conversation

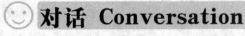

① A：哎，小红要嫁到外国去了，真不错！

Hey, Xiao Hong is going to go abroad to get married. It's wonderful!

B：瞧把她美的！不就是去外国刷碗吗？

Look how pleased she is with herself! In fact, isn't she going to a foreign country to be a dish washer?

② A：哎，老李这一评上副教授，连走路的姿势全变了！

Hey, as soon as Old Li was given the title of Associate Professor, he even walked differently!

B：没错，瞧把他美的！有事没事也穿西服，打领带。

Exactly! Look how pleased he is with himself, always wearing a suit and tie whether he needs to or not.

 语境

　　看到别人，特别是熟人有好事情，是为人家高兴呢？还是从心眼儿里气不平呢？这是一个人是否善良的试金石。很多人看不得熟人穷，认为是丢了自己的脸；很多人看不得熟人富，认为自己会一下子没了"面子"。如果用这种心态生活，那就太累了。好好过你自己的日子吧。人家的喜怒哀乐是人家的事，为别人高兴，自己能跟着开心。生人家的气，就大可不必了。

 Context

　　A yardstick by which to measure whether a person is kindhearted is when he/she sees other people, especially friends, being successful. Some are very happy and others are very resentful. Many of them can't be with close friends or relatives who are too poor because they feel that they lose a lot of "face". At the same time, these people don't want to see those friends or relatives too rich either, because they feel that they would then have less "face". It would be exhausting for someone to hold on to these kinds of thoughts all the time. They should, instead, concentrate on their own life and leave other people's pleasure, anger, sorrow and joy to them. If you are able to be happy for other people's happiness, you will have a better life. It's really not necessary to be angry when you see other people's achievements.

古语：回眸一笑百媚生，六宫粉黛无颜色。// 白居易《长
　　恨歌》
雅语：不必张扬
类语：有什么了不起

相当
[considerably]

😊 对话 Conversation

① **A：听说你的签售活动非常火爆？**
I heard that your autograph sales are going very well.

B：不是非常火爆，而是相——当——火爆！
It's not just well, but considerably well!

② **A：你的汉语水平怎么样？**
How is your Chinese?

B：相当不错。
Considerably good!

 语境

　　"相当"的原意是两方面差不多，动词。因为是两方，就有了比较的意思，虚化为副词，表示比较高的程度。这种用法在2006年春节晚会赵本山、宋丹丹的小品演出中达到顶峰。一时间大家都开始用"相当"来取代对方的程度副词，反过来强调己方事物的重要性，是一种心虚的表现。其实，"相当"再怎么用也不能超过"很"（见《现代汉语词典》的解释），何况"非常"呢？当然，小品中的农民怎么用都可以，本来就是开玩笑嘛！由此也可以看出电视媒体对口语的影响。

Context

This phrase originally was used as a verb and meant that two things are "well-matched". Since two parties are being compared to each other, it is now used as an adverb to represent a higher degree. This kind of usage reached its peak in the Short Act by Zhao Benshan and Song Dandan given at Spring Festival in 2006. After that, everybody started to use this phrase as a way stressing their self importance and a way of surpassing the other party. In fact, people use this phrase when they lack self-confidence. No matter how you explain the phrase "considerably", it can't surpass the word "very" (see *A Modern Chinese Dictionary*). In any event, is there another word to match "extraordinary"? Of course, there is no problem with which way actresses and actors might use this phrase in a show. Whatever they say is supposed to be a joke anyway! From this example we can see how massive an influence the media can have on our daily spoken language.

古语：自大宛以西至安息，国虽颇异言，然大同俗，相知
　　　言。//《史记·大宛列传》
雅语：略胜一筹
类语：非常　特别

4.3.8>

宰熟
[to swindle one's acquaintances]

☺ 对话 Conversation

① A：老李为什么在办公室推销商品？
　　Why is Old Li selling stuff in the office?

B：宰熟呗！

He's swindling his acquaintances!

② **A：最近，亲戚们都在骂老李。**

Recently, all of his relatives are blaming Old Li.

B：谁让他宰熟的！

He deserves it. He's always fleecing his acquaintances!

③ **A：这责任只能让老李承担了！**

We have to make Old Li take responsibility!

B：是啊，只能宰熟了。

That's right. We have to deceive an acquaintance.

👉 语境

　　"熟"指关系比较近的人，"宰"是欺骗、伤害的意思。按照传统，如果对生人不好，关系不大；如果对熟人不好，那是最没"面子"的事。所以，俗话说：兔子不吃窝边草。因为，"面子"主要是在熟人之中。奇怪的是，很多人开始"宰熟"！因为，骗熟人比骗生人容易。 在①中，老李骗同事；在②中，老李骗亲戚；在③中，A 和 B 让老李做替罪羊。

👉 Context

　　This phrase means to cheat and deceive someone who has close relationship with you. According to traditional logic, if you are deceitful to someone that you are not familiar with, that's okay; but if you are deceitful to someone who has close relationship with you, you have absolutely lost "face". It is like the old saying: Rabbits don't eat the grass next to their home. It's because of "face" that people care about is within the circle of people they know. The strange thing is that people now start to swindle their acquaintances, because it's easier to cheat the people you know than a stranger. In conversation (1), Old Li cheats his colleagues. In conversation (2), Old Li cheats his relatives.

In conversation (3), A and B use Old Li as a scapegoat.

古语：以邻为壑 //《孟子·告子下》
雅语：虚情假义
类语：坑朋友　骗哥们　害自己人

汉语革命与文化复兴／代跋

虽然学、用、教了一辈子中文，但是，对于汉语的看法，却是在对外汉语教学之余才逐步形成的。出于对该领域的既成教材的不满，就自己动手写了一本《汉语流行口语》（即本书的前身），2000年由华语教学出版社刊行，5年内已印刷3次并告罄，而且，该书译本已于2003年在日本、韩国，2006年在俄罗斯面世。

《汉语流行口语》这本书，为什么能够走红呢？关键之一是"口语化"。具体而言，该书走的是语境教学的路子，行的是掌握成句的方法。所谓"语境教学"，特指从历史的、文化的、心理的势态方面给予交待，让外国朋友明白其所以然；所谓"掌握成句"特指绕开词汇、语法等元素和规则，着力解决在特定情境中，中国人到底是什么意思，外国朋友应该如何应对。该书的一大特点是以模式化的体例组合一个个话语环境，当外国朋友对这句话的整个背景彻底了悟之后，就可以在类似的生活场合中选用不同风格的表达，去完成同一的交际目的，并在其中体味到汉语的幽默意味。

窃以为，就非母语学习而言，只有达到幽默的层面，才算大功告成。因为，那才脱离开外在性的模仿，体验到运用中的乐趣，那第二语言才真正成为你的仆人。遗憾的是，这种妙境，往往被字、词、句方面的死抠，扼杀在初学阶段而再不可得！

基于以上教学与成书的实践，深感要跳出来研究一下汉语本体的问题。从孟子到司马迁，从韩愈到曹雪芹，从胡适到汪曾祺，汉语言文字在中国历史文化社会的漩涡里打了几千年的滚儿，总的趋势应该是越来越简化。然而，汉字总数已达86000以上，广大使用者的表达与理解能力却呈负增长之颓势。时至今日，典雅之路已然断流，低俗之境又着实不堪！据此，是不是该提出一个"汉语革命"的口号，并探测方向，考虑步骤，逐步地把这件"补天"一般的事情操作起来呢？

按照过去的说法，汉语是中国文化的核心载体，本着当下的认知，汉语就是中国文化的核心。想来还是后者比较靠谱，因为如果汉语不是这个样子，那么汉文化乃至于"全民素质"也不会是这个样子。兹事体大。中国历史上提出过很多不同的救国方略，可就是没听说过"语言救国"！如是，此役纯属创新！问题是"语言救国"比往日的"工业、农业、科技、国防、教育、艺术、体育"等等"救国"之路，优长在哪里呢？

我们的主旨是改革，我们的方法论是"环境、人、语言的三点定位"。具体而言就是：在语言和环境之间的是人，人有问题怎么办？要改造十几亿人的精神及肉体谈何容易！在人和语言之间的是环境，环境有问题怎么办？要改造几十亿年以来形成的自然生态环境和几千年来形成的文化心态环境谈何容易！注意，这回可要进入正题了：在人和环境之间的是语言，语言有问题怎么办？改呗！人类历史上的语言文字改革不算少，人家另起炉灶也不过几十年搞定。我们不过小改小革，理应问题不大。如果从语言入手，结果却推进了人和环境的改造，那又何乐而不为呢？

话说回来，我们的人有什么问题？答曰：处来处去就是个复杂。我们的环境有什么问题？答曰：活来活去也是个复杂。我们的语言有什么问题？答曰：用来用去还是个复杂。

如果三个问题的答案都是"复杂"，那么，解决问题的办法当然不再复杂，因为那仅只是一个词的重复：简化、简化、再简化！其实人们早就在做简化的事情，如"简化字"。可惜的是，其简化的对象单单为"字"，反而破坏了汉字的系统和规律。我们的目的则是简化汉族人用来思维和表达思想感情的工具——语言！这就是釜底抽薪的法子。我删除掉你赖以要面子、绕弯子、玩心眼儿的基本元素——垃圾语言！让你不得不像留学生那么单纯，只好跟山沟里的农民那样善良。

我们希望，从幼儿呀呀学语开始，就通过简单的话语来表达鲜明的态度。从而取代那些虚情假意、自吹自擂、尔虞我诈、文过饰非、斤斤计较之类的劣根性言辞。试举六例：

①使用"让我试试"，剔除"包在我身上"那种自欺欺人的大话。

②使用"不好"，剔除"好是好，但是"那种暗藏贬斥的句式。

③使用"你真棒"，剔除"你比我强多了"那种阿谀奉承的诤言。

④使用"算了"，剔除"再说吧"那种模棱两可的托词。

⑤使用"我不会"，剔除"我哪儿会呀"那种死要面子的反诘之辞。

⑥使用"谁对听谁的"，剔除"你听他的还是听我的"那种让人左右为难的选择问句。

其实，以上翻来覆去说了半天也就是两句话。一是中国人教外国人说的汉语要简化。二是从这一简化中觉悟到：中国人自己说的汉语更需要简化。当然这两种简化不是一回事，前者是为了促进国际文化交流；后者是为了强化处于交流状态之一方的文化品质。

前文中已然涉及到我们汉文化的复杂性问题，这个问题当然不是"复杂性"三字了得。但是，也正因为此事关天、关地、关系当下每一位中国人的生命质量，关系日后子孙万代的活动空间，所以，汉民族文化的复兴是不是该在"集体有意识"的前提下，提到改革的日程上来呢？

或许时机还不成熟，大概条件远不具备。但是！作为热爱祖国语言文字的我们，却觉得可以从汉语革命的角度，来催动中华文化复兴的旷世工程。

李杰群 李杰明

2006 年 9 月

于北京西郊红果园

An Evolution of Chinese Language and Cultural Renaissance / Postscript

Although we have studied, used and taught the Chinese language all our lives, really learning to understand Chinese was related to teaching Chinese as a foreign ; language. Since we were unhappy with the textbooks on the market, we wrote one ourselves entitled *Popular Chinese Expressions* (the first edition of this book), which was published by Sinolingua in 2000. This text has been reprinted three times during the past five years and translated into Japanese and Korean in 2003 and Russian in 2006.

Why has this book been so popular? The major reason is that it is written in conversational style. In a practical way, it teaches the readers to understand the context of the phrase and then shows the readers how to create a sentence using it. By "context education" we mean an education that takes account of the historical, cultural, and psychological background of the phrase in order to relate why it is used as it is. By "creating a sentence" we mean by passing the vocabulary and grammar regulations, and explaining the meaning of the phrase under certain circumstances and how to respond to this kind of usage. This book offers examples under different contexts. When a foreign speaker understands a comprehensive background for each phrase, they can select various styles of expression to both communicate and appreciate the humor in Chinese language.

In our humble opinion, you should understand the humor in any language that you learn, if you do not, you can't say you fully know the language. In addition, the pleasure of knowing a foreign language can't remain at the level of imitation but must extend to the creation of sentences by oneself. Unfortunately, this pleasure is often killed in the beginning when you learn to follow rigid rules of grammar for a particular language.

Based on such teaching and writing practices, we felt there was a need to jump out of the endless circle of merely teaching the Chinese language, to teaching how to think in the Chinese language. From Mencius to Sima Qian, from Han Yu to Cao Xueqin, from Hu Shi to Wang Zengqi, Chinese characters have twisted around the whirlpool of Chinese historical culture for thousands of years. The main tendency during this time is toward simplification. Despite the fact that the total number of Chinese words has reached 86000, Chinese people's ability to use and understand them is declining. Today, we don't see many people who are refined in manners and language, because what is popular is often the vulgar use of language and manners. Perhaps we should call for a "Revolution in Chinese," and search for ways to gradually save the ancient Chinese language.

Traditionally, people believed that Chinese language was the carrier of Chinese culture, but we think Chinese language is the core or nucleus of Chinese culture. If the Chinese language was not in such decline, the nation's ethics and cultural quality would not be as depressed as they are today. This is indeed a serious matter. There have been many ways the nation has been saved in Chinese history, but we have never heard of using language to save our nation. What are the advantages of using this opportunity?

Our main purpose in reforming the Chinese language is repositioning the relationship among the environment, people, and the language. Within these three realms, people and environment are the most difficult to change, but the Chinese language has been reformed countless times. It would be a great contribution, if we could begin a reform within the Chinese language that would drive the reconstruction of our environment and people.

We all agree that reforming anything is a complicated process and we would like to simplify it. But it can't be done by merely simplifying Chinese characters. The result would be to destroy our system and its regulations. We want to simplify Chinese language — as a tool of expressing people's thinking and feeling. This reformation would strike at the root of horrific social customs. It will slough off the nonsense use of language used to save face, spread confusion, and play tricks on others. By doing so, people will be pure in thought and kind to each other.

We wish to simplify the Chinese language beginning when a little child learns her or his first word, and make our conversations flattering, crystal clear, true, humble, honest, and open. For example:

1. Say "let me try it" rather than "leave it all to me";
2. Say "it is not good" instead of "it is good all right, but...";
3. Say "you are excellent" instead of "you are much better than I am";
4. Say "let it go at that" instead of "let's talk about it later";
5. Say "I don't know that" instead of "how should I know that?"
6. Say "listen to who's idea is correct" instead of "do you listen to me or listen to him?"

In fact, all of the above contains two messages. The first one is that we should teach the Chinese language to foreigners in the simplest way. The second is that Chinese people should simplify their own language. Of course, these two forms of simplification contain very different meanings. One promotes international communication, and the other serves to reform our people's moral character.

We have mentioned before that Chinese culture is a complicated phenomenon with a long tradition. But the complication is not an excuse for failing to reform. Chinese reformation is intimately related to everyone's quality of life and future generations' breathing space. Given this importance, shouldn't we put the Han nationality's cultural reformation on our daily work schedule?

Perhaps the opportunity has not yet arrived and the conditions are not met. But, we who love the Chinese language, are ready for an evolution of Chinese language and a cultural renaissance.

Li, Jiequn, Li, Jieming
September 2006
Hongguoyuan, Xijiao, Beijing

出版人：王君校
责任编辑：曲　径
封面设计：李　戈　李白迪
插　　图：郭晓丹
版式设计：吴　铭
印刷监制：佟汉冬

图书在版编目(CIP)数据

汉语流行口语：最新版／李杰明等编著. —北京：华语教学出版社，2007
ISBN 978-7-80200-100-8
Ⅰ.汉... Ⅱ.李... Ⅲ.汉语－口语　Ⅳ.H193.2
中国版本图书馆 CIP 数据核字（2006）第 147858 号

汉语流行口语 最新版

李杰群 李杰明 主编

*

© 华语教学出版社
华语教学出版社出版
（中国北京百万庄路 24 号　邮政编码 100037）
电话：(86) 10-68320585
传真：(86) 10-68326333
网址：www. sinolingua. com. cn
电子信箱：hyjx@ sinolingua. com. cn
北京市松源印刷有限公司印刷
中国国际图书贸易总公司海外发行
（中国北京车公庄西路 35 号）
北京邮政信箱第 399 号 邮政编码 100044
新华书店国内发行
2007 年（特 16 开）第一版
（汉英）
ISBN 978-7-80200-100-8
9-CE-3776P
定价：43.00 元